ARCTIC NATURALIST

Self-portrait sketch of Dewey Soper on horseback in Alberta during the winter of 1919 at twenty-five degrees below zero, by J. Dewey Soper.

ARCTIC NATURALIST
The Life of J. Dewey Soper

Anthony Dalton

DUNDURN PRESS
TORONTO

Copyright © Anthony Dalton, 2010

All rights reserved. No part of this publication may be reproduced, stored in a retrieval system, or transmitted in any form or by any means, electronic, mechanical, photocopying, recording, or otherwise (except for brief passages for purposes of review) without the prior permission of Dundurn Press. Permission to photocopy should be requested from Access Copyright.

Copy Editor: Allison Hirst
Design: Jennifer Scott
Printer: Transcontinental

Library and Archives Canada Cataloguing in Publication

Dalton, Anthony, 1940-
  Arctic naturalist : the life of J. Dewey Soper / by Anthony Dalton.

Includes bibliographical references and index.
Issued also in an electronic format.
ISBN 978-1-55488-746-0

1.Soper, J. Dewey (Joseph Dewey), 1893-1982. 2. Naturalists--Canada--Biography. 3. Natural history--Canada, Northern. 4. Natural history--Prairie Provinces. I. Title.

QH31.S62D35 2010   508.092   C2010-902305-6

1 2 3 4 5   14 13 12 11 10

We acknowledge the support of the **Canada Council for the Arts** and the **Ontario Arts Council** for our publishing program. We also acknowledge the financial support of the **Government of Canada** through the **Canada Book Fund** and **The Association for the Export of Canadian Books**, and the **Government of Ontario** through the **Ontario Book Publishers Tax Credit program**, and the **Ontario Media Development Corporation**.

Care has been taken to trace the ownership of copyright material used in this book. The author and the publisher welcome any information enabling them to rectify any references or credits in subsequent editions.

J. Kirk Howard, President

Printed and bound in Canada.
www.dundurn.com

Cover Images:
Front cover (top): Dewey taking a sun shot for latitude, while standing on the granite seabed of Foxe Basin near Cape Alberta, surrounded by stranded sea ice at low tide. August 11, 1929. *Roland Soper Collection*. Front cover (bottom): Dewey wearing his furs after a winter surveying expedition on the Foxe Peninsula. *University of Alberta Archives 79-21-34-175*. Back cover (left): Watercolour of walrus on ice in Foxe Basin near Nuwata, by J. Dewey Soper. *Courtesy of Roland Soper*. Back cover (right): Sketch of the CGS *Arctic* working through icebergs in Baffin Bay, by J. Dewey Soper. *Courtesy of Roland Soper*.

Dundurn Press	Gazelle Book Services Limited	Dundurn Press
3 Church Street, Suite 500	White Cross Mills	2250 Military Road
Toronto, Ontario, Canada	High Town, Lancaster, England	Tonawanda, NY
M5E 1M2	LA1 4XS	U.S.A. 14150

*For all those who appreciate the wonders of strange lands —
and of beautiful creatures everywhere*

Canada map showing Dewey's main areas of exploration.

Also by Anthony Dalton

A Long, Dangerous Coastline

The Graveyard of the Pacific

River Rough, River Smooth

Alone Against the Arctic

Baychimo, Arctic Ghost Ship

J/Boats, Sailing to Success

*The Best of Nautical Quarterly, Volume I:
The Lure of Sail* (with Reese Palley)

Wayward Sailor, In Search of the Real Tristan Jones

I went to the woods because I wished to live deliberately, to front only the essential facts of life, and see if I could not learn what it had to teach, and not, when I came to die, discover that I had not lived.
— Henry David Thoreau, *Walden* (1854)

Contents

Acknowledgements		13
Introduction		15
1	A Young Naturalist	21
2	Into a Western Wonderland	35
3	First Expedition: Into the Foothills of the Rockies	39
4	Ontario Again	55
5	Building and Learning	71
6	Expedition to the Eastern Arctic, 1923	83
7	A Second Arctic Expedition	105
8	Exploring Baffin Island	123
9	The Nettilling Lake Expedition	139
10	A Winter Traverse	149
11	Cape Dorset Summer	155
12	A Brief Prairie Interlude	163
13	Baffin Island, 1928–29	169
14	In Search of the Blue Goose	183
15	Lake Harbour, 1930–31	195
16	Two Decades of Stellar Service	207
17	An Attempt at Retirement	231

18	Researching the Mammals of Alberta	239
19	A Second Attempt at Retirement	255

Appendix I	Awards and Honours	269
Appendix II	Scientific Discoveries	271
Appendix III	Clubs and Associations	273
Notes		275
Works by J. Dewey Soper		299
Selected Bibliography		303
Index		307
About the Author		313

Acknowledgements

First, I must express my heartfelt gratitude and love to my friend, mentor, and favourite modern poet, Bernice Lever, who had the foresight to introduce me and my writing to her friend Kirk Howard, publisher of Dundurn Press. Without that important connection, this book might not have been written.

Roland Soper, Dewey's son, gave me his approval for the book and helped me with photographs, maps, and many anecdotes about his father. Also, Roly's son Trent — himself a naturalist — gave me new insights into his grandfather. I will long treasure the hours the three of us spent around Roly's dining-room table in Calgary one day, looking at family photograph albums and discussing their memories of Dewey's life. Thanks so much to you both. Philip Soper shared his memories of his grandfather with me by phone from his Toronto home and brought yet another perspective to the story. As a raconteur he proved to be the equal of both Dewey and Roly, and of his younger brother Trent. That long telephone conversation was informative, fascinating, and great fun. Likewise, an equally long telephone conversation with Mary Lou Austdal (at home in Edmonton) gave me a host of anecdotes about her father. I thoroughly enjoyed talking with the members of the Soper family and I will be forever grateful for their help.

On three occasions I passed many fruitful hours at BARD, the Books and Records Depository at the University of Alberta in Edmonton. The archivists there, especially Raymond Frogner, were always helpful and never failed to locate any file I wanted to view. When it came time to request copies of photographs, Raymond responded immediately. You have my appreciation.

My thanks go to Trisha Carleton at the Arctic Institute of North America for information on the ownership of Dewey Soper's watercolours, and to Sharon Bell at the City of Edmonton Archives. Once again, as with earlier books, the staff at the Archives of Manitoba/Hudson's Bay Company Archives in Winnipeg were extremely helpful in my research, as were the people at Library and Archives Canada in Ottawa; I must thank the Library and Archives Canada for permission to quote from Dr. Soper's report of the 1923 Arctic expedition, also for permission to reproduce certain photographs. Thanks to Patrick Hayes at the University of Saskatchewan Archives for permission to quote from *Canadian Arctic Recollections*, and to Robin Weber for help with photographs from the NWT Archives in Yellowknife. Equally, Vincent Lafond of the Canadian Museum of Civilization in Ottawa helped with photographs.

During my early visits to Edmonton for the initial research into Dewey Soper's life, my sister —Pamela Kurmey — fed me, gave me a bed, allowed me to use her computer, and occasionally loaned me her car. Her thoughtfulness and care is greatly appreciated. And my gratitude, as always, goes to my wife, Penny, for her ongoing support — for my adventures and for my literary projects.

My appreciation and thanks go to Constance Martin from the Arctic Institute of North America for permission to use the quote on the back cover of this book. The quote comes from Constance's essay in *Recollecting: J. Dewey Soper's Arctic Watercolours* (page 34).

I am proud to work with the wonderful staff of Dundurn Press and would like to express my gratitude to Allison Hirst, my editor for this book. As an editor, you are an author's delight.

Introduction

Martin Frobisher, a tough British sea captain, in command of the small sailing ship *Gabriel* and a handful of sailors, came in sight of the misty, craggy coast of a land he named Meta Incognita in 1576. It was the first of three voyages the intrepid navigator made to the subarctic regions west of Greenland, initially in an unsuccessful search for a convenient northern navigational route to the riches and spices of Cathay, and later in a misguided quest for gold. He didn't find any precious yellow metals, but he did discover the extensive bay that bears his name.

Frobisher was the first of many Europeans to venture into the unknown and dangerously ice-riddled Arctic seas and touch upon the coast of what would become known as Baffin Island. He was followed by the brilliant navigator John Davis in 1585. On his first of three Arctic voyages, Davis crossed the Arctic Circle between Greenland and Baffin Island, then turned south, making a rudimentary chart of Baffin Island's east coast as he went. Davis probed deep into Cumberland Sound, certainly as far as Pangnirtung Fjord.

A quarter of a century later, the sad figure of Henry Hudson forced the fifty-five-ton *Discovery* through the turbulent tidal rips and ice floes of what is now Hudson Strait and into the eponymous bay in 1610. There, thanks to a mutinous crew, he met his fate.

ARCTIC NATURALIST

William Baffin, astronomer, explorer, and navigator, who idolized John Davis, arrived on the as yet to be named Baffin Island's rocky south shores in 1615. His superb navigational skills took his ship through a wild, ice-choked channel to Foxe Basin[1] and as far west as the Frozen Strait, between the mainland and Southampton Island. Baffin named many of the island groups, including the Savage Islands in Hudson Strait. Two centuries later, Sir William Parry, who followed Baffin's course through Hudson Strait, gave Baffin Island its name.

Frobisher, Davis, Hudson, Baffin: these are all names to conjure up in the annals of the exploration of the icy waters around the southern coasts of Baffin Island. They were quite different from one another, yet they all had something in common: a passion for exploration and discovery, combined with uncommon courage. They were among my earliest heroes and indirectly responsible for leading me down a lifelong path of adventure. Three decades before I was born, they, and others of their ilk, were the inspiration for another young man with the northern wilderness on his mind. He, like me, was always happy camping out, often alone, far from urbanization. He, like me, was fascinated by the Arctic.

Half a lifetime ago I walked the shores of Frobisher Bay on Baffin Island on a relatively warm summer day. There were still patches of ice on the placid sea and some cold, scruffy, greyish bits littering the pebbly beach. A few gulls circled low overhead, hoping, perhaps, that I had food to share. A pair of eider ducks paddled away as I stepped too close to where they foraged for food. Other than the birds, I was alone, heading for the old Hudson's Bay Company fur-trading post to take a photograph. By ignoring the nearby town and concentrating on the sea, it was easy to imagine myself on the Baffin Island of a century before.

I had travelled to Frobisher Bay (the town that would eventually be renamed Iqaluit) for a couple of days as the guest of a business acquaintance. Together we later flew northeast in a small single-engine airplane, over the high land and across Cumberland Sound, to land in the claustrophobic confines of windy Pangnirtung Fjord. From there we hiked up into the mountains for a few days, crossing the Arctic Circle into a magnificent wilderness of snow, ice, and granite. At that time I had no idea I was walking in the footsteps of one of Canada's foremost Arctic explorers and naturalists. By

Introduction

the time I left Baffin Island a week or so later, I had fallen under the spell of the Arctic and the subarctic, just as he had done so long before.

Although my work as an adventure guide took me to the Sahara and the deserts of the Middle East for most of the year, I went back to the Arctic whenever I could. Over the next decade I eventually travelled as far north as Resolute, on Cornwallis Island, and experienced much of the southern half of Victoria Island.[2] In 1984 I went farther to the west, taking a small boat alone far along the Arctic coast of Alaska.[3] Twenty years later I wrote two books about the Arctic[4] and was actively seeking material for a third. When I found an idea, it happened by accident.

The Hudson's Bay Company Archives in Winnipeg is a treasure trove for historians, researchers, and biographers. Hidden away in the deep recesses of the interior are the minute details that make up much of the history of Canada. It was there that I first found the name of J. Dewey Soper. Appropriately, it was a bitterly cold and snowy February day: distinct Arctic conditions outside. I was researching a story about Hudson's Bay Company ships, particularly those that plied the Arctic waters. Dewey Soper's name was on a passenger list for part of one of the RMS *Nascopie*'s[5] annual round-trip voyages from Montreal to the eastern Arctic. Beside his name was the word *naturalist*. Intrigued, I filed the name away for future reference, thinking, perhaps, that there might be part of another story there.

A few days later, at home in British Columbia, I typed Soper's full name into an Internet search panel and discovered bits and pieces of a fascinating story. Bits and pieces were all I could find, plus a slim autobiographical narrative of his Arctic expeditions between 1923 and 1931.[6] I dug deeper. The more information I uncovered, the more fascinated I became with this apparently little-known and largely unheralded Canadian scientific explorer, and the more I knew I wanted to be the author to tell Dewey Soper's life story, for it was his footsteps I had unknowingly dogged up in the Pangnirtung Pass more than thirty years before. And so it began.

Starting in about 1911, the eighteen-year-old Dewey Soper began keeping and maintaining written records of his outdoor wanderings and the wildlife he encountered. Those initial jottings increased to become copious daily notes made during his many field trips. After he graduated from amateur naturalist to professional, his writings increased dramatically. During each expedition, spread over the next few decades, he recorded every wild creature he saw. Following the major expeditions he wrote long and detailed reports, some of which were eventually published as newspaper and magazine articles, in addition to the scientific papers. Occasionally, however, those versions of his travels conflict with one another in small ways: a potential minefield for a biographer and, indeed, for a researcher.

For example, in 1956 he wrote an autobiographical sketch of roughly 16,500 words on forty-six letter-size pages.[7] In 1969 he expanded that to a fifty-thousand-word autobiography.[8] Neither were published. In 1928 the National Museum of Canada published his *A Faunal Investigation of Southern Baffin Island*. The beginning of that book is a much abbreviated narrative of his Baffin Island expeditions of 1923 and 1924–26. The rest is valuable scientific data. Decades later, in 1981, the University of Saskatchewan published Dewey's *Canadian Arctic Recollections*, written as a popular story of his Baffin Island expeditions between 1923 and 1931. Perhaps it is not surprising that there are a few inconsistencies between the pair of unpublished manuscripts and between the two professionally edited publications. In such cases, I have erred on the side of caution and taken the earliest version as the most accurate, based on the belief that, like most people, Dr. Soper's memory probably served him better when he was in his thirties than in his seventies and eighties. If, in doing so, I have incorporated mistakes into this book, then those errors are mine and mine alone.

Dr. Soper understood that his books were destined to be the works that later scientists and other writers would use and build upon in their own research. In the prologue to his classic four-hundred-page opus, *The Mammals of Alberta*, he wrote, "The present volume represents the first complete guide, of this scope and detail, to the native quadrupeds of Alberta. In a sense it is a pioneering effort — actually a pre-planned foundation upon which new knowledge and improvements can be gradually built in the years to come."[9]

Dewey Soper was a Canadian naturalist cut from the same cloth as his distinguished international forebears, the brilliant Carl Linnaeus (known as the father of taxonomy) and the equally laudable but much misunderstood Charles Darwin. As Linnaeus and Darwin both travelled far from home for long periods of time on their individual quests to increase the world's

Introduction

scientific knowledge of fauna, avifauna, and flora, so too did Dewey Soper. The records of his Arctic expeditions show a singularly determined man, prepared to challenge the most hostile of elements to achieve his purpose.

While most people today consider the killing of wild creatures distasteful — and certainly with so many species now on the endangered list there is a valid argument there — it should be remembered that the collecting and research conducted by Dewey Soper and other naturalists strengthens the ability of today's scientists to preserve and protect them all. He did not kill for sport, only for science or for food.

Dewey Soper was as much an explorer as he was a naturalist. He supplied the first accurate charts of important sections of the west coast of Baffin Island. He named many of the most prominent features of the southern half of the island. His own name is on a river, a lake, some highlands, and a bird sanctuary — all on Baffin Island. They are well-deserved honours.

It should be noted that, unless stated to the contrary, all distances are in statute miles and all temperatures are in Fahrenheit. I have maintained all other measurements in imperial, as this was the system in use during the time of Dewey's explorations and research. For convenience, I have included the Latin names of wildlife only the first time the species is mentioned.

1

A Young Naturalist

More than 650 feet above the frigid waters of Melville Bay, the great bluish white glacier trembled at the end of its long snail's-pace journey from high up on the northern expanse of the Greenland ice cap. Decades old crevasses probed deep into its darkening depths while other more embryonic fractures scarred its breadth as far back as the eye could see; all watched over by pristine clouds. With a thunderous roar, a gigantic slab of glacial ice broke free and toppled into the sea. Freezing spray and large chunks of blue flew skyward as the ice plunged toward the seabed. Despite its enormous weight, it stabilized underwater, and then gradually ascended until it settled with only a small portion of its bulk visible above the surface. Rocking lazily from side to side, bobbing with the energy of the sea, the new iceberg slowly rotated and began to move north and west along with others of its kind, obeying the prevailing wind and currents.

Passing Cape York, still in loose formation with other bergs, large and small, its voyage turned westward into Baffin Bay. There the iceberg collected the cold Canadian Current and, denying its Arctic heritage, it turned south, as did its companions. Its speed steadily increased to over five knots to match the current as it passed Devon Island and joined the outflow from Lancaster Sound. Shrouded in mist, the iceberg and its frozen companions drifted in a roughly southeasterly direction, a few nautical miles off Baffin Island's eastern shore. For a few weeks the bergs moved relentlessly with the current, making for their own inexorable destruction in the much warmer waters of the Gulf Stream in the North Atlantic Ocean. Separately, yet in a never-ending, scattered convoy, they passed out of sight of the deeply indented Labrador coast.

On the foredeck of a Canadian government ship, thirty-year-old expedition naturalist Dewey Soper, on his first visit to the Arctic, leaned against the starboard rail near the bow, his blue eyes staring with eager anticipation into the gloom. The ship, CGS *Arctic*,[1] moved cautiously north, washed by drizzling rain and shrouded in fog. Ice bumped alongside the hull, keeping all onboard alert. Every few seconds the ship's foghorn blared its lonely message into the clammy greyness. On the bridge, Arctic veteran Captain J. E. Bernier[2] listened for the telltale echo off a big berg. Frozen lookouts on the bow and at the masthead kept watch, ready to bellow at any sign of danger. At dawn on July 20, 1923, the fog cleared, showing icebergs, growlers, and bergy bits[3] littering the ocean. Captain Bernier turned his ship to the east, carefully picking a route through the broken ice to distant open water. Once clear, *Arctic* turned to port again, on course for Greenland's west coast.

Dewey Soper wrote of his impressions as the ship carried him north into polar waters: "Along the northwestern horizon we now saw a peculiar wall of light reflected from the middle ice-pack of Davis Strait. It was perhaps 25 to 30 miles distant, a singular feature known as 'ice-blink.'[4] It is a curiously structured phantom atmosphere like a pillared curtain of white flame, held in strange immobility. An hour later it had disappeared completely."[5]

During the next decade, as he succumbed deeper and deeper to the mystical draw of Canada's immense and seasonally frozen northland, he would experience many more new and unfamiliar phenomena.

After a last vicious gale, which wrought havoc on ships and boats on nearby Lake Ontario and tore branches off trees and ripped tiles from roofs, spring came quietly to the farmlands north and west of Toronto. It was not before time. The winter of 1892–93[6] had been bitter and hard, with much snow, frequent storms, and stronger than normal winds. The temperature dropped so low that, by mid-January, ice along the shores of the great lake — between Toronto, Hamilton, and the frozen Niagara River — had accumulated to a foot in thickness. It stayed that way for the next two months. Throughout March and into April the cold and storms continued. As April's rambunctious weeks faded into memory, the winds died down, the sombre clouds drifted away, the sun beamed its early warmth on the land, mammals cautiously emerged from hibernation to break their winter fast, birds began to return, and the last of the ice and snow melted. With the spring came new life, as birds and mammals introduced their young to the world. New life also came to a small southern Ontario country family. In a log house on tidy farmland set among hardwood trees at the northern apex of a triangle, with its base connecting Guelph and Acton, Joseph Dewey Soper was born on May 5, 1893.

Dewey's paternal grandfather, Samuel Soper, had emigrated from England in the early 1800s. He arrived in Upper Canada (the forerunner of the province of Ontario) in time to fight with General Sir Isaac Brock in the border war of 1812–14, and was said to have been close by when Brock was killed by a sharpshooter on October 13, 1812. Once peace was established between the two young nations, Samuel was free to go his own way. He soon carved out a homestead in Erin County and became a farmer. When he eventually married, Samuel sired four sons, the second of whom he named Joseph. On a nearby farm, the McLaughlin family, originally from the Highlands of Scotland, had a daughter, Ilona. Farming side by side, the children of the two families of British background grew up together. It was, apparently, no surprise that Joseph and Ilona became firm friends and eventually married. In time they, too, produced four children: Edith in 1890, Joseph Dewey in 1893, Cecil in 1896, and Roy in 1903.

Under the semi-pioneering conditions prevalent in the final decade of the 1800s, while farming offered a certain stability, it was labour-intensive and offered little financial reward. Joseph Senior augmented his meagre income by learning to erect the framework of barns and to generally assist local builders. Still, it wasn't enough. He wanted and needed more. Hearing of building opportunities in Huntsville, Joseph and Ilona Soper moved north with their two young children in the spring of 1894, leaving Joseph's older brother in charge of the family farm. For the next three years, as the babies grew, Joseph built houses and barns in the Muskokas. In his early sixties, Dewey Soper recalled his first impressions of life as a boy of three in Huntsville: "There is a dim recollection of a boyish fight with a young bully along the street; of walking along the margin of a stream not far from home; and of becoming angry one day and leaving this house with the intention of heading for the wild bush-lands on the outskirts of town."[7]

He doesn't tell us the outcome of the fight or of his findings by the stream. Of his adventure into the wilds he only noted that, once his parents became aware of his absence, they sent search parties to comb the nearby woods, and soon found the boy. Dewey added, "The incident appears, in some degree, to have forecast the instinct for the wanderlust, the wilderness, and far-off places which became such a dominant trait later in [my] life."

Joseph Soper (Dewey's father) with rifle.

By the end of 1897, Joseph Soper had developed itchy feet again. He now had three children to feed and money continued to be scarce, yet in preference to working for someone else, Joseph needed to be his own boss — and that meant returning to work on the land. In January 1898 he rented the hundred-acre McAllstrome Farm, between Guelph and Rockwood. For the next four years the family lived and worked on the land while Dewey and his siblings attended a nearby school. Dewey's memories of this period in his life are vague. The only incident to stand out for him was his first personal experience with chewing tobacco:

> [Father] sent me down the line to a nearby cross-roads store to purchase a couple of plugs of McDonald's black chewing tobacco. I had always been impressed with his

evident enjoyment of the weed and speculated on its taste. On this day curiosity got the better of me; I cunningly removed a little of the leaf on the edge of the plug and jauntily marched for home chewing and spitting in the regular manner. Before very long I was very sick and in dire trouble. Unable to navigate I spent considerable time sprawled in an angle of a rail "snake" fence. There is a dim memory of bloodroot and hepaticas in bloom and the plaintive singing of Vesper Sparrows. Eventually wending my way home, the truth was soon known, followed later by a time-honoured method of chastisement by father in the woodshed. This was the first and last time that I was ever led into such temptation by chewing tobacco.[8]

One of Joseph Soper's brothers, Lew, lived in Mitchell, South Dakota. Early in 1902, Lew wrote describing the building boom in the vicinity and urged Joseph to join him there. In March that year, Joseph gave up farming and uprooted his family again. Travelling by train, they arrived in Mitchell in April, and Joseph immediately found work in the building trade. Although he did well at first, the move was not a success. Before long the building boom collapsed and the family struggled to survive. In early June 1904 they packed their belongings and returned to Ontario. Dewey, who was almost nine when he arrived in South Dakota, later claimed to remember little of his two years in the Mitchell area. He did recall learning to ride a bicycle there and, in the summer holidays, he showed early interest in studying nature.

Writing about an element of the South Dakota sojourn in 1915, only eleven years later, Dewey showed revulsion to the cold-hearted boyish slaughter of wild creatures, particularly those that lived underground: "Considerable activity of the local boys was spent on hauling water to the burrows and emptying the pails of water down the holes to half drown them and force the creatures to the surface; as they emerged they were clubbed and killed. It seemed to me a cruel practise …"[9]

Unfortunately, writing about the same event in an autobiographical sketch just over forty years later, Dewey shows inconsistencies in the story, suggesting he believed he might have been involved in the killing:

We youngsters roamed the surrounding shortgrass plains and got casually acquainted with some of the wildlife. One of the commonest species was the plentiful "flicker gopher," or Richardson Ground Squirrel [*Spermophilus richardsonii*]; these animals particularly excited our curiosity and stimulated sadistic inclinations advanced by means of buckets of water poured into the burrows and dispatching the creatures when they blundered half-drowned to the surface.[10]

The Sopers' return to Ontario added little to the family's stability. Soon after they arrived, Joseph took a building job in the village of Monticello. That lasted until the end of the year, when the Sopers again moved, this time to Grand Valley, where it was said there were more job opportunities. As the winter of 1905 became 1906, and the building trade ground to its annual halt for the winter, Joseph once more decided that farming was a better option than building. Accordingly, he took a four-year lease on the 150-acre Burns Farm, a short distance from Rockwood. There, at the age of thirteen, Dewey Soper really became an amateur naturalist. "The area was a delightful one for a boy with natural history inclinations," he wrote in an unpublished January 1956 autobiographical sketch.

One hundred acres of the Burns Farm had been cultivated, the rest left fallow. For Dewey the untamed area was a wonderland. When he wasn't at school or working on his daily farm chores, he roamed a large "stand of virgin hardwoods, tracts of cedar swamp, bubbling springs and meandering brooks, rolling fields and brushy fence rows."

The farm and its environs offered the fledgling naturalist a rich variety of birdlife and a host of fur-bearing mammals for future study, such as weasel, fox, raccoon, skunk, and a few mink and muskrat specimens for good measure. At first Dewey concentrated his attention on the birds. He wrote, using the third person as was his habit, "The interest in them was like a divine fever of excitement."[11]

To assist his studies, he sent to a mail-order house for a bird identification book and a two-dollar telescope, the latter made from elongated cardboard tubes with the requisite lens at one end and an eyepiece at the other. From the time they arrived, Dewey matched the birds in his book with the live versions, quickly learning to identify all the most common species. With increased knowledge came additional confidence. He began to venture deeper into the bush and the swamplands where rarer birds rested and fed during autumn and spring migrations.

As his understanding of avifauna expanded, so Dewey broadened his interests to encompass the local fur-bearing mammals. By 1908, at the age of fifteen, he had developed an interest in trapping and general woodcraft. His enthusiasm, however, was not limited to scientific study. As he freely admitted, Dewey took up trapping in part to earn extra spending money for his hobby. He realized his first success on Christmas morning 1908 when he found a Bonaparte weasel (*Mustela cicognanii*) in one of his traps. That was, without doubt, the best Christmas present he could have had. For the rest of the morning he bounced around full of excitement. His enthusiasm stayed with him long enough for Dewey to recount the important achievement to his favourite uncle, Nelson McLaughlin, at Christmas dinner on the McLaughlin's farm later that day. Perhaps as a reward, Nelson presented him with a single-barrelled 12-gauge shotgun, old but in excellent condition. Dewey said his joy was indescribable. That winter Dewey trapped several ermine (*Mustela erminea*) to add to the weasel. As soon as they were ready he shipped the furs to Funsten Brothers of St. Louis, Missouri, and received a welcome cheque in return. Some of the money he spent on Chester Reed's two-volume set of bird guides, which covered the water, game, and land birds of North America east of the Rocky Mountains. Much of the balance, one assumes, went to help his family.

Dewey now began to regularly tramp the two miles each way into Rockwood to borrow books from the small public library. In particular, the wildlife tomes of Ernest T. Seton created a strong impression on him. About this time he also ordered two special volumes for his own library collection: *Science of Trapping*, by E. Kreps, and Francis H. Buzzacott's *The Complete American and Canadian Sportsman's Encyclopedia of Valuable Instruction*. Those two books added immeasurably to Dewey's ever-increasing understanding of the science of outdoor wildlife study.

By 1910 Dewey had replaced the cheap telescope with a "four-power opera glass" and the list of birds he had identified with his various optics had grown to a considerable length. He noted that "The longer this list became the prouder and more enthusiastic I became."

After spending his trapping proceeds on a powerful air gun, Dewey went out looking for birds and returned home upset at his subsequent actions. He explained:

> An incident happened through my ignorance of birdlife that grieved me for some time. The lust of killing had surfaced; it was a very cold day with fresh snow. Several ringing whistles rang out and a couple [of] dozen birds flew past me and landed in a big spreading birch tree where they began feeding. Hurrying to the tree I could see immediately that they were Pine Grosbeaks [*Pinicola enucleator*], the males in their gaudy plumage; then I shot one to have a good look at it; in the end it filled me with remorse — this taking a life for practically nothing. If I had taken it for scientific purposes it would have been different, but I had not yet begun to mount birds.[12]

The experience hurt, but it was a good lesson for Dewey. Never again would he kill without a scientific purpose, other than for food. In spite of his devotion to birds, he continued to study and collect small mammals. He explained, "I had become a genuine farm boy trapper, expanding operations every fall and early winter as I became older, more experienced and ambitious."

The income from selling his furs helped, too. He saw it as offering him "more moral independence and freedom, augmenting a meagre allowance, and providing more money for books, traps and other materials." Selling furs also bought him his own .22 rifle.

Apart from the obvious benefits of the income the work provided, the teenage naturalist loved trapping. He considered it "a basic experience in acquiring a knowledge of mammals that could not be obtained in any other way." His parents, failing perhaps to understand the depths of his interest and passion, were concerned that he might end up as a "common trapper." In fact, Dewey's early trapping experiences paved the way for his later professional observations, and a career that spanned six decades. Inevitably though, in the early days, trapping caused troubles at home.

Skunks were plentiful in southern Ontario and their pelts were a valuable source of income. Skunks, however, use a highly pungent secretion to deter predators, including young trappers. Stored in two walnut-sized glands in its anus, a skunk can direct the toxic spray well over three feet. At worst the spray causes nausea and retching and can simulate the effects of teargas if it hits the eyes. At best it has a disgustingly foul odour. Clothes sprayed by skunks invariably retain the noxious smell despite repeated washings. Unconcerned, Dewey checked his traplines early each morning before doing his farm chores and before breakfast. Often he arrived home reeking of skunk musk after being sprayed by his angry, panic-stricken victims. Instead of breakfast on those occasions he was banished to the woodshed. No punishment, however, could deter the young man from setting and checking his traplines and snares. He wrote, "This was all part of the game. None of it quenched my desire for the trapline in the smallest degree." A few lines farther on, Dewey explained, "Trapping skunks and other fur-bearers ... was the breath of life to me in those days."

Somehow, considering he had to attend school and was expected to work on the farm, Dewey found time to fill a series of notebooks with his observations on birds, mammals, flowers, and trees, plus his trapline experiences and natural phenomena. Sadly, most of those notebooks disappeared during one of the family's moves. The only one to survive into Dewey's adulthood was *Book of Woodcraft and Woodlore, 1908*, which he described as "done in a very boyish style." That, too, was eventually lost.

Dewey did not always hunt alone. In a short unpublished manuscript written in 1915[13] he reminisced about hunting with his father and his Scots Collie:

> A thing of great delight to me then was to go "coon" hunting with my Dad on a beautiful moonlight [night] in the fall when the animals were feeding in the cornfield flanking the woods. How still except for the trailing bark of the dog and so exciting! I held the lantern so as to shine the "coons" [sic]

(that had now made its way well up a big sugar maple) eyes for Dad to shoot it. With one blast from the old 12-gauge down the animal came to hit the ground with a thud, when the dog then had a few minutes to maul it. Those were alluring times.

Much as he loved his open-air wildlife observatory in the southern Ontario farmlands, by his mid-teens Dewey had begun to look ahead to exploring more distant terrain, including the Arctic: "Many a time I had daydreams while looking at northern lights and the pole star. I knew well that in that direction lay lands that I so deeply desired to travel over and observe. The first man I ever met from the North was an old prospector from the Algoma country of Northern Ontario. His tales of gold, Indians, traplines and wildlife filled my mind with indescribable longing."[14]

It is possible that Dewey's initial interest in the polar regions was inspired by news reports of discoveries and successes that took place during the first decade and a half of the twentieth century. At that time there were still many "firsts" to be claimed by those with the courage to risk their lives and the tenacity to suffer immense hardships. In September 1906, when Dewey was thirteen years old, the Norwegian explorer Roald Amundsen completed the first transit of the Northwest Passage after a three-year voyage in Arctic ice. In January 1909 Ernest Shackleton reached a point only 111 miles from the South Pole. Three months later Robert Peary[15] claimed to have reached the North Pole. Another American, Dr. Frederick Cook,[16] claimed to have reached the North Pole a year before Peary. The claims of those two explorers sparked a controversy that became big news.[17] In mid-December 1911, Roald Amundsen achieved a second triumph when he and his four companions became the first men to reach the South Pole.[18]

Library books on Arctic exploration certainly galvanized the young Dewey Soper. He read the exploits of the Dane, Peter Freuchen, and the Norwegian, Fridjtof Nansen, the tales of the British Antarctic explorers, Ernest Shackleton and the doomed Robert Falcon Scott, as well as those of the Icelandic-Canadian Vilhjalmur Stefansson. He yearned for the day when he, too, could visit the north polar regions: "And the more I read [of the Arctic], the stronger was my desire to get to the land of the Eskimo where many renowned explorers had made their mark…. The longing kept right on unabated."[19]

The breadth of Dewey's reading material at this time was considerable. In addition to the Arctic and Antarctic tomes, he read three of E.T. Seton's books: *Two Little Savages*, *Wild Animals I Have Known*, and *Lives of the Hunted*. He also became a devoted fan of Charles G.D. Roberts, devouring *Kindred of the Wild*, *Children of the Wild*, and *Red Fox*, all of which he kept and re-read years later.

In April 1910, after four happy years on the Burns Farm, the family moved yet again, their lease having expired. The move was a short one of only a few miles to another farm, north of Guelph this time, with the Speed River running through the southern section. More than four decades later, Dewey wrote, "On the day of our arrival I have a very clear recollection of appraising the qualifications of this farm from a natural history viewpoint…. All that came into view was very encouraging. The stream and wild bushlands augured well for the future; birdlife would be abundant and exciting and there would be many species of mammals…. It was not disappointing."[20]

With such a positive attitude it's not surprising that Dewey quickly settled into his new habitat on the Speedside Farm. Being April, he focused his attention on the spring migration. Carrying his notebooks with him when working in the fields, he was able to identify and record the commoner birds. The only drawback for him was his inability to study lesser-known species of woodland birds. He soon made adjustments to accommodate that need. Never afraid of rising early, Dewey began leaving his bed long before the rest of the family awoke and well before he was due to start work on farm chores. That extra hour or so spent observing birds added much to his burgeoning collection of information. During the fall migration he varied his pattern by spending the final hours before dark in the woods and along the riverbanks.

He continued his trapping through the fall and early winter, too, as much for the thrill of the hunt as for the data he was able to record. He also admitted he wanted the additional money his traplines could provide. In the fall of 1910, for example, he earned $150 from selling his furs, commenting, "This was more money than I had ever realized before."

He spent some of that income on more books and a new pair of 6-power Bausch and Lomb field glasses, a vast improvement over the cheap telescope and opera glasses he had used for years. Another aspect of nature study, the preservation of specimens of mammals and birds, prompted him to add more skills to his repertoire. As the winter of 1910–11 came to a close, Dewey enrolled in a correspondence course offered by the Northwestern School of Taxidermy in Omaha, Nebraska. With an already heavy workload of farm chores, plus field and book studies, he now pushed himself further with more education. Eager to indulge in the new and exciting opportunities advanced by learning to preserve his specimens, he quickly spent his trapline earnings on instruments and preservation materials. He later commented that his busy daily schedule drove the weeks and months to pass much too quickly.[21]

That softly worded comment begs a few questions about Dewey's boyhood: did he have friends of his own age? There are few mentions of him with other boys and none of any friendships with local girls. Did he spend all, or most of his time, either working on the farm, at school, or alone in the woods? Based on his daily schedule, it seems most likely that he did just that.

Compared to modern methods, Dewey's first attempts at taxidermy were probably quite primitive, yet effective enough for him to be proud of his growing collection. "My first mount was a Blue Jay [*Cyanocitta cristata*]; it was far from perfect, but the work steadily improved," he wrote, adding, "To begin with, all my specimens were mounted with glass eyes and wired to perches, or dressed-up bases. In due course quite a collection resulted, with wide dispersal throughout the house; later they were housed in a large glass-fronted cabinet."[22]

As his taxidermy skills developed, Dewey occasionally took on paid freelance work for sportsmen. Among the birds he mounted for others were a "Snowy Owl [*Bubo scandiacus*], Goshawk [*Accipiter gentilis*], Prairie Grouse [of the family *Tympanuchus*] and well-plumaged ducks."

While other farm boys shot cottontail rabbits with their .22 rifles, or snared them with fine brass wire,[23] Dewey studied the creatures through his binoculars. One day, while alone, he found a cottontail's ground nest in a strawberry patch. The berries were just about ripe and the nest contained several young rabbits. Dewey noted that "the mother was rather nervous and somewhat excited as it hopped here and there among the vegetation." Dewey left that family in peace; but he later caught another cottontail in a box trap and kept it alive to study its habits. "It was an interesting pet that consumed considerable green stuff like lettuce, turnip tops, etc.," he noted.

By the fall of 1911, as a result of the combination of study and his field activities, Dewey had begun to accept that his future career should be bound up some way in ornithology and mammalogy. He was then eighteen years old. The man who would one day be recognized as one of Canada's foremost naturalists was beginning to emerge. In the meantime, he continued to study birds. Unlike most budding ornithologists, however, Dewey never felt the need or wish to build a personal collection of bird's eggs: an attitude which he said persisted throughout his life. Professionally, of course, once he later established himself on the staff of the National Museum in Ottawa, he collected eggs from a large number of species for that august body.

Earlier in 1911 Dewey's sister, Edith, had fallen in love with a local man, William East. After they married, in late December that year, the couple moved west to Strathcona, Alberta, on the south bank of the North Saskatchewan River, opposite Edmonton. That migration precipitated a new upheaval in the Soper family. Edmonton and Strathcona were experiencing a real estate and building boom. Edmonton had been growing steadily for many years. Since the railway had arrived on its doorstep in 1902, the population had increased enormously and the town had spread out along the river and farther to the north.

Although there had been two fur-trading forts roughly on the site of present-day Edmonton in the late eighteenth century, the development of the future city is said to have begun in 1871 when Edmonton was incorporated as a village. In 1892 the village officially became a town and elected its first mayor. Twelve years later, Edmonton had grown into a city, and in 1905 was named as the capital of the newly created province of Alberta.

Nearby Strathcona was first settled by Europeans in 1891. For many years a young but strong rival to Edmonton's commercial status, Strathcona became a city in 1907. Strathcona and Edmonton then amalgamated under the City of Edmonton name on February 1, 1912. That same year, the Alberta Legislature Building, the provincial parliament, was erected at 97th Avenue and 108th Street, overlooking the North Saskatchewan River. Built in the Beaux Art style, it is a magnificent example of Canadian architecture, reminiscent of some of the stateliest of European buildings. The High Level

Bridge was under construction in 1912, too. It was completed later in the year, providing access to the downtown core via the Canadian Pacific Railway for the first time.[24]

With so much expansion in one area, the restless Joseph Soper saw opportunities afresh for himself and his sons in the building trade. With some persuasive assistance from Edith and William, Joseph made up his mind to follow his daughter and son-in-law to the West. In March 1912 the Soper family auctioned off their farm implements and livestock and prepared to move again.

2

Into a Western Wonderland

Joseph Soper soon found construction work in Edmonton and persuaded Dewey to work with him. As an apprentice homebuilder, the nineteen-year-old's wage would be thirty cents per hour — half that of a journeyman carpenter.

Although building houses in Edmonton and Strathcona was a far cry from Dewey's passionate interest in nature, he proved to be good at construction and enjoyed the work. The long hours he spent toiling on building sites and learning the trade would stand him in good stead later. For Dewey, though, the employment was really a means to an obvious end — the procurement of money to further his wildlife studies. Consequently, he never wrote about his construction work, but did keep a few photographs. Subsequent construction jobs, after he completed his apprenticeship, when he bought land and built houses on a speculative basis for himself, financed his continuing education as well as some of his expeditions, and gave him a good stake for the future.

Dewey was too excited by the birdwatching opportunities offered by the wide open spaces of Alberta to spend much time looking at the plethora of construction sites on both sides of the North Saskatchewan River. Most of his waking hours, when he wasn't at work, that spring, summer, and fall were spent exploring the surrounding countryside. He used up a lot of those off-duty hours at McKernan's Lake,[1] which he described as "A big slough-like body of water." The roughly thirty-acre lake stood a short distance south of the Soper home on University Avenue and was accessible by tram as well as on foot. In winter it froze completely and was a popular open-air ice-skating and curling venue.

For Dewey, in 1912 and 1913, McKernan's Lake was a naturalist's paradise in spring, summer, and autumn. He remembered the lake being "rich in native ducks, grebes, black terns and other species," and he noted that "it offered a prime opportunity for an initial study of western water birds at close range — vastly superior to any of my previous contacts with waterfowl."[2]

In the middle of that first idyllic Albertan summer, Dewey used his carpentry skills to build a small flat-bottomed rowboat to help him get closer to birds on the lake. Sculling quietly and almost always alone, he studied their movements and their nests. He sketched them and he photographed them. He admitted that "[the] hours passed all too swiftly in that magic environment."

In late autumn, as the temperatures dropped and the threat of snow loomed, most building work ceased for the duration of winter. Dewey went back to trapping to earn an income. He set up a trapline along the south bank of the North Saskatchewan River and south along Whitemud Creek, primarily for weasels (genus *Mustela*), with a wide swing back via a string of sloughs on the upper plains for muskrats (*Ondatra zibethicus*). He estimated the line required him to walk fifteen miles each day. Along Whitemud Creek he discovered several hundred hares (*Lepus americanus americanus*, or American varying hare) occupying an area of approximately thirty acres. For trappers, Dewey included, hares were considered a scourge, as they sprung traps set for much more valuable fur-bearing creatures.

In spite of the proliferation of hares, November and December yielded good catches until the real cold set in just before Christmas. Dewey then lifted his traps and spent the remainder of the winter studying and mounting specimens for his private collection. When the weather co-operated, he still went out on birdwatching treks, as evidenced by his report of witnessing a bird chase:

> I was snowshoeing through a beautiful belt of brushy woodlands that usually supported a pretty fair population of winter birds and an occasional weasel and Red squirrel. My attention was presently drawn to two birds, one of which was in hot pursuit of a smaller species. Upon closer scrutiny I soon discovered that a Northern Shrike [*Lanius excubitor*] was trying to catch a Black-capped Chickadee [*Poecile atricapillus*].[3]

Dewey followed as the birds zigzagged through the trees, with the chickadee maintaining its lead into the open. "The pace lasted for a while longer in the furious pursuit then the chickadee darted into an especially dense stand of low shrubbery." With some satisfaction, Dewey noted that the shrike then gave up the chase and the chickadee lived to forage for its own food for another day.

With evident reluctance, Dewey buckled on his tool belt and returned to the building sites in the spring of 1913 when construction resumed after the winter. Happy though he undoubtedly was as a carpenter and builder, the creatures of the wild continued to call him, and the calls were getting louder. Dewey answered at every possible moment. In a brief unpublished article he wrote, "Trying to make a living definitely interfered with birdwatching and doing some collecting for the cabinet."

As an adjunct to his collecting and studying, he took up photography, spending fifty dollars of his earnings on a new camera.[4] He was quickly rewarded by having a photograph of a least flycatcher (*Empidonax minimus*), including nest and eggs, published in the *Family Herald and Weekly Star*'s Natural History Club[5] section, along with his essay on the subject, in late summer or early autumn.

3

First Expedition: Into the Foothills of the Rockies

As with most Canadian provinces and territories, Alberta covers a lot of ground. It stretches 765 miles from the common border with the United States on latitude 49, all the way to the Northwest Territories at latitude 60, and 413 miles from east to west. The province covers 255,285 square miles.

Alberta is a land of great rivers: the Peace and Athabasca flow north to spill their waters into the Arctic Ocean as the northern extremity of the mighty Mackenzie River; the North and South Saskatchewan rivers flow out of the Rocky Mountain glaciers to cross the province and irrigate its farmlands en route to Saskatchewan and Manitoba.

Along Alberta's eastern boundary, where it makes the transition into Saskatchewan, the land is flat — wide open prairie farmland. By contrast, on its western side, where it shares a substantial part of the Rocky Mountains with British Columbia, it is decorated with high granite peaks. Mount Columbia, in the southwest, is the highest, reaching up to 12,294 feet.[1] The mountains then, as now, were home to many species of wildlife. Dewey knew about them but, not having had the opportunity so far to explore the mountains, he had never encountered those creatures in the wild.

For some time he had been thinking of expanding his animal studying horizons farther to the west from Edmonton. In particular, he wanted to go exploring in the foothills of those mighty Rocky Mountains. A chance meeting with Jack Coker, an old acquaintance and fellow wilderness wanderer from Ontario, gave Dewey the opportunity he required. After visiting each other a few times, Dewey suggested an extended hunting trip to the West. Coker agreed immediately. They planned to travel by train to Hinton and have their outfit transported to their intended campsite by pack horses.

"Our chief concern in the venture was to simply enjoy wilderness life and adventure. However, in order to pay expenses, and considerably more, if possible, we went fully equipped to take all the fur-bearers that we could."[2]

Dewey was certainly capable of handling the planned adventure. He was a lean, muscled young man of five foot, nine inches tall and weighing about 165 pounds.[3] The two young men quit their jobs early in October and began the exciting task of putting together their "outfit," the equipment and basic food supplies they would need. Considering the apparently casual rationale for the trek, the expedition was, in reality, a serious undertaking. Once

A collection of Dewey's hunting, trapping, and camping equipment beside the family garage in Strathcona, Edmonton, 1913.

accumulated, their total outfit weighed in at about eight hundred pounds. The food alone weighed 525 pounds. Dewey's list[4] is detailed:

Flour	150 lbs	Sugar	40 lbs
Cornmeal	50 lbs	Black tea	6 lbs
Baking powder	9 lbs	Raisins	6 lbs
Fine salt	20 lbs	Rice	12 lbs
Bacon	35 lbs	Maple syrup	20 lbs
Salt pork	15 lbs	Black pepper	1 tin
Lard	6 lbs	Ginger	1 tin
Butter	18 lbs	Mixed pickles	3 jars
White beans	60 lbs	Saccharine tablets	150
Pot barley	12 lbs	Soap, toilet and laundry	10 bars
Split peas	10 lbs	Matches	5 boxes
Dried apples	20 lbs	Candles	10 dozen
Dried prunes	25 lbs		

On top of that load, they each had "a waterproof match box, sheath knife, pocket compass, light belt axe and a heavy 4-pound chopping axe." Toiletries and a first-aid kit added to the weight in their backpacks. In addition, they would carry steel traps, "cord and wire to make snares, and a few bottles of Funsten's[5] animal lures." To keep warm at night, they each had two double blankets: "genuine 3½ point Hudson's Bay [Company] blankets, of which there is no superior." For protection from the elements they added large sheets of waterproof canvas and a light tent. Dewey listed their armaments: "Jack was equipped with a .303 Ross rifle and a Stevens 10-inch .22 pistol, while I took a .30-30 Winchester carbine and a Stevens pistol the same as Jack's." Primarily used to shoot game birds, such as grouse, for meals, they wore their pistols, cowboy style, in leather holsters on their belts.

Raised on the relatively flat farmlands of southern Ontario and later living and working on the prairies, Dewey had never seen a real mountain range, but he was keen to do so. He was not disappointed: "As the train rolled around a curve, just east of Hinton, I looked upon the glorious Rocky Mountains for the first time in my life. It would be hard to describe the thrill of those moments as the great peaks, white with snow, soared high against the blue of the sky — no doubt one of the most sublime spectacles in the world."[6]

In Hinton, Dewey and Jack hired a local outfitter named Ernie Harrison to supply six pack and saddle horses for the trek into the interior. That cost them forty dollars. To avoid having to pay more for two extra saddle horses, they chose to walk with the pack animals. At first, after crossing the Athabasca River on a CNR construction ferry, they followed the Grande Prairie Trail northward. About mid-morning on the second day the trail split. The Grande Prairie Trail continued north and the Soper–Coker pack train turned north-northeast, roughly following Fish Creek. Dewey described the ups and downs of that day:

> The country here was very wild and rugged. The trail followed a tortuous route up and down hills, over stones and gravel, through grassy meadows and over uplands of coniferous forest and ghastly areas of considerable windfall that had a few years back been swept by a forest fire. On several occasions we came pretty close to Fish Creek.... It was only twelve to fifteen feet in width, but in most places fairly deep. Twice during the day it was necessary to ford this stream where the trail beyond was situated on more favourable terrain, and all steep climbing was avoided.[7]

They camped that night beside the forks of Fish Creek and the Hay River (later to be known as the Wildhay River). The Hay was considerably wider than Fish Creek and, as Dewey saw it, "Clear, cold and fast with many rapids." They would learn just how cold the next morning when they had to ford the river twice. Dewey and Jack removed boots and socks, rolled their pants up above their knees, and waded across with the horses. By the time they reached the opposite bank their feet and legs were numb with cold. Clean socks and brisk walking soon generated warmth and comfort again.

Dewey's notes from the expedition are rich in wildlife sightings. Always observant, on the walk in he counted a variety of hares, caught a glimpse of a weasel, and noted occasional Canada jays (*Perisoreus canadensis*) and

First Expedition: Into the Foothills of the Rockies

Hudsonian chickadees (*Penthestes hudsonicus hudsonicus*). Shortly before reaching the site of their planned expedition base camp, he saw his first hawk owl (*Surnia ulula*) and immediately added it to his collection with the aid of his pistol. Soon after, they reached their destination:

> At 11:00 a.m. we swung around a bend along the river, through a heavy local growth of spruce and stopped inside a beautiful natural clearing of about 400 square yards on the edge of the river. It was here that Harrison was heading for, as the place was highly favourable for the erection of a log cabin; medium-sized spruces for the walls were in good supply, dry wood existed in abundance, and, of course, we had some of the world's finest water right at our door.[8]

While Harrison organized his horses for the return journey to Hinton, Dewey sat down to write a letter as their outfitter was preparing to leave them. He obviously had a strong connection to his parents and that is reflected in his writings. Close to forty miles north and west of Hinton, and cognizant of the fact that he would not be able to communicate with his family for more than two months, and knowing they would worry about him, Dewey wrote the second of two letters sent from the last semblance of civilization he and Jack would see for many weeks. The letter is full of news about their trek upcountry from Hinton and finishes on a warm note:

> The packer is waiting for Jack and I to finish our letters home and then he will start back with all the horses for Hinton. So I will have to close for this time. Much as I dislike to do so. You will see us about Christmas time, I expect; possibly a few days before. I will have lots to tell you when I get home; there is little yet as compared with that which is still to come! With the best of fond regards to all.
> Your loving son, Dewey.[9]

For the next eight to ten weeks the two young men would be on their own with no access to the outside world without a long cross-country walk. Daunting though the prospect might have been to some extent, they were excited and ready for an exceptional wildlife experience. As Harrison and the horses left, Dewey noted, "Our last link with civilization disappeared around a bend in the trail. Our isolation was now complete and in our present mood we were thoroughly ready for it."

Mindful of the immediate need for shelter and warmth, their first task was to erect a lean-to tent, the floor of which they carpeted with a thick layer of soft spruce boughs. Between them they cut a pile of firewood large enough to last for a few days, built a fire in front of their camp, and settled in under a full moon. They could hear foxes "yipping across the river on a ridge to the north" and a few hares hopped hesitantly into the clearing. Dewey was in his element. He wrote with all the fervour of his youth, "There is a tingling excitement in a wilderness night like this."[10]

In contrast to the wonders of their initial night outdoors at their chosen camp, the first full day alone was a miserable one due to heavy rain. It started well enough with a walk along the river during which they noted many signs of fur-bearing mammals. The rain started in mid-morning and turned into a downpour that lasted until late afternoon, when it turned to snow. Fortunately, despite the dreadful weather, they were able to keep the fire going and derive a modicum of heat from it. They spent an uncomfortable and restless second night, though Dewey's laconic comment about it hardly does justice to the discomfort. He wrote, "The situation was not of the best."

The lean-to was a temporary measure, nothing more. The plans had always included building a log cabin at the outset and living in relative comfort. After a cold and snowy night, followed by a hot breakfast, they stayed warm by cutting and trimming logs for the cabin walls. By the end of the day they had cut forty-six logs plus trimmed the requisite wood for both a window and a door frame. The clearing that was to be their home until sometime in December had been enlarged and the detritus of a miniature logging operation lay scattered over its area: "Spruce boughs lay in every direction, while the air was filled with their fragrance."

Dewey and Jack were extremely happy with the results of their first day's endeavours, but there was much more to do before they could call the

First Expedition: Into the Foothills of the Rockies

planned cabin a home, albeit temporary. It took them eight days of hard work over long hours before they were able to move in and make themselves comfortable. They were just in time. Soon the temperature dropped and ice began to form on the river "about three-quarters of an inch thick extending out from the bank for about six feet."

Dewey showed off his building skills by fabricating a masonry stove for cooking and to heat the cabin, mixing the mortar from clay and wood ash. He noted that "the stove performed in fine style."

The log cabin Jack Coker (left) and Dewey Soper (right) built near the Wildhay River on the Rocky Mountain foothills expedition, October–December 1913.

With the cabin feeling like home, they chopped enough firewood to keep the stove fed for two months, and piled it against the outside walls. Finally they were ready to begin hunting, trapping, and exploring. Snow fell, and soon their wilderness was covered in a layer of white. Many species had already gone into hibernation for the winter but there were more than enough remaining alert and foraging for food to keep Dewey and Jack busy. The snow, too, made their work easier, as tracks were much more visible.

Although neither of them was particularly religious, Dewey and Jack Coker took most Sundays off from hard work during the expedition, including while building the cabin. When possible, they reserved Sundays for taking hot baths, shaving, donning clean clothes, writing their journals, reading, and baking squaw bread[11] (also known as "Indian maiden bread"). The latter was a skill that Dewey had learned from Harrison on the trek in from Hinton.

Despite knowing only too well the risks involved in being alone, the two separated for a day, setting out their traplines in different directions. Jack followed the river to the east, setting lynx traps. Dewey meandered west across a meadow and through stands of spruce, making ten sets for weasels before returning to the cabin. Dewey commented regularly on the large numbers of hares in the vicinity. He and Jack shot a few of them with their pistols to use as bait for lynx in the steel traps and snares, and they almost certainly used them for food. When they checked their sets the next day they were disappointed to discover both traplines to be empty. Rather than setting more traps, they went hunting instead. Jack collected two muskrats and a couple of spruce grouse (*Dendragapus canadensis*).

Now they began trapping in earnest. With Jack following one riverbank and Dewey working on the opposite, they set long lines. Dewey recorded "fifteen sets for lynx, ten for ermine, one for mink and one for fox." That day he collected two ermine (*Mustela erminea*) from his earlier sets. He described them as "blood-thirsty little creatures." The ermine, relatively common in the region, were already dressed in their winter whites for camouflage, with only a black tip on their tails for contrast. On that foray, while preparing a trap for an otter (*Lontra canadensis*), Dewey was astounded to discover a balsam poplar (*Populus balsamifera*) twenty-six inches in diameter which had been felled by beavers. It was, he said, the largest tree cut by beavers that he saw throughout the foothills expedition.

Jack managed to wound a mature red fox (*Vulpes vulpes*), which still found the strength to elude him for a while and hide among some rocks. He found it, dragged it out, and finished it off with a blow to the head. That fox was the most valuable pelt they had collected to that point.

As the days went on they often found hares in traps, occasionally even blue jays, where they had hoped to see ermine or lynx. Dewey did manage to bag an otter with a clean shot from his .30-30 carbine. At that time, otter fur was a valuable entity, so when he saw it out on the river ice eating a wild duck, he was elated to make the kill. Getting to it was another matter. Dewey had no choice but to undress and wade out up to his waist in icy water to retrieve it. He did not enjoy the experience but was excited to have the otter and, being young and fit, he soon warmed up with exercise.

Gradually, as day succeeded day, without the pair really profiting much from their endeavours, they began to accept that the local Mountain Cree[12] had effectively trapped out the area as far as valuable fur-bearers were concerned, except for the ubiquitous ermine. That fairly obvious fact did not deter them. They continued to extend and maintain their traplines and occasionally discovered spectacular results.

Jack came back into camp one morning with the news that he had found a big golden eagle (*Aquila chrysaetos*) caught in one of their fox traps not far away. He had hurried back to tell Dewey in case he wanted a photograph. When they reached the trap they saw that the eagle was only caught by two toes and hardly hurt at all. Dewey took his photographs, Jack released the bird, and it spiralled quickly into the air before flying south. Dewey wrote of the eagle with even greater than usual enthusiasm: "What a noble and majestic creation!" One day later they caught their first fox in a trap.

A contingent of Mountain Cree rode past the cabin on pack horses about that time. Unfortunately for the young trappers, the horses accidently sprung all the red fox traps along that trail, but, as Dewey gratefully noted, "The men were honest enough that none of our double-sprung No. 2 traps were stolen." Resetting the line took only a minimal amount of time for Dewey and Jack.

There were other Natives trapping in the general area. One built a line of lynx snares, with one set less than fifty yards from the cabin. Dewey and Jack recognized the less than subtle hint that they were living on someone else's traditional hunting grounds. There wasn't much they could do about it, however, as the cabin couldn't be moved, so they continued as before.

The scarcity of fur-bearing animals began to worry both men. The other trappers in the area obviously had some impact but not enough to completely explain the lack. Dewey wrote in his journal, "There was great cold and silence on the land." After just over a month, they had only collected furs from twenty ermine, nineteen muskrats, two foxes, one mink, and one otter.

It was abundantly clear that the advice received in Hinton was not as accurate as they had believed. Moving out of the area, however, was never really an option. That would have meant abandoning the cabin and building another one somewhere else. They simply did not have time for that; instead, they persevered, and found their tally of muskrats and ermine slowly increasing each day.

Tracks of deer and moose often marked the snow, though Dewey and Jack never did see any at close enough quarters for a shot. That in itself was not a problem. They always had fresh meat for the pot due to the abundance of spruce grouse and hares.

When Jack shot a pileated woodpecker (*Dryocopus pileatus*) with his .22 pistol, Dewey was truly happy. It was the first of the species to join his bird collection, though preserving the specimens was not easy. The correspondence course he had taken in taxidermy before leaving Ontario now paid off. "All I could do with the bird skins was to temporarily salt them and pack them flat in a box until I arrived home; then I cleaned the skins and made them up into full mounts ..."

Most days they walked anywhere from twelve to twenty miles checking their traps, usually getting back to the cabin by about 5:00 p.m. In spite of the snow, freezing temperatures, and the distances, they seemed to find the almost daily treks invigorating. Dewey said, "[the long walks] always put us in fine fettle for a bountiful supper."

Being so far from help, the two men had to be careful not to get hurt. They did not always succeed, and this was early winter, with temperatures mostly well below zero. On the edge of a lake, Jack broke through the ice and submerged his feet and legs to his knees. Dewey quickly built a roaring fire to dry Jack's clothes and to warm him, but the trousers were frozen stiff by the time it was hot enough. On the same day, Dewey froze his ears and suffered greatly as they swelled up to way beyond their natural size and proved impossible to sleep on due to the pain. He also sprained his foot and had to remain at the cabin for a few days to rest it while Jack tended the traplines. Typically of Dewey, he did not waste his time while alone, nor did he do much resting. On the first day by himself at the cabin, apart from preparing meals, he washed and mended clothes, wrote his journals, and split wood. Then, thinking of the near future when they would have to find a way to

First Expedition: Into the Foothills of the Rockies

transport their outfit, furs, and specimens back to Hinton, he put his carpentry skills to use and built a sled. Six feet long and fourteen inches wide, it would suffice to help haul their belongings back to the railway.

Jack returned in the late afternoon and was pleased to see the result of Dewey's supposed resting. They did no more work that day. Instead, they tested the sled in the snow, dragging each other around the clearing on it. It is unlikely that the horseplay did much good for Dewey's injured foot, but the rough handling of the sled showed it to be sturdy enough for the job it was designed to do. With November rapidly coming to a close there is a sense of urgency in Dewey's notes. The traplines were not productive, especially the lynx and red fox lines. As a result, they lifted those lines and set new ones, concentrating on ermine now as the most likely to be caught, due to their abundance.

Meeting up with a Native (probably Cree) named Martani they had encountered before, Dewey and Jack arranged to trade all their steel traps for an equivalent value in furs when they were ready to leave. That sensible arrangement guaranteed them an unspecified number of furs and probably saved them weight at the same time.

In early December, both needing a change of scenery and activities, they embarked on a sled journey toward the Rockies. The plan was to be away four or five days, man-hauling the sled beside the Hay River where the terrain was level and on its ice elsewhere. Nature now turned against them. Just when they needed the cold to maintain crispness in the snow, the weather became mild. By mid-afternoon the snow had become soft; in consequence the sled became harder to drag as it settled into the near slush. Anxious to reach the mountains, they worked together, struggling hard to keep the sled moving. By dark they were appreciably closer to their goal, but not close enough. To add to the difficulty, a Chinook (a warm dry wind off the Rockies) rolled in from the west overnight. At daybreak the ice on the Hay River was covered in water as far toward the mountains as they could see. Hoping for another change and a quick freeze, they stayed put — Dewey quite happy to watch birds and try a little hunting. Even that was not so successful. By the end of the day they had only shot two spruce grouse, both of which went into a pot for stew.

Although their expedition farther into the mountains was proving unlikely to be successful, the resilience of the two young men shines through Dewey's notes. After dark they listened to an owl hooting from somewhere on the opposite bank of the Hay River. They cooked up a large meal over a big, hot log fire. Sated, they reminisced about their experiences, entertained each other with tunes on a harmonica, and listened to the gentle calls of nocturnal creatures.

The temperature did drop a little overnight, but it was not enough to freeze the water covering the river ice upstream. Continuing was virtually impossible. There was no choice but to return to the cabin. Dewey wrote a colourful description of that early morning:

> The winter dawn was a thing of gorgeous quality; the air was clear as crystal; the spruces were of the deepest green; underfoot the river ice was pearly white and bluish-green and the arch of the sky could not have been more blue. The east was seamed and splashed with fiery crimson, lilac and orange in softest harmony — the colours often reflected with spectacular effect on the river ice over which we travelled.[13]

After no more than three miles of this magnificence they reached a stretch where the Hay River had overflowed far beyond its banks. As it was impossible to drag the loaded sled through the flooded bushland, they had no choice but to wade through the water flowing over the river ice. Their boots and socks were soon soaked through and their feet chilled. At midday they built a fire and dried everything, but that proved to be nothing more than a temporary respite. Seven more times that long afternoon they had to take to the more than ankle-deep water on the river ice to avoid large flooded areas of adjacent land. By the time they reached the cabin, after travelling many miles with dangerously cold and wet feet, they were worn out. Still they had work to do. Dewey remarked, "It called for real will power and determination to crawl about and get the fire going, carry water and get something to eat."

As the traplines produced fewer and fewer fur-bearing catches, there was little game for the pot. Provisions were running low. With this in mind, they agreed to continue trapping for ten more days, mostly in pursuit of the easier to catch ermine, and then begin their long trek back to Hinton. They snared

First Expedition: Into the Foothills of the Rockies

a few, but not enough to warrant staying on longer. On Monday December 15, Martani and his son came to collect the steel traps and hand over furs in exchange. It was almost time to leave.

After a final night in their cabin, Dewey and Jack ate a large breakfast in front of a roaring fire — the last real warmth they would have for many days. Outside the air was cold and crisp. Snow was hard-packed on the ground. Together they carefully loaded the sled and tied everything down under a tarpaulin. Leaving the fire to burn itself out, one of them closed the cabin door for the last time. Side by side, each harnessed to the sled by a rope, they began sliding the heavy outfit to the southwest.

Dewey had desperately wanted to trap at least one mink. More than two months after the start of the expedition, he still had not achieved that goal. Some weeks before they had set three mink traps along the creek leading to Fish Lake. They now retrieved them as they passed and were overjoyed to find a large mink in one of them. Jack skinned it that evening and stretched the pelt onto a board while Dewey baked squaw bread.

The nights by now were so cold that the only way the two could keep from freezing in their sleep was to awake regularly and pile more wood on the nearby open fire. By morning their blankets were covered in thick frost and far from comfortable. Morning routine now demanded that they stoke up the fire, get their bodies and extremities thoroughly warmed, and eat a hot meal before setting out as soon as it was light enough. Dewey referred to the morning activities on the southbound trail with casual understatement: "It may be said that breaking camp in excessively cold weather is rather trying, as everything is too cold to handle, but one can always warm hands and feet at the fire just before leaving."[14]

December 17 was a difficult day. It was bitterly cold and snow lay thick on the ground. Beyond the lake's southern shore they had hoped to follow the frozen creek for a while. In any event, it was too narrow and winding; overhanging willows added to the obstacles. In an attempt to speed up their journey, the only option was to move into the forest and force an alternative route. When the trees thinned out into open meadows of snow, the icy wind became the enemy, punishing them badly. They stopped at midday, scavenged for dry wood, built a fire, and ate a hot meal. The afternoon, they knew, would be unpleasant.

It was worse than they expected: "The trail became so difficult that we could not pull the whole load on the sled and were obliged to relay with half loads; this was all very slow and laborious, as it entailed three times as much travel for every mile of advance."[15]

The following day was no better. Once again they were forced to haul half loads using the relay system. The temperature had dropped to around forty below zero and a wind made it feel so much worse. During the morning they found it necessary to stop and light a small fire to warm up their hands and feet before they could continue. Later, as they ate lunch, Dewey heard the distant moan of a locomotive whistle to the south. That mournful sound, harbinger of civilization, spurred them on.

Late in the afternoon they traversed a small frozen lake without having to relay part of the load. That, too, gave them renewed energy. As darkness fell they camped on the far side of the lake and built a roaring fire, which they kept burning all night long to prevent themselves from freezing. Dewey noted, "By this time we were fully impressed with the fact that it was no sinecure camping out in the open with only a shelter tent and open fire and blankets, and devoid of warm fur parkas and fur mitts. It was very evident that we were not properly equipped to meet this intensity of cold."[16] It was not a mistake Dewey would ever make again. In the morning, he reported, "the cold had a sinister intensity that was hard to overcome. The trees were cracking with the frost."

Ill-equipped though they were, they had to keep moving to survive — and they had to move fast. Their physical fitness and mental toughness got them through. At midday they crossed a ridge, and there in the distance was the welcome sight of the Athabasca River. Being on snow-covered land, as opposed to frozen lakes, meant they were still relaying loads and getting tired of the additional exercise. Unfortunately, they could not afford to leave anything behind, so they persevered with all loads and reached the river just before darkness fell. When they made camp that evening in a grove of spruce trees, they had all their goods with them, and they were satisfied that they had left nothing behind but their footprints and the tracks of the sled's runners: a stellar achievement. Their remaining food supplies were down to beans, some squaw bread, and a little bacon. With darkness the temperature dropped even lower. As with the previous night, they huddled around a fire in their blankets to keep a semblance of warmth in their bodies.

First Expedition: Into the Foothills of the Rockies

They had reached the river; Hinton was not far away — no more than a few hours. There was a problem, however. The construction ferry they had used at the beginning of the expedition did not operate in winter: the ice made sure of that. Unfortunately, the Athabasca River was not yet completely frozen. Although ice stretched out from opposing banks, a wide-open lead existed down the middle. To attempt a crossing there would be suicidal. Yet, to survive, they had to find a way to cross the river.

Leaving their outfit at the camp, Jack went east, following the downstream flow. Dewey walked west, upstream. Jack was disappointed in that he never found an ice bridge across the river. Dewey's quest, however, proved more successful. About a mile upstream he found a location where the ice stretched from shore to shore, and it was thick enough to support their weight and that of the loaded sled. By one o'clock they were camped in a grove of spruce trees near the Hinton railway station. After a quick meal they shaved and cleaned themselves up enough to head into town and meet people again.

The next train for Edmonton was due to come through Hinton at midnight. With hours to spare, Dewey and Jack moved their outfit to the railway station and stacked it beside the track. They spent the evening having dinner at the hotel, then chatting with men playing billiards in the warmth of the pool room. In 1912, Hinton was not a regular stop on the railway line. Boarding a train meant signalling it to stop. As midnight approached, the owner of the pool hall loaned Dewey and Jack a lantern to wave at the train as it rumbled in from the west. When the locomotive steamed to a halt, they hastily tossed their outfit into the baggage car and climbed in beside it. Within a few hours they were in the comfort of the Soper home and regaling the family with their adventures.

4

Ontario Again

As a direct result of the Rocky Mountain foothills expedition, Dewey had his second short article published. "Bird Notes from Western Alberta"[1] appeared in the *Family Herald and Weekly Star* early in 1914. He also showed an entrepreneurial bent by opening a small taxidermy business, which helped bring in a little money, as there were no building jobs available. For a year or so Dewey had also been studying piano. As the winter drew on, he practised whenever he could. Playing the piano was a comforting pastime for when he could not get outdoors. There wasn't much else for him to do anyway. In 1914 the Edmonton building boom came to an abrupt end. Men walked the streets begging for work. No one had money to pay for luxuries such as taxidermy. Through a friend, Dewey secured a position as delivery boy for a grocer — at twelve dollars per week.

The First World War broke out in August.[2] By then the employment situation in Alberta had become hopeless. Joseph Soper decided to return to Ontario with his family and go back to farming — the only sure way to make any living. Dewey, twenty-one that year, chose to go with them as his father's partner.

The family left Alberta in September, with most of them crossing the country directly to Guelph. Here Joseph had rented a house while he looked for a suitable farm. Dewey stopped off at Broadview, Saskatchewan, en route to do some carpentry work for his rancher friend Dave Bettschen. That job lasted almost two months and gave Dewey much needed funds to help his family. Winter was coming and there was still no work.

Impressed by the poetry of Eric A. Darling, especially his lyrical piece, "The Old Canoe,"[3] about this time Dewey began scribbling his thoughts in the form of prose poems. At first they were extremely amateurish, yet they have a certain appeal as they, sometimes clumsily, relate his experiences. "The Trail,"[4] dated 1914, is almost certainly his homage to the Rocky Mountain foothills expedition of 1912 with Jack Coker:

Dewey became an accomplished pianist after practising for several hours each day. He also demonstrated pianos and was, briefly, a salesman for a piano manufacturer.

> As we bare our chests to the cold and storm
> Tighten our belts on the hunger trail;
> Under the glowing moon our sleeping forms
> Find peace far beyond the city's turmoil,
> Off by the streams and forest with insidious lure
> Called by the wilderness solemn enticements and beauty
> We gladly enter the great solitudes for joy and freedom
> Of the Creator's great masterpiece, what a home for wildlife!
>
> To the foot-wide trails we hike by foot or saddle horse
> Threading the valleys and high divides — such flawless scenery,
> And past beetling cliffs and dizzy drops on risky slopes

Ontario Again

Where but one slip in a bad place and fate decides the future.
But what a thrilling grandeur prevails in the awesome vastness
Where the trail gradually unfolds past crag and spur
And one presently thinks of preparing camp for another night.
If it is cold and windy, a roaring fire is badly needed.

In the grey, cold dawn camp is rather cheerless and frosty,
And not pleasant in turning out of the warm blankets
And getting into frigid clothes and stiff shoe-packs —
    another day!
A grateful fire, then a sourdough's enticing meal of bacon,
A stack of flapjacks, butter, syrup and plenty of hot coffee.
This is good survival fare on the long and picturesque trails,
If on foot, the pack is sure to gall and a noon halt is heaven.
Now we are in the spell of the primeval forest that once
    filled dreams
And our bodies are now hard as nails and crying for action.

By day and night we are truly guided right with charts
Through grasslands, river valleys and the great dim forests
Where numberless secrets are, as yet, well hidden away
But how good to thread the lonely forest aisles hunted by
    marten,
And the compass keeps telling us we are not going astray.
The trails are the ones we wanted leading to the lands of
    dreams
With the sincere hopes that this can sometime be repeated.

Around the same time, obviously missing Alberta, he wrote "The West,"[5] the first half of which expresses his feelings well:

Adieu my fair expansive West
So often it possesses one's memory

That it cannot be less than the best
For a fairer land would be hard to imagine.
It is not constructed for weaklings
But for men of stubborn will and aspirations.
Vast riches can be contrived from its plains
It's smiling hills, ridges, prairies and meadows;
On and on through forests and muskegs to the Rockies,
And how haunting are those sublime snow peaks
That one never tires of gazing on hour after hour.

Away from the attempts at poetry, Dewey's field notes from late January to the end of July 1915 are filled with brief glimpses of his mostly solo wanderings in search of specimens for his collection.[6] Meticulous to a fault, he recorded each sighting. None were too insignificant for him. The snow was close to knee-deep on January 27, but that didn't stop Dewey from exploring along the frozen Speed River a couple of miles southwest of Preston. He didn't see much wildlife that day, except a flock of redpolls dining on cedar berries, and the tracks of an ermine.

Two days later he went out again, this time on skis. It was windy and very cold and, again, little to be seen except "an English sparrow impaled on a thorn bush, no doubt the work of a shrike." He also recorded a few red squirrels foraging for sustenance among the cedars beside the river.

February dawned with an ice storm that coated the trees with delicate crystals, bending the branches down and turning the landscape into glistening surrealistic patterns of white and grey. The weather apparently kept Dewey indoors most of the time because, unusual for him, he failed to make any notes between February 1 and February 8. When he did get out again, he buckled on his skis and glided around the meadows and through small pockets of trees for several hours. His trained eyes often discerned minute tracks in the snow: ermine, squirrels, and wood mice. Generally, though, there was little activity. He wrote, "It is really quite notable how empty of wildlife the woods can be at this time of the year."

When the weather made work in the outdoors impossible, Dewey spent long hours practising the piano; he studied the natural sciences and continued to read books about exploration.

Ontario Again

In mid-March the birds began to reappear. The first skunks came out of hibernation. He caught a female screech owl near a barn and surprised a muskrat swimming in a creek with a trout in its mouth. At this time, Dewey's often sterile notes are coloured with musical descriptions such as the "soft lisping" of golden-crowned kinglets (*Regulus satrapa*); the "nasal yank, yank, yank notes" of white-breasted nuthatches (*Sitta carolinensis*) and the "sweet warblings" of eastern bluebirds (*Sialia sialis*). At the beginning of April, with spring in the air, the Sopers were able to rent a farm a few miles north of Preston, between Kitchener and Guelph.

The Soper home on the farm north of Preston, Ontario, in 1916, with a pear tree in the foreground. The Soper family lived here from 1915 to 1919.

Work on the farm now took up many hours each day, leaving Dewey little time for his nature studies. Joseph was getting old by this time. More and more the responsibility for the hard work fell on Dewey's shoulders. Although he often found farm work laborious, most of the time he was happy enough. His rather selfless stated goal at that juncture was "to make the life of my parents as happy as possible."

Despite the time constraints, he continued with his quest to turn himself into an efficient and professional naturalist. He changed his modus operandi from collecting mammals and birds for mounting and display to dedicating himself to the task of building a private collection. To this end he prepared his specimens to scientific museum standards with accompanying labels and corresponding catalogue entries, and he housed them in proper cabinets with multiple drawers. He noted that the first specimen in the new and much upgraded collection was a male swamp sparrow (*Melospiza georgiana*) he took at Preston on April 26, 1915.

By this time he was communicating, albeit on an irregular basis, with other naturalists, including E.T. Seton,[7] W.E. Saunders,[8] Dr. R.M. Anderson,[9] and P.A. Taverner.[10] He donated study specimens, sometimes requested, often as gifts, to museums and to their staff naturalists.

Throughout the spring and into early summer, Dewey spent as many hours each day collecting as he could. Based on the breadth of his field notes, he probably carried his .22 rifle, telescope or binoculars, and notebooks with him wherever he happened to be working on the farm. It is unlikely that any birds flew over that he did not stop to identify or collect. It is equally unlikely that he could resist stopping work to watch field mice, voles, rabbits, and other small mammals whenever they showed themselves. At that stage in his life, despite the hard work, living on a country farm, with its attendant wild creatures, was rewarding and educational. Each day something would spark his interest:

> May 5, 1915. [His 22nd birthday] Found the nest of a Horned Lark in a meadow; it was located in a small depression in the ground lined with fine dead grass. It measured 2 [inches] deep and 2.5 [inches] wide. It was partly overhung by a tuft of grass and contained four eggs.[11]

> May 14, 1915. Was much interested in watching a pair of chickadees cleaning out a hollow rail in the fence for a nesting site. They were so tame as to allow me to approach within a few feet of them as they worked …[12]

Writing about male bobolinks (*Dolichonyx oryzivorus*) on May 28: "Their rollicking songs over meadows and hayfields are most welcome on these beautiful spring days."[13]

The summer months rolled past and winter returned to carpet the land with snow. Dewey's notations on wildlife observations became fewer and fewer. That situation lasted until summer when, in mid-July 1916, and obviously frustrated, he moaned, "Unfortunately, my time is so taken up with more mundane activities that it has been difficult or practically impossible to pursue zoological collecting and general observations of NATURE which is so dear to my heart. Sometime in the future I expect to be giving my life to this work. At least this is my avowed intention at the present time."[14]

The next entry is dated October 30, and is more upbeat, probably because of the content: "On October 28 a neighbour shot a large female Goshawk while it was attempting to carry off a chicken. I was given this beautiful bird which I mounted instead of making it up as a study skin."[15]

After a long hiatus, in February 1917 the entries in that book resumed, continuing through the spring and summer. That spring Dewey built a canvas-covered canoe, which he named *Wanderlust*. Fifteen feet long with a high

Dewey built this canoe in 1917, named it *Wanderlust*, and first used it on the Grand River, east of Kitchener, Ontario. He later used it on two expeditions on the Ridout River, on the Moon River in the Muskokas, and on rivers and lakes in the Temagami region of northern Ontario.

prow (Ojibway style, he explained), he used the new transport to paddle about on the Grand River and smaller waterways to study the local waterfowl and wading birds. He planned to use the canoe for a much more ambitious venture in northern Ontario as soon as he could arrange time. Until then, apart from exploring local waters by canoe, he also occasionally went on excursions by car with his naturalist friend Will (W.E.) Saunders from London, Ontario.

On October 20, 1917,[16] Dewey and his cousin Herb Allen travelled by train to Ridout in northern Ontario for a late-season wilderness canoe trip. *Wanderlust* went with them: all told, their outfit for a two-week expedition weighed eighty-seven pounds. After a more than twenty-four-hour journey, which included a six-hour stop in Sudbury, they reached Ridout. They went, Dewey wrote, "In search of adventure, wildlife and general allurement of the boreal forest."

When they stepped off the train at Ridout, with night fast approaching, the weather was "cold, sleety rain." Not exactly what they had hoped for. The conditions dampened the enthusiasm of the two young men for a time, but later, while acknowledging the gloomy climate, Dewey wrote, "The scenery was attractive — the rushing rivers, the solemn forests of pine and spruce and the endless timbered hills and ridges, spectacular to some extent. The country is typically boreal and brings to mind the Ojibway Indians, the renowned Hudson [sic] Bay Company and the romantic fur trappers."[17]

The station master took pity on them that night and allowed them to sleep in the waiting room instead of having to make camp in the nearby woods. The morning dawned bright and sunny and the two adventurers were happy to be setting off warm and dry. Had they known what was in store, they might have turned for home on the next southbound train.

For much of the first day Dewey and Herb enjoyed themselves immensely as they paddled along the river. The peacefulness of the wilderness, the calls of the wild creatures, and the beauty of the Ridout's setting soon had them relaxed. Late in the afternoon they began to encounter rocky outcrops. The hills closed in and suddenly they met the first rapid. Up to this time, neither of them had attempted to run whitewater in a boat of any kind. *Wanderlust* helped them run that initial short stretch of turbulence with no problem. Ahead, just around a bend in the river, they could hear another, much wilder torrent. It proved to be far too dangerous for their almost non-existent whitewater skills.

They portaged the complete outfit but managed to hand-line the canoe down to the safety of a large flat rock where they could reload. A series of beaver dams then slowed their progress, making it necessary to half unload the canoe before they could haul it over the biggest ones. As the sun began to set, they could hear the roar of another rapid. That one necessitated a portage of roughly one hundred yards. Another, higher beaver dam caused them to take to the bush. Back on the river, a few more minutes of quiet paddling led them to another rapid. Like the previous one, it was impossible to run. A portage being the only possibility, and night rapidly coming on, they camped beside the head of the rapid to wait for daylight.

That night, their first outdoors on this trip, proved cold, so cold, in fact, that the still water where they had hauled out the canoe had frozen to a quarter of an inch thick by morning. The portage was the longest they had yet taken: it stretched for a few hundred yards to calm water. Later, paddling downstream, Dewey often heard "the broken calls of a Red Squirrel," and spotted a lone chipmunk on the riverbank. Soon the thunder of another rapid announced the next portage. Due to their inexperience, they almost left it too late to get off the river. At the last second Dewey reached up and grabbed an overhanging branch and held on long enough for Herb to get ashore and tie the canoe to a tree. They had come close to disaster and they knew it. An important lesson learned.

Following the rapid, the river began to make sharp turns, which impeded progress even more, as it became necessary to round the bends slowly in case of more whitewater beyond. At mid-morning they reached the final rapid on the Ridout: "This last portage-rapid was the wildest of the lot. The current approached the vital area very casually and then suddenly bursting loose roared madly over boulders and down rocky ledges. The sight was singularly awesome."[18]

The current was too strong for them to hand-line the canoe down to a less turbulent level. That meant it had to be carried along the winding portage route with the other freight. When they relaunched the loaded canoe in a sheltered eddy they were faced with an unusual sight: "The foam danced away from an abrupt falls in wild convolutions that farther down filled the surface of the stream from bank to bank.... As the canoe rammed through the foam it piled up on both sides, got higher and higher until finally ... [it] toppled over into the canoe in big, fluffy heaps ..."[19]

Not long after, *Wanderlust* pointed its high prow out of the Ridout and onto the much wider Wakami River. Now the hills became higher, some rising almost vertically from the river, cloaked in stands of pine, fir, and spruce. Giant boulders often dominated the riverbanks, causing Dewey and Herb to rest their paddles and study them from the canoe. They went ashore at least once on this stretch so Herb could climb a boulder twice his height. The landscape of forest and rocks prompted Dewey to note that the region should be rich in "fur-bearers such as lynx, marten, fisher, mink and weasel." He also imagined it to hold a resident population of black bear and moose.

In the afternoon they entered a lake, which they crossed, aiming for a large island on the opposite shore close to where they expected to find the continuation of the Wakami. The river's new mouth was wide, an estimated two hundred yards, and, to their consternation, was covered in new ice. Late on day two of their expedition their progress was blocked. For the remainder of daylight they paddled around small islands, finding bays frozen over and ice thickening along the shoreline. They walked inland, possibly looking for a way past the ice so they could travel farther. There was no way forward. As the temperature dropped they made camp on the island, and Dewey cooked up a mulligan stew using the meat from a ruffed grouse he had shot the day before as the main ingredient.

A bitterly cold night had Dewey wide awake by 5:00 a.m. and adding fuel to the dying fire. As daylight broke, he saw that a thick mist lay heavy over the lake. When he went to investigate, he found ice. In the night the lake had frozen from one side to the other. Winter had hit suddenly and the camp was some twenty miles from the railway line and safety. Fortunately, having experienced far worse conditions in the foothills of the Rocky Mountains a few years earlier, and with many years of short forays in all weather behind him, Dewey was a competent winter wilderness traveller. He woke Herb and told him they had to start for the railway immediately after breakfast.

They were disappointed at having to retreat, yet they continued to enjoy the experience. For a few hours, keeping to the lake ice, but close to shore, they dragged the canoe to the Wakami River. There, much to Dewey's relief, they found it free of ice and were able to reload and paddle against a slight current. They began to look positively on their chances of getting out with all their equipment. That all changed again within a quarter of a mile. At a bend in the river they ran into more ice. In the bow, Herb smashed at the ice with a strong birch club while Dewey paddled with all his might. As the hours passed, progress upstream alternated between easy going in patches of open water and the hard work of breaking ice. Inevitably the canvas canoe suffered and had to be repaired regularly. Dewey's concern for the situation shows in his comment, "We resolved sometime during the forenoon that, if necessary, we would keep on paddling all night if it would do any good."[20]

They hadn't seen anyone since leaving the railway and they had not heard any shots, but they discovered they were not the only ones in that part of the wilderness: "By quite a coincidence the spot we selected for lunching was the scene of a kill, the animal shot freshly having been a bull moose with fine antlers; both hind quarters and one front quarter had been taken. The remainder of the body had been raised off the ground with supporting poles."[21]

It is probable that they carved a couple of steaks off the remains because Dewey wrote "after an appetising meal we loaded up again and made a fresh start."

Constant encounters with ice and repeated punctures in the canoe's canvas sides and bow required regular stops for repairs. Once they reached the Ridout River, with its considerably faster current, they found long stretches between rapids with no ice. The portages and beaver dams, of course, required greater effort than before as they were now going uphill. On turning a bend after the first two portages they ran into ice again. This time it blocked the river for a few hundred yards and was too thick for Herb to smash through with his club. Taking to the land, it took them three hard and sweaty trips to portage everything to the next stretch of open water. Tired and cold, they camped that night in a glade surrounded by willows. Sitting by the campfire, they listened to wolves howling in the distance and the hunting call of a great horned owl (*Bubo virginianus*) closer by.

By morning the river had frozen close to the banks. The ice was too thick to paddle through, but too thin to walk on safely. On land the bushy willows prevented them from portaging the outfit along the banks. Determined to keep moving, they tried another approach: "After a time we pushed the canoe out on the ice, Herb creeping into the bow while I very cautiously got into the stern. Suddenly the craft broke right through the ice; as one foot was outside, my shoepack got soaked. However, we went on and got to open water in the middle of the river."[22]

They persevered throughout the day and into the evening, reaching their fourth portage of the return trip about 8:30 p.m. The moon was full and yellow and bathed the river and forest in a bright light. While Dewey again repaired the canoe, Herb made one carry to the end of the portage. When he returned, they both shouldered heavy loads and made another trip. This took care of most of the outfit, except for the canoe. Normally one man could carry the eighty-pound canoe by himself. Coated with ice as it was, *Wanderlust* was far too heavy and the men were too tired. Working together — and resting every few minutes — they manhandled the canoe to the far end of the portage.

They had not eaten since the moose steaks at lunchtime. Still they kept moving, concerned that the river might freeze completely before they could get out. At midnight, exhausted but still going, they were treated to a magnificent display of northern lights: "The whole heavens were alive with streamers of green, blue, red and gold. Great thrusts of light would shoot to the zenith, flickering in great majestic waves of even greater power and radiance. Again the fiery tongues flickered and waned with astonishing speed, then into more brilliance. What an awesome performance!"[23]

Once again they had to beach the canoe to effect repairs to avoid it sinking. At 12:30 a.m., after twenty-two hours of working their way upriver, they called a halt in favour of a warm fire, a hot meal, and a few hours of restless sleep. Over breakfast in the morning they discussed the possibility of leaving the canoe and most of the outfit in the woods and making a dash for the railway at daylight. They also considered staying put for a few days in the hope that the temperature might rise and temporarily free the river of ice. Common sense and a warming morning sun told them to keep going, and to take the canoe and outfit with them. The railway could not be far away.

That final day on the trail was a repeat of the previous one. Thick ice alternated with thin ice. The sun added its warming effect and the ice melted. The two tired men kept paddling, repairing, and portaging. After a hard struggle, they finally reached the railway at about 6:00 p.m. Now that they were safe, the weather improved; the temperature rose. With plenty of time in hand, they decided to continue their holiday by staying in the Ridout area for a few more days, though there is no written evidence that Dewey collected any specimens: "So we paddled extensively up the river to the south and learned more about the birdlife, saw several moose and White-tailed Deer, sighted several beavers and muskrats and saw a grayish form in the stream-side forest that I deemed was a lynx. And how we loved the beautiful forest and our peaceful luncheon campfires."[24]

The result of a successful moose hunt for Dewey on the Ridout River in northern Ontario in late September 1918.

The following autumn, Dewey and Herb returned to the Ridout River on a moose-hunting and small mammal collecting expedition. Once again, *Wanderlust* went with them as primary wilderness transport. This time they left in September to avoid a repeat of the harsh weather of the previous year. Unfortunately, the only records of that journey to survive are a few dated photographs with captions in Dewey's hand and half a paragraph in his unpublished biography: "The objective was successfully reached as we canoed and camped along [the] Ridout River and adjacent lakes. One moose was secured and I also collected 55 specimens of small mammals and birds. This was the grandest experience of this kind that I had known for many years. The northern fastnesses are in a class by themselves."[25]

Dewey's standing as a naturalist to be recognized continued to rise. In March 1919 he joined Will Saunders in London and together they went on a short collecting trip to Point Pelee, on the north shore of Lake Erie. There they were joined by Dr. R.M. Anderson of the National Museum in Ottawa. The main objective of the visit was to collect specimens of the beach mouse (*Peromyscus maniculatus bairdi*). This they achieved, along with other species. On the way home they stopped at Jack Miner's bird sanctuary near Leamington, where hundreds of Canada geese stopped over on their northern migration. Dewey was impressed by their size and numbers. He wrote, "Up to this time I had never seen such a spectacular aggregation of wildfowl."

It's probable that the Sopers had someone else to help with the farming by this time, as that summer Dewey took a train west again to spend time in Alberta. His sister Edith and her husband Will East had moved from Edmonton to Islay, close to the Saskatchewan border and just south of the Vermillion River. Although his primary reason for being there was to collect and preserve wildlife specimens, to make money he took a harvesting job for a few weeks and helped on a couple of building sites.

Pen-and-ink sketch of a black-footed ferret, by J. Dewey Soper.

Dewey stayed from late August until the onset of winter in late November. During that time, by working late many nights, he was able to preserve thirty-nine specimens, mostly mammals. On weekends, when work allowed, he studied waterfowl at the nearby Island Lake (later Kenilworth Lake), south of Islay, and on Laurier Lake to the north. Those solo winter rambles on the snow and ice in Saskatchewan — during which he often covered quite a few miles — were useful training exercises for his future long-range Arctic expeditions.

Ontario Again

Back in Ontario, and again living with his parents on the farm, by early 1920 his piano-playing skills had progressed to the stage where he was almost ready to take the ACTM degree examination for the Toronto Conservatory of Music.[26] Instead, he all but abandoned the piano to dedicate more time to ornithology and mammalogy. Even so, his knowledge of the instrument and his ability to play well would soon provide another source of income.

5

Building and Learning

Joseph Soper sold his holdings in the farm in April 1920 and retired with Ilona to a house in nearby Guelph. With no job, and money running out after the winter, Dewey purchased a pickup truck and ventured into the cartage business. It didn't take him more than a few months to discover his mistake: "It was not profitable, consequently I sold out and went back to the familiar business of building which represented pure income."[1]

Some time before the cartage business, Dewey had earned his certificate as a journeyman carpenter, joined the appropriate union, and was qualified to earn the highest wages in that profession. At that time, this amounted to between sixty and seventy cents per hour. The advantage to Dewey was that he could take jobs as he wished and still give himself free time for exploring and wildlife collecting without going broke. He did, however, take some time off for nature studies. With Will Saunders, he spent a few days in August studying small mammals in Proton County.

At the end of the month, once again with Herb Allen, he embarked on another canoe trip in northern Ontario. Their goal this time was to paddle a loop from the small town of Temagami, west across Lake Temagami to Tern, Obabika, Wakimika, Diamond, Willow, and Lady Evelyn lakes, and so to the long finger of Lake Temiskaming by way of the turbulent Montreal River. Successful in their objectives this time, the pair observed

Dewey Soper writing his journal at an open overnight camp on the Temagami Lake adventure, August 30, 1920.

152 species of birds and returned with thirteen specimens. Commenting on the low number of study specimens taken, Dewey said that the combination of "travelling and camping were so demanding every day that it was difficult to find time for putting up specimens. Most of those taken were preserved by the campfire after dark."[2]

The rapids caused serious concern, prompting Dewey to write, "Up to this time the wildest and most dangerous white water that I ever encountered by canoe was on the lower reaches of the Montreal River."[3]

Although Herb had run rapids and portaged past them on the Ridout River, Dewey felt his cousin was not experienced enough for the Montreal River. Neither was he, but he conveniently ignored that fact. As a consequence, he asked Herb, in the bow, to cease paddling. Dewey then handled the heavy load by himself. He admitted "it was a nerve-wracking and lucky descent to Lake Temiskaming."

The corollary to that traumatic run down the rapids was that Dewey suffered a profound nightmare a couple of days after returning home. In the course of his dark mental disturbance he turned his bedroom into a wreck and suffered cuts and bruises in the process. "For a few moments Mother and Father wondered if I had gone completely berserk!"[4] Whatever happened to Dewey's mind that night, it was a one-time event, never to be repeated throughout many years of hard and often dangerous travels, on rivers, on land, and on subarctic seas.

That dramatic episode did nothing to deter him from wilderness canoe trips. After a few weeks of carpentry work on a new house in Guelph, Dewey was restless again and could not resist the primeval call of forests. He persuaded his younger brother Cecil to take a deer-hunting trip with him in the Muskokas in late October. The plan was to paddle the Moon River from Bala to Georgian Bay and back again, hoping to collect a deer close to the banks. It is to Dewey's credit that the fearful descent of the rapids on the Montreal River did not frighten him away from the Moon River. The Moon runs downhill in an often dangerous succession of falls and rapids and requires constant vigilance, as well as above-average canoe-handling skills.

They failed to shoot a deer and, surprisingly, Dewey did not collect any specimens for his collection. He did, however, add considerable new material to his written wildlife records. Most important for him, he was truly happy being in the woods and far from civilization. He didn't know it then, but the Moon River excursion was to be his last real outdoor experience in Ontario.

Over the winter of 1920–21, with no building work available, Dewey became a salesman for the Mason & Risch Piano Company. On weekdays he travelled his assigned territory visiting musical outlets; on weekends he worked in the company's Kitchener office, demonstrating and playing pianos. With his daylight hours filled, he did not get much opportunity for wildlife watching over those months. He wrote of the music business, "It cannot be said that I was happy in this work; I longed for greater freedom, the wide open spaces of a less settled region and the wildlife that it harboured."[5]

Having had some small success with naturalist articles submitted to newspapers and magazines, he enrolled in correspondence courses to improve his use of the English language and for creative writing. As the winter turned to spring, his longing for the wild spaces of the West, particularly Alberta, became too much to ignore. Whenever he could, he was already roaming away from the pianos to the Grand River to check on the spring bird migration. Toward the end of April he quit the job, packed his carpentry tools and his specimen-preserving materials, and headed west.

Cecil and Dewey Soper camped beside the Moon River in the Muskokas in early November 1920 while canoeing from Bala to Georgian Bay and back again.

Throughout May and into early June, Dewey worked on a construction job for Dave Bettschen at the Sunny Acres Farm near Broadview, Saskatchewan. In his spare time he collected and preserved a further twenty-five specimens of small mammals and birds and continued to add to his wildlife journals. He noted that his "data on the spring arrival of birds was particularly good." On one outing he had watched a pair of Swainson's hawks (*Buteo swainsoni*) harassing a prairie hare (*Lepus townsendii*). He added the encounter to his field notes: "One [of the hawks] was seen to dive rapidly and fly over [the] fleeing Prairie Hare, but did not attempt to make a strike. It could be seen that the hare was badly frightened and all out to escape and finally disappeared into the protective seclusion of a thicket of silverberry [*Elaeagnus commutata*]."[6]

While at Sunny Acres, Dewey wrote enough to fill eighteen pages of his eventual typewritten notebooks, and included two sketches of wild plants and a list containing eighteen distinct species of birds he observed during his stay.

Building and Learning

Once his work for Bettschen was done he moved on to his sister's home in Islay, Alberta, where he had arranged to stay for the remainder of the summer. There he invested his savings in a piece of land and built a modern bungalow as a speculative venture. He followed that with contracts to either build or help to build houses in Islay and nearby. By the time he'd finished the construction work, winter had arrived. Dewey moved to Edmonton and enrolled in the University of Alberta. He knew that, to get his name known and to eventually be accepted as a professional biologist, he needed the higher education that only a university could offer. He started late in the year but, with diligent study over the next few months, he gradually caught up with the other students. He was fortunate in that his zoology professor, William Rowan, recognized his passion and his already considerable knowledge. Rowan was an avid birdwatcher, as was Dewey. As a result, once they got to know each other, they often went on field trips together.

When he wasn't studying, Dewey found time to write a fifty-thousand-word book manuscript he called *Lore of the Wild*. It was subsequently rejected by two publishers and, in fact, never did get into print. The original manuscript is now in the University of Alberta Archives.[7]

During his first winter at university, Dewey met and became friends with Frank Farley, an amateur naturalist from Camrose, Alberta. Learning of Dewey's skills as a builder, Farley advised him to consider building houses in Camrose, where there was a current need. Accordingly, at the end of spring term, Dewey loaded up his tool chest and moved the forty-five miles southeast. He purchased two lots side by side in the town and set to work to build another two modern bungalows; this time assisted by his father, who had again moved west.

During the construction months, Dewey and Frank Farley often took time off from their respective jobs to go on weekend field trips together in the latter's car: consequently, Dewey added another seventy-five specimens of birds and mammals to his collection and much to his notes. The building work took a little over four months but proved to be a worthwhile venture. As soon as they were completed, Dewey sold both properties for a respectable profit. He was then well set financially for the balance of his time at university and possibly beyond.

He still had a few weeks left before returning to his studies. The experiences of the 1912 expedition into the foothills of the Rocky Mountains

One year after building a house at Islay, Dewey built two bungalows in Camrose, Alberta, to help finance his continuing education at the University of Alberta.

with Jack Coker had left Dewey with a desire to see more of the region. Accordingly, as the summer of 1922 began making way for autumn, he made plans to return on a solo venture. This time he would explore a region well to the south of the previous expedition and close to the boundary with British Columbia. He was armed with a letter of introduction to Arthur Griffin, Chief Forest Ranger, from Benjamin Lawton, the Chief Provincial Game Guardian and Forest Officer for Alberta.[8] Once again, and this time accompanied by a somewhat more professional outfit for a naturalist, Dewey took a train west. At Edson, he left the mainline train and changed to another to take the spur line southwest toward Coalspur and beyond to Mountain Park.

Griffin arranged to help Dewey take his sixty pounds of equipment and provisions by pack horse to a forestry cabin about eight miles to the southwest. That would be his base for the next two weeks. It was unfortunate that Dewey was suffering from a heavy cold at this time, and combined with the long walk in, on far from level terrain, it made for a trying day. The increase in altitude, added to the cold, made his breathing erratic and slowed him down. That aside, as soon as the horses had been unloaded, Dewey immediately set out a trapline for small mammals.

Building and Learning

This log cabin, situated at Cardinal River near Rocky Pass, Alberta, was Dewey's shelter for two weeks in the fall of 1922. He was on a solo collecting expedition in the foothills of the Rocky Mountains at the time.

Over the next few days, while Griffin worked on clearing the local trails, they left the horses to their own devices in the long grass of an adjacent meadow. Dewey went out for up to ten hours each day, setting and checking traplines, and exploring new routes. Often he worked his way high into the foothills, climbing craggy ridges and up through Rocky Pass to the border of Jasper National Park. He returned each day with specimens that he then had to skin and preserve for a variety of museums.

Once, in the middle of the night, Griffin woke Dewey to tell him there was an animal in the cabin. Dewey lit a candle and looked around. On the table, trying to get into a pot of beans, was a large grey woodrat. Dewey reached for his pistol but wasn't quick enough, and the rat dropped to the floor and vanished. Griffin told him to wait. "The rat," he said, "maybe two of them," would be back. A few minutes later he was proved correct. Dewey fired once with fine number 10 shot and added the rat to his collection tally for the day.

On one climb to above the treeline on the summit of the pass, Dewey found the wind gusts to be so violent as to make it almost impossible to make headway. At times it was necessary for him to lay flat to avoid being bowled over. Seeking shelter in a rocky draw he discovered a flock of white-tailed ptarmigan (*Lagopus leucurus saxatilis*). Already they were losing their summer brown in favour of winter white. On one, the transition had finished: it was completely white. Dewey added that specimen to his collection. Often on his daily explorations he would stay out too long and have to take seemingly unnecessary risks of injury to his ankles and legs over difficult terrain to get back to the cabin after sunset.

Although he had no formal training in botany, Dewey was fascinated by the diversity of trees and small shrubs on the mountain slopes between six thousand and 6,500 feet in altitude. He collected many for later identification by a botanist associate.

In a hanging valley near Mount MacKenzie he trapped mountain long-tailed voles (*Microtus mordax*), a species he had not collected before. He also took a pair of gray-crowned rosy finches (*Leucosticte arctoa tephrocotis*). Higher up he was rewarded with a golden-mantled ground squirrel (*Callospermophilis lateralis*) and, near a rock slide, his first Rocky Mountain pika (*Ochotona princeps*).

Harry Spence, a friend of Griffin's who happened to be in the area, occasionally went out with Dewey on his daily hunting trips. Dewey found him to be good company but inclined to boasting, which he found distasteful. When Griffin left after about a week, his trail work completed, Spence left, as well, and Dewey was alone. At first he admitted to being lonely, but the

---

Following Page: Map of the location of Dewey's Rocky Mountain foothills expedition of 1922. His earlier expedition cabin, shared with Jack Coker, was at the location to the NW marked 1913. From Dewey Soper's notebook. Map origin unknown.

Building and Learning

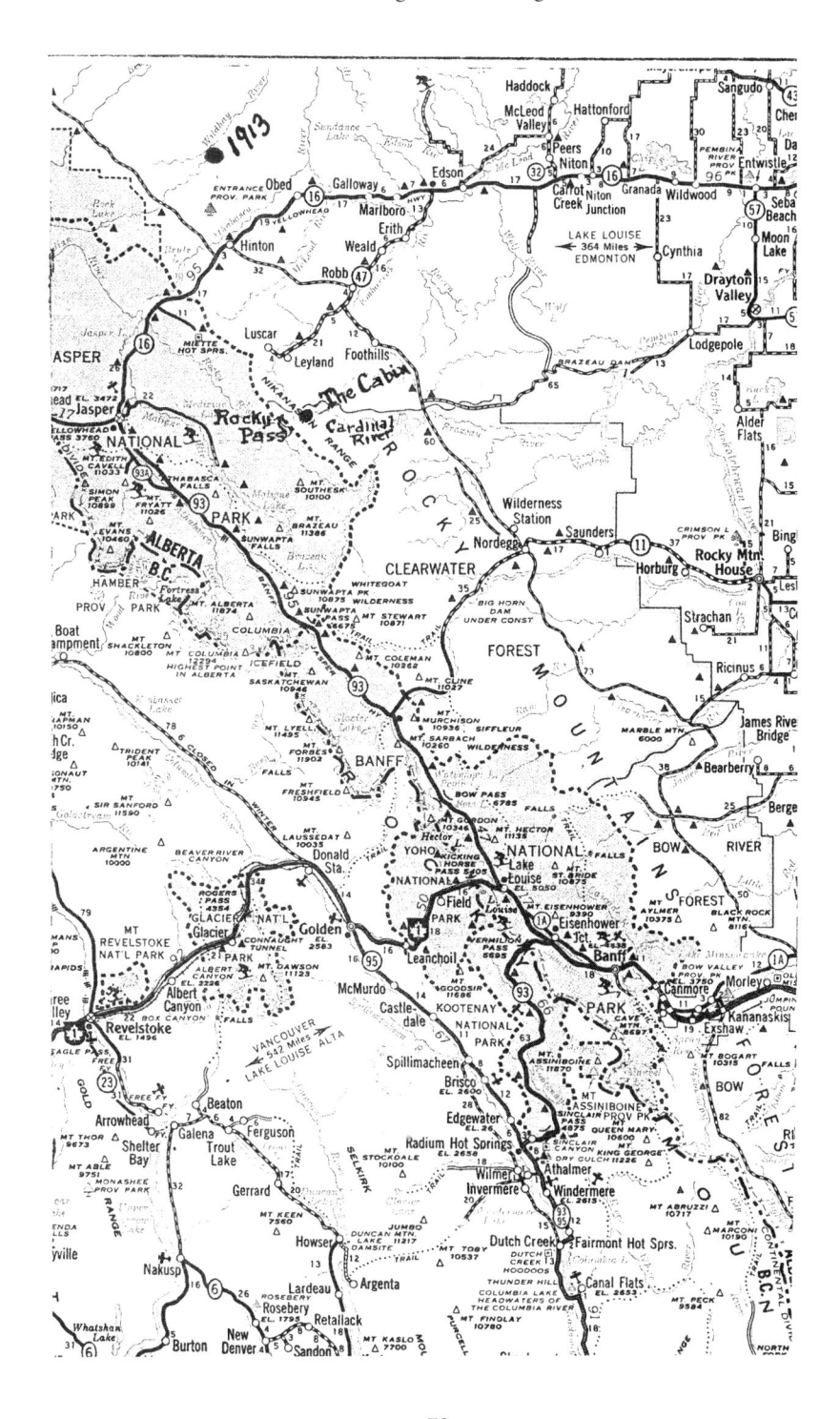

accumulated work of preserving specimens and writing up his notes kept him busy for long hours at the cabin in the evenings. A few days later he awoke one morning to find the ground covered in white. The first snow had fallen and it was time for him to prepare for his own departure. That snow obliterated many of the location signs he had left pointing to his traps, so he lost a few, unable to find them.

He had expected either Griffin or Spence to return for him with a pack horse or two to carry his outfit and accumulation of specimens back to the railway station at Mountain Park. When neither of them arrived, and with time running out, Dewey loaded a backpack and set off alone, hoping to find horses himself. Moving fast, considering his load, he made it to Griffin's home base in a little over two and a half hours. There he learned that Griffin was away fighting a forest fire. He met up with Spence and a packer who owned horses, but none was available at the time. There was no alternative

Sketch of little northern chipmunk, by J. Dewey Soper.

but to return to the cabin, pack everything tidily, and carry out what he could. The rest would have to be picked up later by Griffin and shipped out to Edmonton as freight. To avoid travelling after dark, Dewey cut across the bends in the trail, estimating he saved himself two miles in the process. He spent the night preparing his equipment and shutting down the cabin and was back on the trail before first light to catch his train at 9:00 a.m. Less than two days later he was home, and the remainder of his outfit arrived safely a few days after that. For Dewey it had been an extremely satisfying two weeks. He was then ready to return to his studies for the winter. He explained the nature of the courses he took:

> Shortly after arriving home from the Rocky Mountains.... I again enrolled at the University of Alberta for the winter. I was more or less independent in relation to the studies as I was only taking a limited number of subjects without working for a degree. However, I was seriously anxious to get a good training in textbook and laboratory zoology (especially in relation to mammalogy and ornithology), in general ecology and evolution; in relation to the latter, of course, I read everything that was available re: the writings of Charles Darwin, Huxley, etc. I was also enthusiastically eager to become skilled in English literature and writing and also went to classes in geology throughout the winter.[9]

His science studies obviously paid off, but even he could not foresee the eventual honours the university would bestow on him.

Whenever possible, while good weather held, he took time out for pleasure, and that meant being outdoors. On October 27 he and his father spent the day on a birdwatching canoe trip down the North Saskatchewan in *Wanderlust*. They put in at the Low Level Bridge early in the morning and raced downstream, identifying ten different species en route. Dewey enjoyed the day. He wrote, "The river is excellent for canoeing throughout. Between Clover Bar Bridge and the Fort four mild rapids, 'swifts' occur which are navigable without any trouble by staying in mid-stream. At such places the current is about 10 miles per hour — about twice the average speed. The last one, about three miles west of the Fort bridge is the strongest, throwing up waves about a foot high in places."[10]

Just under one month later the temperature dropped so drastically that the North Saskatchewan River froze completely over.

6

Expedition to the Eastern Arctic, 1923

In January 1923 Dewey received a letter from his acquaintance Dr. Anderson, Chief of the Biological Division, National Museum of Canada in Ottawa. Anderson offered him the position of naturalist on an expedition into the eastern Arctic for the coming summer. Now almost thirty years old, Dewey's boyhood dream of exploring in the Arctic was about to come true.

Well aware that an Arctic voyage held the potential for being frozen in and having to spend a winter in the North, Dewey's planning for the summer voyage had to take that possibility into consideration. Therefore he had to assemble his outfit accordingly. On the scientific side, his preparations included facilities for collecting birds and mammals, as well as "specimens of marine invertebrates, fish, insects, and plants … [plus] ethnological specimens …" He also had to consider the photographic work he wanted to accomplish and the detailed coloured sketching necessary to record the "perishable parts of birds." Beyond that grand scope, he had chosen to take regular readings of sea and air temperatures en route, and he anticipated the possibility of banding sea birds in the northern rookeries.

Ordered to be in Ottawa by mid-June to take care of final arrangements, Dewey travelled first by train to Winnipeg and Port Arthur (now part of Thunder Bay), Ontario. There he boarded the SS *Huronic* for a forty-hour cruise on Lake Superior and Lake Huron to Sarnia, and spent a few days visiting friends and relatives in southern Ontario. He arrived in Ottawa on time and got down to the serious business of preparing for an expedition. Once he was ready he took the overnight train to Quebec City for the scheduled sailing of the CGS *Arctic* on July 1. She was a scruffy old ship that had seen better days and as such was hardly a good ambassador for Canada. But she was tough; up in the ice that would be all that really mattered. If *Arctic*'s appearance concerned Dewey in any way, he failed to mention it.

Due to a slowdown getting freight to the ship in time, the departure was delayed twice. The ship finally set sail at 4:30 p.m. on July 9. On land the air had been hot and humid. Out on the river and underway, the ship's movement soon created a cooling breeze. Famed Arctic sailor and explorer Captain J.E. Bernier was in charge of the ship while the expedition commander was J.D. Craig[1] from the Department of the Interior. Craig's wife, Gertrude, was also onboard. Although her name was never added to the ship's roster, she was aboard for the duration of the voyage: photographs taken in a variety of locations, with her in them, prove that. Dewey must have known she was there but never mentioned her in any of his reports. Captain Bernier was not on the ship when it sailed from Quebec City. He joined the vessel a few days later at Father Point on the river's south shore. Until then, Commander Craig, plus the First Officer and a St. Lawrence River pilot took charge on the bridge.

The passenger list included a couple of RCMP officers as well as the six-man scientific party, of which Dewey was a member. In addition, the ship carried a legal team of five men en route to Pond Inlet to officiate at a murder trial.[2] Among them was Crown Prosecutor Adrien Falardeau, a Quebec City lawyer; Leopold Tellier, also from Quebec City, who would be counsel for the defence; and Judge L. Rivet. With the crew of twenty-six, the ship's manifest showed she carried a total complement of thirty-nine persons on departure. Four hours later two members of the crew were lost when the ship was hit by a sudden squall off Île d'Orléans. Third Officer Wilfred Caron (Captain Bernier's nephew) was swept overboard, and Craig's secretary, Desmond O'Connell, drowned while trying, unsuccessfully, to rescue Caron from a lifeboat.[3] The tragic event naturally threw a pall of sadness over the ship, but nothing could keep the enthusiastic Dewey Soper down for long.

When Captain Bernier came aboard from a tug on the evening of July 10 he was shocked and pained to learn of the two deaths, especially as one

Expedition to the Eastern Arctic, 1923

Captain J.E. Bernier, master of the CGS *Arctic* and famed Arctic sailor.

was a relative. The expedition voyage, however, had to go on. The pilot left with mail on the same tug. With that changeover, CGS *Arctic* was, at last, truly ready for her expedition. But she still had to detour[4] to make a call at Gaspé, Quebec, to pick up members of a geodetic survey bound for Rigolet, deep in Hamilton Inlet, on the Labrador coast.

The out-of-the-way stop at Gaspé gave Dewey most of one day to ramble through the woods to the north of the village and collect a few specimens. He noted that "birds did not seem particularly abundant. The commonest species were Herring gull [*Larus argentatus*], double-crested cormorant [*Phalacrocorax auritus*], white-throated sparrow [*Zonotrichia albicollis*], junco [*Junco hyemalis*], Lincoln sparrow [*Melospiza lincolnii*], savannah sparrow [*Passerculus sandwichensis*], golden-crowned [*Regulus satrapa*] and ruby-crowned kinglets [*Regulus calendula*], robin [*Turdus migratorius*], and olive-backed thrush [*Hylocichla ustulata*]."[5]

From Gaspé, *Arctic* crossed the unusually calm Gulf of St. Lawrence with all sails set, and fetched the Newfoundland coast off Table Point on the afternoon of July 15. The weather there was considerably colder than it had been on departure. Some of the higher hills still had patches of snow on them. That evening they sighted the coast of southern Labrador and entered the Strait of Belle Isle, gateway to the North Atlantic. The following morning, midway through the strait, Dewey saw his first icebergs: "A dozen or more were in sight simultaneously, some being fully 100 feet in height. The average, however, would not exceed 50 feet."[6]

Throughout that day the ship coasted through random fields of ice. The sea temperature had dropped from 50° in the gulf to 40° in the strait. Dewey happily recorded seeing flocks of Atlantic puffins (*Fratercula arctic*), a few murres (*Uria aalge*), and was delighted when a large flock of kittiwakes (*Rissa*

Sketch of an Atlantic puffin (*Fratercula arctica*), by J. Dewey Soper.

trydactila) took off from a pinnacled berg and flew in a wide circle before landing on another berg. Those three quite different birds were almost certainly the first he had ever seen of each of the species. He also noted, but did not offer scientific identification for, porpoises (probably harbour porpoises — *Phocoena phocoena*) that habitually play in the bow waves of ships, plus, "Pinkish shrimp-like creatures about two inches in length [that] were very numerous in the strait."

Thick fog and scattered floe ice slowed *Arctic* to a crawl as she turned north, paralleling the Labrador coast. Fulmars (*Fulmarus glacialis*) now joined the murres and puffins, and red phalaropes (*Phalaropus fulicaria*) moved up and down with the gentle motion of the sea in the shelter of icebergs far from shore. The ice concentration became thicker as the ship navigated slowly north. The need to land the geodetic survey party at Hamilton Inlet compelled Captain Bernier to force his way through the ice. Having a specially strengthened bow, *Arctic* shouldered some floes aside and rode directly over others. As darkness fell, the captain ordered the ship anchored to a large floe until the morning light and he could once again see what lay ahead.

Bernier, a blue-eyed, barrel-chested Quebecer of seventy-one years, had been at sea since he was a boy, and he had captained his first deep-sea ship when he was seventeen. At the age of fifty-two he made his first voyage to the subarctic waters of northern Hudson Bay — in the CGS *Arctic*. Two years later he took *Arctic* as far north as Lancaster Sound. Despite his age, Bernier had sailed the ship into the Canadian Arctic regularly since then, mostly on government business. A little ice off the Labrador coast was not likely to slow him down for long, or give him much cause for concern.

With daylight, the view from the masthead showed the icefields covered many miles out from the coast. It was not closely packed so the ship could move through it, albeit with the utmost caution, but it was not without its dangers. Dewey passed the hours watching for sea birds and marine mammals. Throughout that day, Bernier expertly conned his charge, slowly making headway through the floes. Time, however, was wasting. By late afternoon the ship had only progressed as far as Gready Island. Unable to guarantee passage through the pack ice to Hamilton Inlet, Commander Craig and Captain Bernier decided to land the survey party at a small fishing village on the island and leave it up to them to find an alternate means of covering the remaining one hundred nautical miles to their destination in the inlet.

During the brief stop to offload the small party, Dewey managed to get ashore for an hour and collected nine birds and some forty plants. He wrote, "The chief birds here were pipits [almost certainly the water pipit — *Anthus spinoletta*] and horned larks [*Eremophila alpestris*], both of which were tending young out of the nest."[7]

Underway again and heading out to sea, *Arctic* soon cleared the ice to find open water. The next port of call was to be Godhavn, west Greenland, on Disco Island in the Davis Strait. Rough seas characterized the early part of the crossing causing many onboard to succumb to seasickness. Dewey, apparently, was spared that suffering. With huge waves breaking over the forecastle and even the bridge at times, the ship rolled alarmingly, registering thirty-seven degrees off the vertical at one point.

RCMP constable Tom Tredgold and Dewey Soper had fun modelling winter fur clothing onboard the CGS *Arctic*.

Expedition to the Eastern Arctic, 1923

Once the weather relented and the seas lessened, Adrien Falardeau threw a bottle into the sea west of Cape Farewell, Greenland, on July 21, 1923. Presumably it carried some kind of identification message because the following year he learned that his bottle had drifted across the Atlantic to be found on a beach in the Outer Hebrides. It was picked up at Port of Ness, Isle of Lewis, Scotland, on March 7, 1924, and, according to Dewey, the find was reported in a newspaper article headed BOTTLE FROM THE ARCTIC[8] on April 1, 1924.

Dewey found the eight-day, open-sea voyage from the Labrador ice pack up through Davis Strait quite monotonous, enlivened only by the occasional icebergs. He did, however, become friends with Constable Thomas Tredgold of the RCMP. That friendship would stand him in good stead once he was able to go exploring on land again. When the lookouts sighted Greenland's mountains, it coincided with the crossing of the Arctic Circle. An excited Dewey wrote, "When we arrived in sight of the Greenland coast I beheld my first truly Arctic landscape. Already we had arrived in the weird 'Land of the Midnight Sun.'"[9]

With land close by and birds again in sight, the naturalist went back to work. He took note of pomarine jaegers (*Stercorarius pomarinus*) and purple sandpipers (*Calidris maritime*), and mentioned the regular sightings of "small black whales, popularly called Blackfish by the sailors …" They were almost certainly long-finned pilot whales (*Globicephala melas*).

Two days after crossing the Arctic Circle, *Arctic* dropped anchor in the harbour at Godhavn on the south side of Disco Island. Given a permit to collect specimens by the local authorities, Dewey, with Thomas Tredgold as his assistant, spent an afternoon and part of the evening tramping far inland. By the time they returned to the ship they carried "a couple [of] dozen birds, many small rock specimens and plants that made up 87 herbarium sheets, the majority carrying one or more duplicates."

The original plan had been to cross Baffin Bay directly to Pond Inlet to land the judicial team. In a memo to his superior in Ottawa, J.D. Craig explained his reasons for taking the expedition north to Ellesmere Island first:

> We had intended going direct from Godhavn to Ponds [*sic*] Inlet so that the trial might be held while we were attending

to our work farther north. Mr. Rivet [trial judge], however, asked that we attend to our northern work first, partly so that he might be able to see more of the country, and partly so that the "Arctic" might remain at Ponds [sic] Inlet during the trial, the ostensible reason for this being that a jury might be selected among the officers and crew of the ship.[10]

This rather suggests that Judge Rivet might have been more interested in a northern holiday cruise than in the task he had been assigned. Had the ship kept to the original itinerary, it's probable that Dewey would have added further to his bird collection. He commented on that possibility in the introduction to his official report: "The season for the best collecting had already fled before we reached these points on August 21st. [Pond Inlet] and September 11th [Cumberland Gulf] respectively …"

From Godhavn the ship steamed cautiously north through thick fog, with lookouts on watch for icebergs around the clock. The fog suddenly came to an end at Latitude 75°N, on the southern edge of Melville Bay and there on the sea and flying in small flocks were thousands of dovekies (*Alle alle*), the first seen so far. With Cape York in sight, *Arctic* turned due west back to Canada. On the crossing of the northern extremity of Baffin Bay, with no ice in sight, Dewey saw a large male walrus (*Odobenus rosmarus*) in the sea — his first of that Arctic species.

Passing through Glacier Strait, between Cobourg Island and the southeast coast of Ellesmere Island, the passengers and crew watched as glaciers on the islands, large and small, overflowed into the sea. By this stage of the voyage, icebergs and floes were no longer a novelty, yet the views and activity around him prompted Dewey to write,

> This is the home of the iceberg and the theatre of the most beautiful and awe-inspiring scenery in the world. Perhaps nowhere is there drawn together in a single panorama such a variety of circumstances, such vast accumulations of ice and rugged mountains of unqualified desolation, sea and sky unspeakably blue. Strange indeed is the lure of the

north. Such unmitigated desolation and emptiness, chilling in its silence and vastness, yet possessing a charm elsewhere unequalled and unknown.[11]

Arctic struggled through heavy field ice to call in at the RCMP post at Craig Harbour[12] on Ellesmere Island. The object of visiting Craig Harbour was to take onboard RCMP Inspector Wilcox and his six policemen, who had been at the remote outpost since its installation the previous summer. In 1923, Wilcox and his men were scheduled to set up a new police post at Buchanan Bay, on Ellesmere Island, in the southwest corner of Kane Basin. The ship only stayed a few hours, just long enough to load the RCMP contingent and their sled dogs and close down the post. Once they were onboard, *Arctic* cruised north, past the Carey Islands, toward Etah, Greenland. En route Dewey collected his first polar bear (*Ursus maritimus*) specimen from heavy ice near the ship. They later saw more polar bears and walruses.

At Etah, *Arctic*'s personnel met the crew of *Bowdoin*, a beautiful eighty-eight-foot LOA[13] schooner under the command of Captain Donald B. McMillan.[14] *Bowdoin*, well-acquainted with the Arctic, was waiting for ice conditions to improve so she could cross the narrow ice-choked channel of Smith Sound to erect a memorial at Cape Sabine to the men of the ill-fated Greely Expedition[15] of 1884.

Dewey and Tom Tredgold, in company with RCMP Corporal T.R. Mitchelson, again went ashore for the day collecting specimens. Among other birds, they saw thousands of dovekies — so many that Dewey described the congregations as "thick as gnats at sundown."

Being considerably larger and stronger than *Bowdoin*, *Arctic*[16] had a better chance of making headway through the pack ice. Consequently, she weighed anchor, and Captain Bernier forced her bow into Smith Sound. *Arctic* soon ran into heavy ice. Following a wide lead, she managed a few more miles of northing before the ice closed in on her, trapping her for several hours. When a new lead opened in the right direction, Captain Bernier boldly followed it, only to be trapped again, this time for two days. Cape Sabine, on Pim Island, which marks the entrance to Buchanan Bay, could be clearly seen about ten miles distant. The ice, however, was too thick, making further progress impossible. The crew used dynamite to blast their ship free and she fled under full sail and steam, back to Craig Harbour, taking the Mounties with her to reopen the police detachment. The planned Buchanan Bay RCMP post would have to wait for another year. In Glacier Strait, Dewey spotted a polar bear hunting seals on a large pan of ice and collected the beast for the National Museum.

Dewey spent three days ashore at Craig Harbour while the ship explored west to Fram Fjord and beyond in Jones Sound. At that time Craig Harbour was said to be the most northerly police post in the world, although, other than maintaining an official Canadian presence, there really wasn't much policing to be done. Tom Tredgold remained ashore with Dewey and worked with him as he investigated the flora and fauna and added to his growing collection of specimens. The only birds collected during this stop were ruddy turnstones (*Arenaria interpres*), a few gulls, kittiwakes, guillemots (*Cepphus grylle*), and eider ducks (family *Somateria*). Dewey and Tom also made their own explorations of the coast in a canoe. They encountered walruses, one of which gave them cause for concern when it showed far too much interest in their canoe. On land, they discovered the ruins of an old Inuit village overlooking the sea ice.

After *Arctic* returned to collect Dewey, only three of the RCMP detachment stayed at Craig Harbour. The others, including Inspector Wilcox, sailed away with the ship as it retraced its route through Glacier Strait, where Dewey was able to collect another polar bear and preserve its pelt for the National Museum. Turning into Lancaster Sound they passed a large floe with six adult polar bears on it, one with a new cub. They left them alone. Subsequently, they saw many more polar bears, mostly wandering across the ice floes or swimming alone between them, leading Dewey to the belief that Lancaster Sound contained more polar bears than any other region visited on the expedition. They also saw more walruses.

Dewey enjoyed watching the sea creatures from the ship's deck, but he preferred to be on shore, where, with time available, he could explore and collect without being dependant on others. At Dundas Harbour on Devon Island he was free to roam the land for nine full hours. His wide-ranging walk secured him a few birds, some plants, and a variety of minerals. He saw signs of lemming, caribou, fox, hare, and muskox, but was disappointed to not see any of the creatures themselves. Working in the coastal mountains he collected a large polar hare weighing twelve pounds. In notes made at the time, he identified it as *Lepus arcticus groenlandicus*.[17] In a book written many years later he changed the classification to *Lepus arcticus monstrabilis*.[18]

On the coast he came upon a few Native graves and tupik stone rings overgrown with grass and moss: obvious signs of an old encampment.[19] He recorded their locations and, adding to his collection of minerals for the museum, he collected a sample of magnetic sand from the adjacent bay.

It was in this vicinity in September 1818 that Captain John Ross of the Royal Navy made the mistake that would haunt his career and the rest of his life.[20] He confused an Arctic mirage with real mountains, which he decided blocked Lancaster Sound (or "Inlet," as he referred to it), and offered no opportunity for further navigation to the west by that route. The mountains Ross thought he saw he named for John Wilson Croker, First Secretary of the Admiralty. The "inlet" he failed to explore because of the mirage would eventually prove to be the eastern entrance into the Northwest Passage.

From Dundas Harbour the voyage continued west to Beechey Island in Barrow Strait, the westernmost objective of the expedition. Equally important to the history of the search for the Northwest Passage, Beechey Island is a bleak rock fronted by pebbles and a usually frozen sea. Despite its historic associations, Dewey was not impressed with the lonely Beechey Island: "No place visited by us in the Arctic compared to the unparalleled desolation of Beechey. Its sombre coastline bears the stamp of a million sullen years of erosion unrelieved by a single element to assuage its hopeless asperity."[21]

Sir John Franklin and the members of his ill-fated 1846 expedition to find and navigate the Northwest Passage passed their first miserable Arctic winter here. Franklin's two ships, *Erebus* and *Terror*, survived that winter in the ice close to where *Arctic* anchored in 1923. When Franklin's expedition sailed away from Beechey to their eventual deaths off King William Island, they left behind the graves of three seamen.[22] Dewey was deeply affected by those lonely graves: "Standing over the five [sic] graves of the first dead who sleep here in this awful desolation, then and only then, did the full and profound solemnity of their last heroic days come to me, as they battled for life far from the aid and eyes of the world."[23]

Almost all members of the crew and passengers on *Arctic* went ashore on Beechey Island to attend a ceremony honouring Franklin and his doomed men. Gertrude Craig went with them. She was photographed with Inspector

Wilcox, standing in the remains of the wooden yacht *Mary*.[24] That little twelve-ton boat had been left on Beechey Island in 1850 by Sir John Ross as a rescue vessel in the forlorn hope that some or all of Franklin's men might still be alive and able to reach her.

Dewey climbed up the nearby eight-hundred-foot-high hill to a cairn built by Franklin's men as a signal for any potential rescuing force: "I found that the cairn consisted of tons of rock, requiring a prodigious amount of labour to construct."

In the talus slopes close by, he found "as free fragments ... several species of coral." The only wildlife he mentioned seeing while on the island were Thayer's gulls (*Larus thayeri*) and a school of beluga whales (*Delphinapterus leucas*) passing by in Lancaster Sound.

The original expedition plans called for landings on Cornwallis Island and Melville Island. Thick ice in Barrow Strait prevented the ship getting close to either destination. It was a great disappointment to Dewey, who wrote, "Few men had ever seen Melville Island up to that time and very little was known about the fauna and flora."

Blocked by impenetrable ice to the west, the ship crossed the western end of Lancaster Sound to enter Admiralty Inlet, where Dewey, Tom Tredgold, and surveyor Henderson were put ashore in Strathcona Sound. They surveyed the general area while the ship cruised farther south toward the end of the inlet.

Studying the stone remains of a Native settlement, overgrown with turf and moss and of indeterminate age at a site he referred to as Eskimo Point, caused Dewey to suggest that "the excavation of these sites would undoubtedly well reward the labours of an anthropologist."[25] In the absence of scientists, lemmings (genus *Lemnus*) had taken over the site.

Compared to the stark morbidity of Beechey Island, the land Dewey explored in Strathcona Sound was rich in flora. He described meadows of Arctic poppies (*Papaver radicatum*) a foot and more high; concentrations of foxtail[26] and other assorted grasses — most of which were at least knee-high. Patches of saxifrage (*Saxifrageaceae*) in bloom added to the colourful scene, which he carefully photographed. Although he roamed a few miles inland, he saw little wildlife, except occasional flocks of snow buntings (*Plectrophenax nivalis*). A high prominence of sandstone prompted him to climb to the summit, which he measured by aneroid barometer and determined to be 1,425 feet above sea level. There he collected stones and erected a cairn. Later, back on the ship, he was pleased to be able to see the cairn through his binoculars.

Working along the shoreline close to a creek he was surprised to meet a small flock of horned larks (*Eremophila alpestris*) so far north, and took three for his collection. He also saw, but apparently did not collect, ravens (*Corvus corax*), in addition to the usual Thayer's gulls, fulmars, and murres, plus more snow buntings. While Dewey was wandering inland, Tom Tredgold saw a couple of weasels (*Mustela erminea*) on the coast but did not try to catch them.

On the ship again, they steamed down the inlet back to Lancaster Sound before turning into Navy Board Inlet, between Baffin Island's Borden Peninsula and Bylot Island. Passengers and crew looked on in awe at the ice-covered mountains around them. Dewey described the scene:

> Great numbers of glaciers enter this narrow arm of the sea from either side. Some assume rather notable and fantastic shapes. In one place the ice formed a perfect cross on the mountain side, in another an almost perfect "A." A huge complex glacier called the fingers and thumb stretches down to the sea from the inland cap like a gigantic hand on the Baffin side of the inlet.[27]

The constantly snow- and ice-capped mountains on Bylot Island, ranging above six thousand feet, are among the loftiest in the Canadian Arctic. The impressive island is named after Robert Bylot, the mate on Henry Hudson's ship, *Discovery*, in 1611. Bylot was one of the crew of mutineers who set Hudson adrift to his death in the eponymous bay. Pardoned for his skills in getting *Discovery* safely back to England, Bylot returned the following year as a member of Sir Thomas Button's[28] expedition, which reached the Nelson River. Bylot spent the next few years leading exploration voyages in the eastern Arctic and is credited with many first sightings.

Forty years after Soper's visit to the region, renowned British mountain climber and polar sailor Bill Tilman[29] made the first crossing of Bylot Island

CGS *Arctic* at Pond Inlet in 1923.

on foot, with a climbing companion, in the summer of 1963.[30] Starting from Cape Liverpool on Lancaster Sound, they trekked due south to the foot of the Sermilik Glacier on Eclipse Sound, opposite Pond Inlet. The arduous up and over journey on snowfields, glaciers, and occasional ridges of rock, took them roughly two weeks, during which they made their highest camp at about 5,200 feet. There is a sense that Bill Tilman and Dewey Soper would probably have enjoyed each other's company on similar expeditions. They were close in age: Soper born in 1893 and Tilman a few years later in 1898. They both spent a great portion of their lives living rough in remote locations and became hardened and knowledgeable outdoorsmen; also, they were both intellectuals.

CGS *Arctic* was due to remain in the vicinity of Pond Inlet for the duration of the murder trial, but would make short local journeys. For that welcome sojourn, Dewey went ashore and became the houseguest of the RCMP detachment for the next two weeks. He enjoyed the change of faces and the company, and revelled in the opportunities of spending long summer days collecting specimens of flora and fauna.

Dr. Therkel Mathiassen,[31] a Danish archaeologist and cartographer from the National Museum of Denmark in Copenhagen, happened to be in the area excavating ancient stone igloos. His presence afforded Dewey another interesting intellectual for conversational purposes.

Expedition to the Eastern Arctic, 1923

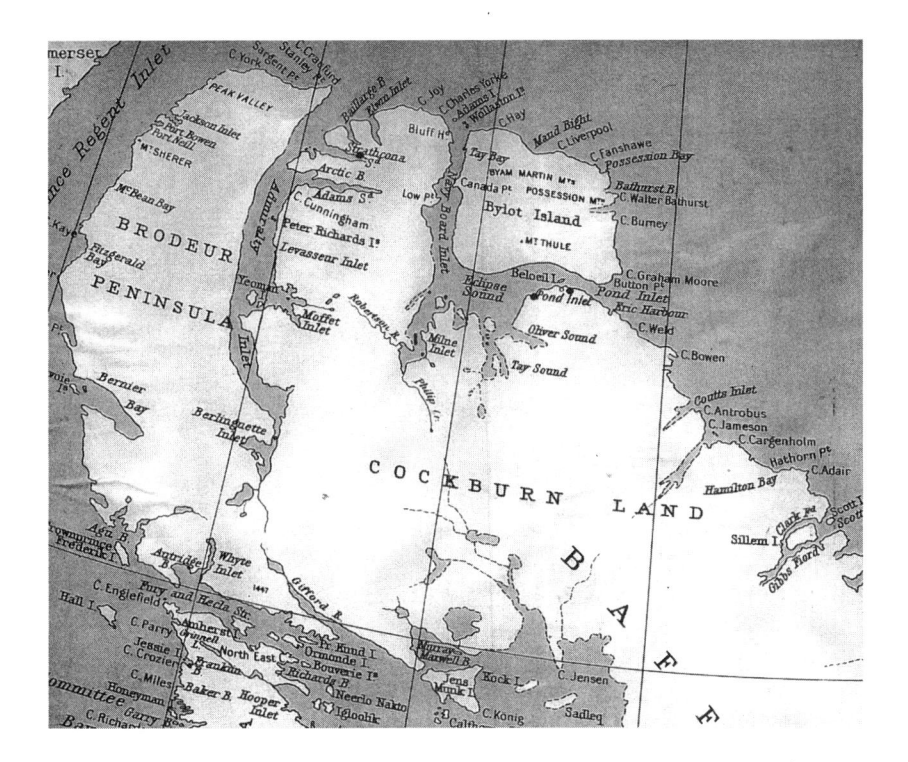

Map of North Baffin Island in 1929. From: A Map to Illustrate Report on Exploration in Southern Baffin Island, 1929. **Source:** Library and Archives Canada/*Southern Baffin Island: An Account of Exploration, Investigation and Settlement During the Past Fifty Years* /AMICUS 4379308/ Map on page 130.

Mathiassen was no stranger to Arctic life. With the famed Danish polar explorer Peter Freuchen,[32] he had been a member of the first stage of Knud Rasmussen's multi-year Fifth Thule Expedition[33] (1921–24). Leaving Rasmussen's party on Danish Island, close to Lyon Inlet in the southwestern corner of Foxe Basin, Mathiassen had travelled by dog team north up the Melville Peninsula and across northern Baffin Island to Pond Inlet that spring. He was staying as a guest of the HBC factor. Mathiassen's journey of close to five hundred miles had been a spectacular achievement and must have impressed Dewey enormously.

Being late in the flowering season, the local flora was past its best. That did not stop Dewey collecting and pressing, including plants he had not previously seen. The birdlife, too, was scarce. The familiar fulmars, snow

Dewey in front of a Native summer tupik (skin tent) while collecting birds near Pond Inlet, August 1923.

buntings, ravens, and Thayer's gulls were there, and occasionally a glaucous gull (*Larus hyperboreus*), but little else of interest. Between August 25 and 27 a substantial migration of Lapland longspurs (*Calcarius lapponicus*) passed through, enabling Dewey to collect a few specimens. He heard of foxes (*Vulpes lagopus*), wolves (*Canis lupus arctos*), and wolverines (*Gulo gulo*) having been seen, but did not meet with any himself. Locals said that Arctic hares (*Lepus arcticus*) had been plentiful the previous year. In the summer of

Expedition to the Eastern Arctic, 1923

Sketch of a snowshoe hare (*Lepus americanus*), by J. Dewey Soper.

1923, few were in evidence. He did manage to secure a selection of lemmings and weasels. Of the larger mammals, he already had his polar bear specimens and was hopeful of collecting a caribou or two farther south. Meanwhile, schools of narwhals (*Monodon monoceros*) regularly cruised past Pond Inlet, many of them being taken by Native hunters. There is no record that Dewey took any specimens of that marine species, not even a much-prized helical tusk, or horn.

Midway through the Pond Inlet stay, the HBC factor, Georges Hérodier, took Dewey along the coast to the Patricia River, about twenty miles away. There he was able to collect plants — some new to him, some familiar — and make extensive notes on the physiography of the land. He was interested to find and study a series of "old raised sea beaches, or terraces, which prevailed one above another to a height of several hundred feet above the sea. Their character and outline was very distinct."[34] Therkel Mathiassen later told him there were other such terraces on north Baffin Island that reached as high as seven hundred feet above sea level.

Departing Pond Inlet on September 3, the trial over, CGS *Arctic* sailed south along the Baffin coast to cross the Arctic Circle again off Cape Dyer; she passed Cape Walsingham and rounded Cape Mercy to probe northwest, deep into Cumberland Sound, taking eight days in total for the voyage. The weather en route alternated between "bright and moderately warm" and "dull, cold and dispiriting.... Heavy, lowering cloud-rack covered land and sea."

When the ship dropped anchor in front of the HBC post at Pangnirtung, the work started immediately. The purpose of the visit was to establish an RCMP post, consequently some one hundred tons of cargo — consisting of provisions for the police officers, coal, and lumber — had to be offloaded and ferried ashore. For Dewey this meant he was free to explore and collect specimens at will. Unfortunately, he was disappointed. He wrote in his report,

> From a zoological standpoint my efforts at Pangnirtung for the ensuing eleven days were comparatively fruitless.... The birds had completely vanished with the exception of a few pipits, snow buntings, ravens and Thayer's gulls. Mammals were scarce also. A few hares were seen, but so wild as to be impossible to approach at this time. Lemming signs were profuse throughout the country, but they had evidently disappeared as prolonged trapping failed to secure a single animal.[35]

There were no caribou to be seen either.

Expedition to the Eastern Arctic, 1923

His disappointment extended to the plant life, which he noted was "far on its autumnal decline. All bloom had ceased." He did comment favourably on the heather, and on various berries, such as blueberry (*Vaccinium uliginosum*) and curlewberry (*Empetrum nigrum*), the leaves of which had already adopted their fall colours.

Although the weather was generally fair for the location (just south of the Arctic Circle), freshwater ponds froze and snow fell on the higher elevations. With collecting opportunities limited, Dewey was uncharacteristically showing signs of boredom. He had hiked the valleys and shores for days, but wanted to do more.

"On September 15 I proposed climbing a prominent mountain northeast of the post and naming it in honour of Mr. William Duval."[36] Dewey and three others set off on the 2,215-foot climb. At the summit, in a snowstorm, they built a cairn around a weatherproof container holding a record of their climb. The snowfall became a blizzard, making the descent difficult and potentially extremely dangerous for the unskilled climbers. When they returned to the ship in the evening they were "tired, wet and hungry," but Dewey was happier for the brief excursion and exercise. The snow continued to fall for a few days, covering the shoreline to a depth of sixteen inches. Winter was setting in and it was time for the expedition ship to sail south.

Arctic loaded another forty tons of rock ballast and weighed anchor on September 22. She blew her steam whistle on farewell, and set course for the Strait of Belle Isle and then directly up the St. Lawrence to Quebec City. The uneventful voyage home came to an end on the afternoon of October 4.

Dewey immediately took a train to Ottawa, where he deposited his specimens with the appropriate experts at the National Museum, filed his reports, and added a further report on the ethnological opportunities waiting for scientists in the eastern Arctic. After describing the various archaeological sites he had visited and any work that had been started or completed at those sites, plus the potential for excavation, and advice on accommodation and sustenance for future archaeologists, he concluded with a rather convoluted but strongly worded paragraph of recommendation and request:

> When facts are examined in the present light of things as illuminated by even such fragmentary knowledge of the

subject as was obtainable on a voyage of such fleeting possibilities, I should strongly recommend the Department to send an ethnologist to the north before it is too late. It [would be] deplorable if we should finally be obliged to go to Copenhagen or elsewhere outside the boundaries of Canada to study Canadian archaeology. A representative collection of the remains to be found in these ancient ruins of the Canadian Arctic Archipelago should certainly find its way into Canada's national collection.[37]

During *Arctic*'s eight-thousand-nautical-mile voyage over three months, Dewey had spent relatively little time on land. In fact, his shore time totalled slightly less than one-third of the expedition's duration. His landings were: Gaspé (Quebec), seven hours; Gready Harbour (Labrador), one hour; Godhavn (Greenland), nine hours; Craig Harbour (Ellesmere Island), three days; Etah (Greenland), eight hours; Dundas Harbour (Devon Island), nine hours; Beechey Island, three hours; Strathcona Inlet, roughly eight hours; Pond Inlet, thirteen days; and Pangnirtung Fjord, eleven days. Yet he arrived in Ottawa with an impressive collection of 821 specimens, made up of:

Zoological	
Birds	131
Mammals	25
Marine invertebrates	30
Fish	6
Ethnological	78
Botanical	470
Geological	76
Entomological	5

Plus, he took 304 photographs, developed the plates/negatives onboard for later printing, and catalogued them. Beyond that, Dewey returned with "numerous water-color sketches, catalogues covering all specimens secured, with data, a daily journal and a daily bird record book [of sightings]." In addition, he had reported, albeit briefly, on a few Inuit sites of interest to archaeologists.

The three months spent on the CGS *Arctic*'s voyage had been at times exhilarating, always educational, and, quite often, frustrating. Most of all, those months in the north had kindled an admiration and respect for the Arctic that would not go away. Dewey knew he wanted to return, as soon as possible, and for an extended stay. With that in mind he began his campaign.

7

A Second Arctic Expedition

The introduction to Dewey's report on the Arctic expedition of 1923 discusses the timing of the breeding season for birds on Baffin Island, and includes the following provocative statement:

> The most gratifying results, and of some phases, the only obtainable result, will be secured by a naturalist going into the north prepared to remain throughout the year. In a region so little known faunally, at least, as Baffin, Bylot and North Devon [Islands], the most noteworthy strides in the natural sciences and the great opportunities there awaiting us like a duty and a privilege can obviously be realized and discharged only by determined workers willing to remain in the country for one or more years.[1]

He added a five-page addendum to the report headed "A Recommendation for Further Zoological and Other Field-Work in Baffin Land and Adjacent Arctic Regions."[2] It was, by his own admission, an attempt "to point out the possibilities awaiting a conscientious investigator."

The addendum begins, "This summer's voyage of the C.G.S. *Arctic* upon which I served as zoologist, has seemed more than ever, despite its limited opportunities, to indicate the great possibilities for further field-work in that little known region north of Hudson Strait. The fauna of Baffin Land and other islands of the Canadian Arctic Archipelago is scarcely represented in the National collection."

Having baited his hook, he later talks of "the great work to be done here by someone." In spite of Dewey's natural humility, there is no doubt as to who he thinks should be sent to Baffin Island for a year. He brings in national pride and patriotism, and again stresses the need for Canada to have "as complete a collection of the fauna, flora and natural resources of the country as possible in the National Museum as a basis for intelligent study by Canadian naturalists." He even goes so far as to remind the report's readers that his mentor, Dr. Anderson, supplied a significant collection of fauna representative of those species on the Arctic coast of the mainland. With that reminder established, he goes back to his main theme: "Until we make adequate collections from the archipelago to the north and north-east, however, many problems of distribution and evolution remain unsolved and the mainland specimens referred to cannot assume the value they will when comparative material is secured from the more northern regions."

He discusses the scientific value of the birds and mammals he collected in 1923 on "so short and fleeting a trip." Then back to the concept of a year-long field study: "How much of importance might one confidently expect from a trained collector remaining in the country throughout the year?"

Again he urges, "For the best results I should heartily recommend that a zoological collector be detailed for work in Baffin Land for at least one year. Broadly, the whole year would necessarily have to be spent in the one place as there is no means of obtaining transportation for any great distances in that region …"

With that thought firmly planted, he goes into detail, suggesting Cumberland Sound as an ideal location for a collector to be based. In 1924, much of the coastline of southwest Baffin Island was still unexplored, with significant gaps on government maps. That, almost certainly, in concert with the known and unknown wildlife possibilities, led him to focus on the Pangnirtung area. Plus, of course, he knew of the HBC and RCMP accommodation already established at Pangnirtung Fjord. He includes William Duval's post, also in Cumberland Sound, and lets it be known that Duval has invited him to use it as a base should he return.

Dewey then furthers his case with specific work to be done: a study of the great caribou migration, whales and seal populations, the large bird rookeries, and for the first time in his writings, we learn of his particular interest in snow geese and blue geese. He mentions unsubstantiated reports of their breeding grounds in the vicinity of Nettilling Lake and Amadjuak Lake, west of Cumberland Sound, and how little is known about the big birds. Adding to his own photographic ability, he argues that a small movie camera should be taken along, with a sufficient number of reels of film to record the activities of all creatures encountered.

Dewey spent the winter of 1923–24 furthering his zoological studies at the University of Alberta in Edmonton. While there, he continued his efforts to be sent back to Baffin Island. To this end, he corresponded with J.D. Craig, commander of the 1923 expedition. Craig apparently wrote back expressing cautious optimism on Dewey's behalf. In a letter dated April 8, 1924, Dewey replied in part,

> Dear Mr. Craig, It was a great pleasure to receive your kind letter of a few days ago…. The kindly encouragement of your words means more to me than I can say. I rejoiced in the news which you imparted in regard to my probable appointment to the Arctic again. Even though, as you said, it was unofficial, it nevertheless carried that little grain of hope and probability that must always be a great measure of comfort to a man who waits patiently for months in uncertainty.

Dewey closed his letter with a slice of blatant self-serving opportunism: "Enclosed you will find a little pencil sketch of Craig Harbour, Ellesmere, which please accept. I fancied that you would be interested in this sketch considering the subject …"[3]

Craig wasn't the only one who felt positive that Dewey Soper would receive the appointment. Dewey also received a letter from Dr. Anderson about the same time. It, too, expressed the belief that Dewey had a better than even chance of being sent to Baffin Island for the year. Soon after, the welcome news arrived that he was indeed invited to go on an extended expedition to Baffin Island for the Victoria Memorial Museum in Ottawa. To be based with the RCMP detachment at Pangnirtung, the expedition would spend not one but two years on southern Baffin Island. He accepted immediately. "At this time," he wrote, "Baffin Island was regarded as one of the largest virtually unexplored land masses in the northern hemisphere."[4]

Once again, on the journey north, Dewey would be a passenger aboard the CGS *Arctic*, only this year Pangnirtung, his destination, would be the first port of call. The ship eased away from King's Dock in Quebec City on July 5, and made way for the Strait of Belle Isle, which they transited six days later. As with the previous year, icebergs, growlers, and drifting floes greeted them as they entered the Atlantic. None caused any great concern or slowed the ship. The wind-driven waves, however, built up to create an extremely dangerous situation for the ship, crew, and passengers.

Navigation in the unpredictable waters off the Labrador coast requires extreme skill from captain and crew, together with, as always at sea, a certain amount of luck. The weather has everything to do with the difference between a smooth voyage and a deadly experience. Dewey described a near tragedy that took place some distance into the North Atlantic:

> Shortly after leaving the Strait of Belle Isle en route to Cumberland Sound a great storm broke that nearly ended in disaster for the ship.... An enormous wave broke over the rail [in the dark of night] and shifted the deck load of 200 tons of coal far over to port. At the same time an immense wave swept over the deck and poured five feet of water into the boiler and drowned out the fires.[5]

As the ship battled waves up to sixty feet high, one hundred nautical miles from the Labrador coast, all hands were called to jettison the deck cargo of coal, lumber, and other supplies. With that considerable weight off the ship, they then stood to the pumps, working four-hour shifts around

Dewey Soper onboard CGS *Arctic* ready to leave Quebec City for the Far North on July 4, 1924.

the clock. Although there is no written evidence that Dewey took his turn at the pumps, it is unlikely that he, of all passengers, would not volunteer his services. He was young, he was fit, and he was not ready to die. There is a telling quote in *Canadian Arctic Recollections* that enforces this observation: "The 13th was a miserable time of fatigue and uncertainty."[6]

For five days *Arctic* wallowed in enormous aggressive seas, without benefit of engines and, due to the excessively high winds, unable to make sail, buffeted by a raging storm and malevolent waves. Each moment could have been the ship's last, with no possibility of rescue for those onboard.

For five days the men pumped until they were exhausted. By July 16 the water level in the hull had been lowered enough that the fires under one boiler could be lit. Once the steam built up pressure, they finally had power for lights and the wireless; the crew could then begin the work of cleaning up the engine room. By the seventeenth, the seas had subsided to a moderate level and the engineer had his engines running again. A shaken but relieved complement of crew and passengers was then able to rest and recover from the beating they had taken.

The storm had gone, the waves reduced to rolling swells. Now fog hid much of the coast from sight for a few hours. Late in the day, about thirty nautical miles off the coast, as the fog dispersed, Labrador's snow-capped Torngat Mountains could be clearly seen. The following morning *Arctic* began the crossing of Hudson Strait. In the distance an excited Dewey could see the outline of Baffin Island's hills. He wrote, "With a thrill I thought about the mysteries dwelling beyond the far ridges and peaks."

Baffin Island is the largest island in the Canadian Arctic and the fifth largest island in area in the world, measuring 195,928 square miles.[7] Only Greenland, New Guinea, Borneo, and Madagascar cover greater areas. It is 960 miles from north to south and 420 miles from east to west at its widest. That width narrows to 150 miles at its waist, roughly along the Arctic Circle. Its topography varies dramatically, with rugged, mountainous terrain dominating the deeply indented eastern coastline of fjords, and rolling lowlands dropping to a level, muddy plain on the western side. In places, particularly in the north, sheer cliffs rise one thousand feet out of the sea. Baffin Island has mountain peaks as high as seven thousand feet in the Cumberland Peninsula, and the considerable expanse of the Penny Icecap is also at an elevation of up to seven thousand feet.

To Dewey Soper, Baffin Island in all its geological forms meant the continuation of the work he had so briefly touched on the previous year. The many and varied land formations each harboured its own species of fauna and avifauna, in addition to the unique Arctic flora. Anxious to get back to work, those

A Second Arctic Expedition

last few hours as *Arctic* cruised up Davis Strait, past Meta Incognita Peninsula, Frobisher Bay, and Hall Peninsula, must have seemed like an eternity to him.

Pangnirtung Fjord probes northeast for twenty-eight miles from Cumberland Sound and is, on the average, over one mile in width. It is dominated by mountains which vary from two thousand feet in its lower reaches to five thousand feet at its head. At high tide the sea level is reported to be as much as twenty feet above the mean.

When Dewey Soper arrived on Baffin Island on July 22, 1924, for his second visit, he already had plans to explore the interior lowlands between his base at Pangnirtung Fjord on Cumberland Sound and the coastline of Foxe Basin. The German explorer and scientist Bernard Hantzsch[8] was the only white man known to have travelled all the way west from Cumberland Sound to Foxe Basin. Two lakes, Amadjuak and Nettilling, flood large parts of the interior. Although difficult to reach, both were extremely attractive to Dewey for their birdlife potential. He wanted to be the second white man to make the crossing. Unlike the unfortunate Hantzsch, Dewey planned to return alive.

Before the western interior and Foxe Basin expedition there was much work to be done in the more immediate vicinity of Cumberland Sound. At the time of Dewey's arrival, most of the flowering plants were in full bloom. He commented on the eclectic variety he encountered during a long hike on

Pen-and-ink sketch of Pangnirtung Fjord, by J. Dewey Soper.

July 25, and noted that bumblebees and butterflies were busy on groups of fireflowers (*Epilobium latifolium*).

One of the distinct advantages to staying with the RCMP was that they had their own boats and they patrolled frequently. Also, Constable Tom Tredgold, Dewey's friend and sometime assistant collector from the 1923 expedition, was now based at Pangnirtung. As one of only eight white men at the Pangnirtung settlement, and there on official business, Dewey was often invited to join the police, and the Hudson's Bay Company traders, on their patrols and business cruises.

The waters of Cumberland Sound are enclosed by mountainous terrain on three sides and the broad expanse of Davis Strait on the open end. The shorelines are rugged, heavily indented, with land heights reaching to 2,500 feet on the southwestern coast and more than double that — up to six thousand feet — on the opposing side. Pangnirtung is the second largest fjord leading inland from the sound. Kingnait is the largest. As a consequence of the enclosing terrain, Cumberland Sound is notorious for its sudden violent wind squalls, as are the large fjords.

Cumberland Sound was discovered by British master mariner Captain John Davis (*circa* 1543–1605) in 1585. A little over a century later, he was followed by the first whalers. Before long, fleets of whaling ships spent the brief summers in Davis Strait and Baffin Bay. Those early visitors always did their best to get out before the winter ice closed in. In the mid-1800s that changed. The relentless whalers[9] set up whaling stations at Blacklead Island, Niantelik Harbour (on the southwest coast of the sound), and on Kekerten Island, farther north. Instead of returning to Europe or New Bedford, Massachusetts, at the end of each season, they began to spend the winters there in order to be on-site and ready to hunt bowhead whales when they returned to the Arctic as the ice began to break up in the spring.

Kekerten Island is among the Kikastan Islands. It is a low-lying island of mostly rock (maximum elevation five hundred feet) south and west of the entrance to Kingnait Fjord, and roughly forty miles from Pangnirtung. A few days after Dewey's arrival, he travelled to the former whaling station[10] in the HBC's motor launch, *Unagava*. He almost certainly enjoyed the visit, but Dewey found little to interest his scientific mind on Kekerten. As was his custom, he roamed widely, noting that the island was "almost destitute of vegetation." He was equally disappointed in the scarcity of birdlife.

He far more enjoyed a similar multi-day excursion to Kingua, on Issortukdjuak Fjord, with his HBC friends a few days later. The HBC boat was going to bring back a large quantity of white whale (beluga) skins. Tredgold was invited along, as well, on the seventy-mile voyage. Keeping to the mostly sheltered waters between the offshore islands and the coast, travelling in the opposite direction from Kekerten, the journey took all night and part of the next day.[11] En route they stopped at American Harbour (or Oshaluk), where they were greeted by William Duval, the trapper/trader Dewey had met in 1923. Duvall, his Native wife, and two daughters entertained the unexpected visitors over coffee.

Arriving at the mouth of the Sermilling River in mid-morning, Dewey and Tredgold went ashore with their camping and collecting outfit. At this latitude they were almost on the Arctic Circle. *Ungava* continued up the fjord to Midlualik Bay, the boat crew agreeing to return to collect the naturalists in just under three days. During that all too brief stop (for Dewey) he added to his collection "many more valuable specimens of both land and sea birds and many desirable plants, some of which I had not observed before."

In summer, large numbers of beluga whales frequented the inlets and bays leading up to Issortukdjuak Fjord and Midlualik Bay. The Inuit captured hundreds at a time by the simple expedient of blocking off their access to the sea with boats, then waiting for the outgoing tide to strand the creatures on the flats. Once the white whales were helpless, they shot them.[12] Dewey and Tredgold were on hand to watch for a while as the Inuit skinned and fleshed a few hundred belugas on the exposed seabed. The skins and barrels of blubber were destined for the HBC. The Inuit retained some of the blubber for their own use, and the dogs benefited from the meat. The baled skins and sealed barrels then had to be loaded into *Ungava*'s hold. While the Natives and HBC men worked at their gruesome task, the naturalists turned away to follow the banks of an unnamed river for a few miles.

Other than birds, such as snow buntings, ravens, water pipits, and a horned lark, Dewey and Tredgold saw little wildlife on their hike. Despite that lack, Dewey was happy to wander inland, watching the river coursing over rapids and falls as they walked upstream. At such times, roaming unknown country, the explorer in him came alive. Had he the time, he would have gone so much farther: "I longed to go on and on in order to discover what lay beyond the nearby [mountain] ranges."[13]

When the heavily laden *Ungava* departed for Pangnirtung, Dewey and Tredgold went with it, but again stopped off at Sermilling Bay, this time taking a freighter canoe with them. *Ungava* was due back at Midlualik Bay in a few days for another load of skins and more barrels of blubber. In the boat's absence Dewey and Tom explored much of the Sermilling valley and climbed high into the hills in search of specimens for Dewey's collection. He had hoped to finally see caribou, but was disappointed again, as he had been the previous year. He later learned that caribou do not migrate out of the interior to the coast until early September or beyond. Land birds again were scarce, as were mammals of all sizes. Though the creatures he hoped to collect did not show themselves, Dewey was acutely aware that he and his friend were roaming on land few if any white men had ever trod.

They climbed a mountain on the west side of the bay and recorded its altitude with the aneroid barometer as 1,800 feet. They duly built a cairn and left a record of their climb, with a notation that they had named the peak Mount Edmonton, after Dewey's preferred home city. The view from the summit must have been quite spectacular, for Dewey described it as "a panorama of wild and rugged grandeur, particularly to the north and northeast facing the Penny Highlands." Looking seaward, they sat for an hour or more watching belugas far below: "In the clear blue-green waters of the bay several hundred white whales swam and frolicked … opposite the mouth of the river."

On the way back to camp, at about one thousand feet above the sea, they stopped by a tarn, or small mountain freshwater lake, and expressed surprise at finding little fish in it. They caught a few, which Dewey preserved for later identification in Ottawa. That eventual study by an expert suggested them to be Arctic sticklebacks (*Pygosteus pungitius brachypoda*).

The return voyage to Pangnirtung, again aboard the HBC's *Ungava*, was a long, rough ride in choppy seas and pelting rain. Later, in his quarters at the police post, Dewey set to work completing his curing of the collected skins of "a few land birds, [plus] several eiders and glaucous gulls." In the field he had only been able to perform rudimentary preparation. They now required more cleaning and liberal applications of salt. Acknowledging the amount of work to be done on the birds, as well as the pressing of plants, prompted

A Second Arctic Expedition

Dewey to observe with wry honesty, "Until all such labours were completed and field-notes brought up-to-date, one could not engage in further sallies afield — that is, with a good conscience."[14]

He did go out, of course, but, it seems, only for a few hours each day, on rambles into the mountains and along the coast, collecting and adding to his list of specimens. Each successive foray into the field, no matter how short in time, added to his workload back at base. To Dewey it was all part and parcel of the job to which he had dedicated his life. He had the interest and he had the energy to work long hours.

Opposite the Pangnirtung settlement there was a valley with protective walls up to two and three thousand feet high. A stream tumbled down from the heights, feeding a few small lakes before running into the fjord. Dewey decided to explore the valley and its sides in the hope of finding new specimens of plants and, naturally, collecting wildlife. The RCMP motorboat *Lady Borden* carried him and Tredgold across, taking with them a sixteen-foot canoe, in which they planned to return later. As a collecting exercise the excursion was a failure. Hiking in the mountains leading out of the valley was too exhausting. Dispirited after a few miles of hard going, they turned back to the coast, planning a quick crossing to home.

Fjords, by virtue of their topography, are notorious for spawning sudden squalls. Pangnirtung Fjord was no exception. Dewey wrote of one he witnessed: "During an autumn gale … Pangnirtung Fjord whipped into a foaming maelstrom that was fearful to behold, hurling its waterspouts into the air to heights of over one hundred feet."[15]

The fjord was calm when Dewey and Tom pushed away from shore to make the roughly five-mile crossing. They were no more than one-third of the way across when a squall struck from out of the north. Whitecaps built up within minutes, and the canoe was soon in danger of being swamped. Paddling under such conditions is desperately hard work and the two onboard were soon tiring. Working together, they angled across the waves, back to the shore they had so recently left. They were fortunate to make it safely, although a few miles south of their starting point. Tredgold fired shots into the air from his .303 rifle, and soon *Lady Borden*'s bow wave could be seen speeding through the white-capped swells in their direction. Both men knew they had had a lucky escape. Dewey wrote, "This experience taught us ... never to make wide crossings of mountain fjords or bays in small craft ..."[16]

That first summer of the second Baffin Island expedition proved to hold a rapid learning curve for Dewey. He had survived a storm on Pangnirtung Fjord. Soon after, he badly burned the fingers of one hand. Stranded on shore late at night with their boat while waiting for the tide to return after hunting Arctic hares, Dewey and two police companions (including Tredgold) brewed a pail of tea. Without thinking, Dewey had grasped the scalding hot metal handle and lifted the pail with his bare hand: "Four of my fingers were burned nearly to the bone by the time I could set the pail down without spilling its contents."[17] Instant immersion in an icy stream for long periods eased the pain. Later treatment at home in Pangnirtung with liberal amounts of carron oil saved his fingers.[18]

In mid-August Dewey sailed again on *Ungava*, making a second visit to Kekerton Island and a first visit to Blacklead Island. The boat, with HBC post manager Nichols, employee Abe Ford, RCMP constable Hugh Margetts, and Dewey aboard, was piloted by a Native named Vevik. Each one of them was well aware that a storm could blow up in minutes and turn a placid sea into twenty-foot waves. Halfway across, the wind surged out of the southeast, quickly escalating in strength to a full gale and big seas. Dewey's first August as a Baffin Island resident, albeit temporary, was proving to be a test of the man and his mettle. Dewey had been through the violent storm off Labrador in the CGS *Arctic*, but *Ungava* was a cockleshell compared to her:

> The violent pitching and rolling ... soon drove us from below and into heavy clothes, clinging desperately to the aft deck. The wind and waves were awesome. Seldom before had I felt the awful grandeur of the sea as I did during those dark, turbulent, and lonely hours. Through it all Vevik stood impassively at the wheel, his long black hair flying wildly in the wind. It was a savage and unforgettable scene.[19]

Vevik handled *Ungava* with consummate skill for ten hours, until he could run her into the safety of a sheltered bay on an unnamed island off the southwest shore, about twenty nautical miles northwest of Blacklead Island. There, tucked away from the elemental violence, the men cooked a hot meal, the first food they had taken since the storm broke. Typically, Dewey, the professional, noted the large number of gulls in the bay when the boat pulled in. More than that, he quickly ascertained that, while some were the common glaucous gulls, others were of a kind he had never seen. It didn't take him long to collect a few and ascertain that they were Kumlein's gulls (*Larus kumleini*).[20]

Once the seas subsided, the boat continued through the island chain to Blacklead. There the weather closed in again and for three days the rain pummelled the island from one direction and the surf pounded it from another. The HBC men stayed at the trading post while Dewey and Hugh Margetts took over an old mission building.[21] The mission had been abandoned long before, yet the two men found it clean and dry as a temporary shelter. They also discovered it contained a library, and the books had been preserved in good condition. The foul weather made working outside impossible; instead, Dewey spent the long hours in the mission, skinning and salting the ducks, gulls, and other birds he had collected on the way to the island.

When the weather cleared, the boat crossed to the southern mainland and stopped for a short break at Niantelik Harbour, once a favourite anchorage of whalers, due to its nearly landlocked aspect. They continued on a southeasterly course, making occasional — apparently random — stops. They learned from an Inuit that caribou were now on the move from the highlands of the interior to the coast. At the deep and extensive Kassigiak Fjord, *Ungava* turned inland, following the southwest branch to its conclusion. There, for the first time, Dewey saw a caribou — a lone, stately buck running up the valley away from the intruders. Leaving Vevik with the boat, the white men set off in pursuit, each armed with a rifle.

After a couple of miles the hunting party came upon three bulls grazing in a meadow. Dewey badly wanted a skin for the museum collection, and the meat was necessary for sustenance. The rifles cracked. The caribou fell. Dewey measured and skinned his specimen on the spot. Loaded down with the hide, skull, and an impressive rack of antlers, he returned to the boat. The other men carried the meat. Dewey went out again that evening, walking along the shoreline, where he saw a few snow buntings, pipits, and one each of Lapland longspur (*Calcarius lapponicus*), Greenland wheatear (*Oenathe oenathe leucorrhoa*), and purple sandpiper.

They sailed at high tide, about 4:30 a.m., to avoid the jagged shoals near the islands. No more than halfway down Kassigiak Fjord, Vevik bellowed, "Nanook! Nanook!" The ill-fated polar bear didn't stand a chance. No matter how fast it swam away from the boat, bullets were faster. Dewey claimed the pelt for the National Museum, expressing some regret that the bear had not had a chance to escape. It was, he said, "truly pathetic." He likened shooting a polar bear from a boat to "shooting down a cow in a barnyard."[22] They saw more polar bears over the next few days but did not pursue them.

Dewey spent the next days in the mission on Blacklead Island, preserving his specimens for packing and shipment to Ottawa. That necessary extension of the collecting process was interrupted when a migration of redpolls (*Carduelis flammea*), purple sandpipers (*Calidris maritima*), and white-rumped sandpipers (*Calidridis fuscicollis*) flew in from the north. To add to his pleasure, flocks of Lapland longspurs arrived. He collected a few of each species and was delighted to also get a white gyrfalcon (*Falco rusticolus*) on September 1.

The HBC steamer RMS *Nascopie*, a veteran Arctic workhorse that was doomed to sink at Cape Dorset under strange circumstances in 1947,[23] arrived for its annual summer visit to the Arctic on September 6, much to the excitement of the Native population of the island and, no doubt, to the white men, as well.

For Dewey, the ship's arrival was significant for different reasons: he could ship out his specimens, send letters home, and an acquaintance from the 1923 expedition was onboard. In the spring of 1923, Major Lachlan Taylor Burwash[24] had travelled by dogsled through an area Dewey wanted to explore. Burwash went from Pangnirtung to Amadjuak on the Hudson Strait coast, via Nettilling Lake and Amadjuak Lake, with two Inuit companions. Now he gave Dewey much useful advice and, as he was to leave the Arctic on *Nascopie* this voyage, Burwash recommended that the naturalist hire his right-hand man, Akatuga, as an assistant for the duration of his time on Baffin Island. As a result, Akatuga and Dewey became a team that lasted right up until the latter left Baffin Island in April 1926.

Ungava departed from Blacklead Island for Pangnirtung on September 8. *Nascopie* followed up the sound the next day. When the ship was preparing to leave, after unloading, Dewey sent out ten boxes of zoological and botanical specimens for the National Museum. That Soper freight joined bales of furs, white and blue fox primarily, plus the beluga whale skins and blubber from Midlualik Bay. *Nascopie*'s departure was the last link the Baffin Island communities would have with the outside world until the next summer.

Only a few weeks at most of good weather remained before the snow fell heavily. Enjoying a warm spell, Dewey accepted an offer from the police to explore the head of Pangnirtung Fjord with them. Neither he nor any of the RCMP detachment had been that far to date. Riding in the police boat, *Lady Borden*, they saw many seals en route, and were suitably impressed by the grandeur of "the lofty mountains and gigantic glaciers." At the head of the fjord, where they moored the boat, Dewey collected a few ringed seals (*Pusa hispida*) and his first bearded seal (*Erignathus barbatus*). He and Tom Tredgold walked a few miles inland and bagged eight Arctic hares. There were so many in sight, and such easy targets, that they could have taken more but chose not to. Dewey kept the skins for the museum and the meat became the main ingredient in a mulligan stew.

In anticipation of winter exploration, Akatuga's wife, Unga, kept busy making Dewey a winter wardrobe out of caribou skins, plus a "heavy lined caribou skin ground robe on which to spread the eiderdown sleeping bag." Meanwhile, Akatuga spent much of his time hunting seals for his family and for the dog team.

In the late summer of 1924 the HBC opened an outpost at Kangertukdjuak on Nettilling Fjord, placing William Duvall in charge. Dewey took advantage of this move to send a load of his supplies to the post by sea, in order to have them on hand for his expedition to the interior in April 1925. This was no small shipment. It weighed one thousand pounds, and included: "hardtack, flour, cornmeal, bacon, butter, tea, coffee, syrup, molasses, rice, salt, powdered milk, soap, matches; 20 pounds of smoking tobacco; 1,500 cigarettes; 15 gallons of gasoline; 8 by 10 feet double silk tent and one duck tent; Hudson's Bay blankets; 18-foot freighter canoe; 1,000 rounds rifle ammunition (.22, .30-30 and .44-40); 900 shotgun shells (12 ga. and .410); a general collection of zoological and taxidermy supplies, and a plant press."[25]

The weather deteriorated rapidly as September came to a close. Snowfalls became a regular occurrence. Pools and lakes froze. Regular gales raged across southern Baffin Island, keeping everyone inside for days at a time. The sea, for the most part, remained open. By month's end, Dewey was wearing snowshoes for his hikes in the valleys and into the mountains. He continued to collect, although most of the summer birds had flown south. His list for those early days of winter included rock ptarmigan (*Lagopus mutus*), a few redpolls, Arctic hares, and, with his small traps set, he snared the first brown lemmings (*Lemmus lemmus*).

As winter set in Dewey kept himself fit by hiking (on snowshoes) or cross-country skiing whenever he could. Often he would take Mac, a white collie (the police mascot), with him. Still looking at plans for winter journeys, he now arranged to ship another supply of provisions to the HBC outpost on Sermilling Bay. The RCMP boat was heading that way on a last patrol before freeze-up, so Dewey and his goods went along for the ride. On his return to Pangnirtung he received the welcome news that a herd of caribou were on the opposite shore. Akatuga and other Inuit hunters went over and shot twelve, of which Akatuga claimed three. The large quantity of fresh meat, which would keep frozen, was greatly appreciated by both whites and Natives. Dewey prepared the skins of Akatuga's three beasts, while the latter cleaned the skulls by the simple expedient of suspending them in the fjord's salt water on the ends of ropes and letting nature's sea creatures clean off the meat.

Another caribou herd came close in late October. This time Akatuga and one of the policemen took ten between them. That meat would feed the police, Dewey, and Akatuga's family for a considerable time. It took them two full days to clean and preserve the skins in the confined space of Akatuga's igloo. With the outside temperature below the freezing point and the caribou legs frozen, the work was hard and far from pleasant. Dewey remembered, "Preparing these specimens proved to be the coldest task on the hands that I have ever endured. However, it was a good job well done by the time the skins were cleaned, salted, and packed in boxes ready for shipment the following summer."

With one more caribou hunt soon after, the men were confident they had enough meat stored to keep the settlement supplied until spring. The timing of that last hunt was opportune. A vicious storm attacked the fjord immediately after the men brought in the meat, and blasted the area for four noisy days and nights. The waters of the fjord were so rough and littered with ice that no boats could go out for a further two days.

November was a trying month for the restless Dewey. The weather conditions prevented any worthwhile excursions, and the sea ice had yet to thicken enough for dog-team travel. He watched and waited as, gradually, the ice crept down the fjord, thickening with each day. By November 20 it was almost at the mouth on the edge of Cumberland Sound, and strong enough to travel on. For the first time, Dewey experienced an Arctic dog team in action when Akatuga took Dewey seal hunting at the edge of the ice. Akatuga hitched sixteen dogs to his sled in fan formation and the excited team raced out onto the ice at eight miles per hour. Dewey was excited, too, and sometimes a little nervous: "On one brief occasion the team ran over some young dark ice that undulated ahead of the sledge runners like so much rubber. For a few moments I thought that we must surely break through."[26]

Seal hunting was serious business for the Inuit. They went out on the ice as often as they could in hopes of bringing in a few for the dogs. Dewey went out with Akatuga frequently, constantly watching the expert and honing his own newfound skills. He learned how to harness and run a dog team. He learned how to hunt seals, and he learned how to build a wind-proof snow house, or igloo. With each new lesson he prepared himself more and more for the winter explorations he was determined to undertake.

8

Exploring Baffin Island

"For several months I had been quietly incubating a scheme whereby an attempt would be made to cross Baffin Island from the head of Issortukdjuak Fjord."[1]

And so Dewey set the scene for a major winter overland expedition to cross southern Baffin Island from east to west. First, to gain much needed experience, he embarked on a series of short winter hunting expeditions with Akatuga. The caribou-skin clothes made by Unga now became standard outdoor wear. Through no fault of his own, Dewey's first short journey, to follow the Kolik River to its source in the mountains, was almost his last.

While helping Akatuga and three other Inuit hunters push a loaded sled up a four-foot icefall, Dewey broke through the thin ice he was standing on and fell shoulder-deep in fast-flowing, icy water. Fortunately he was holding on to a rope at the time, and that held him long enough for the Inuit to drag him to safety. Had they not done so quickly, he would have been sucked under the ice and drowned or otherwise frozen to death. His companions now worked together to keep him alive as his clothes froze in the frigid air. They laid a hair robe on the snow for him to stand on, hurriedly built a windbreak from blocks of snow, and helped him strip naked. He had a clean, dry suit of caribou garments in a waterproof dunnage bag, but he was far too cold to help himself.

"By this time I was chilled to the bone and my hands had no feeling. The Eskimos dressed and buttoned me up. Part of my face was frozen. I started to jog up the valley to increase my circulation but it took hours to become comfortably warm again."[2]

That night, in an igloo built for five, the Inuit took turns slowly drying the wet clothes over lamps fuelled by blubber. Dewey suffered no ill effects from his ordeal, though his face was painful for a few days until the healing process took over. It was a graphic lesson that he would never forget. He knew he had been extremely lucky. Tom Tredgold suffered a similar accident early in December:

> [Tredgold] was returning from a hike ... facing a light head wind at 25° below zero.... He unluckily walked into an area of thin "black" ice through which he immediately plunged up to his chest. The tidal pull nearly sucked him under the older ice. He rid himself of a high-powered rifle and a light pack; then after a fearful struggle, finally managed to pull himself out and onto firm ice.[3]

Tredgold was alone and four miles from home at that point. His lower body and his mittens were soaked and freezing fast. The Mountie was made of stern stuff, however. He wrapped his hands in a dry part of his parka and ran for the settlement. On arrival, his hands were found to be "dead white" and frozen solid. Amputation seemed a certainty — yet there was no surgeon anywhere on Baffin Island. Saving the policeman's hands became a priority. With help from his associates, and exercising great care, Tredgold's hands slowly thawed and returned to life. Potentially tragic incidents such as these did not just happen to the few white men on Baffin. Native hunters, too, occasionally froze their extremities. Having survived one accident, and infinitely aware of the possibility of future life-threatening episodes, Dewey spent time in December typing the reports of his first few months on Baffin and developing and printing photographs — just in case.

The police and HBC employees, plus one white woman (presumably the wife of one of the HBC men[4]) and the resident naturalist numbered nine people. They celebrated Christmas together at the HBC house with a banquet, followed by cigars and wine supplied by the HBC manager. Dewey recalled, "It was a brief, warm touch of civilization and graciousness …"

Immediately after Christmas, Akatuga and his dog team carried eight hundred pounds of dog feed to the HBC outpost at Sermilling as a cache for the forthcoming expedition. He was back in less than a week, having covered 160 miles round trip.

On the morning of January 6, 1925, with a full moon due that night, Dewey and Akatuga loaded the sled again, this time with six hundred pounds of provisions. They fan-hitched the sixteen dogs to it, and sped away from Pangnirtung. The immediate objective was Issortukdjuak Fjord. Beyond that, Dewey had heard from Natives about a substantial lake due north of Nettilling Lake. He wanted to find that lake, explore and survey it, before completing the east–west journey. At the Native village of Nunatuk they had planned to team up with another Inuit with a second dog team and sled. He, Nowanalik, was to have carried mostly dog feed, while Akatuga's sled carried the other provisions. When they arrived at the village, Nowanalik changed his mind due to the soft snow conditions, and refused to go with them. It was too late to find another team and driver. Frustrated, Dewey decided to travel beyond the end of the fjord, deposit a cache of dog feed, then return to Sermilling for more, ready to strike out for the interior. It was an ambitious plan that failed, because, if indeed the lake existed, they were unable to reach it.

No matter how cold the temperature, the task of mapmaking had to be taken care of regularly. Dewey needed an accurate record of his expeditions into hitherto unknown territory. The only way to accomplish that was to take bearings on all noteworthy points. To do so, and to write down the observations, meant having his hands bare. Even for a few minutes at a time, he constantly risked serious frostbite.

The northerly advance to the lake's reported location had to be terminated when deep, soft snow made it virtually impossible for the dogs to pull the sled at more than an estimated two miles per hour, and that was with the two men pulling, as well. Soft snow was more than a hindrance to travel: it was also useless material with which to build an igloo. They had to travel ten miles beyond the fjord before they found a snowbank firm enough to use for an overnight stop.

Disappointment began to set in the next morning. The valley narrowed to a canyon about one hundred feet wide. Trapped within its walls, soft snow lay several feet deep. The dogs and sled could go no farther. Dewey strapped on his skis and continued alone to scout the way ahead, hoping for better conditions. Beyond the narrow canyon he found more deep, soft snow leading to a dead end. There was no alternative but to retreat to Sermilling. Without a second sled and driver, and held back by the soft snow, the expedition could not proceed. To add to the difficulties, the temperature dropped to −48°F.

They rested the dogs and themselves at the Sermilling outpost for two days, then began their return to Pangnirtung, Dewey not wasting the journey. He took the time to explore a long inlet off Issortukdjuak Fjord that the Natives knew as Ekaluardjuak. In a long finger pointing northwest, and a few miles in length, hemmed in by granite walls a thousand feet high, he found open water where, he said, "The tides are so strong … that the sea never freezes over." The tide was turning when they got there and raced back through the opening into Ekaluardjuak with great power.

They took their time going home, stopping at Native villages for anywhere from a few hours to a couple of days in some instances. Close to Pangnirtung Fjord they stopped to inspect four fox traps Akatuga had set early in the month. Two held prey: a white fox and a blue fox. They were added to the specimens destined for the National Museum's collection.

The expedition had not been a success, in that Dewey had not achieved his objectives. However, to balance that negative, he had gained immeasurable experience and had added useful detail to incomplete maps. He also knew he would go back when snow conditions made overland travel less difficult. His story of the journey in *Canadian Arctic Recollections* tells that they covered a round-trip distance of approximately four hundred miles in twenty days. That would have required them to travel an average of twenty miles per day, which seems excessive.[5] We know they stopped for at least four days at en route villages or outposts. They also had days when they covered far less than the twenty miles. A calculation based on Dewey's record of locations from that journey suggests the actual distance was more in the region of two hundred miles. Despite that discrepancy, considering it was Dewey's first major Arctic winter expedition, it was a fine achievement.

Exploring Baffin Island

On his return to Pangnirtung, considerably earlier than anticipated, Dewey hired an additional Inuit hunter, Kilabuk,[6] and his twelve dogs, for a planned hard exploratory journey into the Penny Highlands and on to the east coast via North Pangnirtung Fjord, with departure set for two weeks later. The plan was to use the two dog teams to get the provisions up to the pass. Then Kilabuk and his team would return to Pangnirtung while Dewey and Akatuga pushed on to the coast. In the interim, Akatuga went seal hunting — taking as many as possible. That large amount of meat, chopped and bagged, was to sustain the two dog teams on the hard mountain ascent, and for one team on the subsequent traverse to the east coast. Dewey also spent many hours preparing food for the men.

"The most time-consuming job for me was making large quantities of precooked stew frozen in small cubes." His recipe was made up of basic trail fare, but nutritious: "Smoked buffalo pemmican, white beans, desiccated potatoes, bacon, butter, and seasoning."[7] He said that this concoction was quick and easy to heat up on the trail at the end of a hard day and was enjoyed by whites and Inuit alike.

Dewey's rationale for this new expedition venture was simple: "So far as was known, no white man had ever crossed Pangnirtung Pass …" It was his intention "to run a survey route through it, and [leave] a detailed description of the terrain from sea to sea."[8]

Reaching the head of Pangnirtung Fjord took only a few hours. The flat land of the Weasel River delta gave no trouble either. By 4:30 p.m., with darkness rapidly approaching, their onward passage came to a halt, blocked by a rock moraine. They decided to tackle that impediment to the pass in the daylight, so built a snow house and settled in for the night. The sight that greeted them in the morning was daunting: "Four glaciers emerged from tributary valleys into the Weasel River gorge between rocky ranges in this sector. A scene of wilder grandeur would be hard to imagine. The moraine … spanned the valley to a depth of about 100 feet. It was composed of a great mass of sand, gravel, boulders, and blocks and layers of ice, all in rather awesome array."[9]

They hitched both dog teams to one sled and hauled it to the upper level of the moraine, without unloading, then repeated the exercise with the second sled. A second moraine soon after was dealt with in the same way. This part of the journey took the men up the valley between mountains of four to five

Pen-and-ink sketch of Pangnirtung Pass, by J. Dewey Soper.

thousand feet. As the route turned suddenly to the east, Dewey noted that the walls hemming them in rose almost sheer for a thousand feet or more. Now the river began a fairly steep rise, gaining three hundred feet in half a mile. A third moraine, more of an ice wall littered with stones and gravel, was too steep for the dogs to climb with loaded sleds, and unsafe for the men. To assist their ascent they cut a series of staggered steps in the ice. Urged on by the men, the dogs then dragged the empty sleds to the top. Dewey and the two Inuit made multiple climbs, carrying the loads on their backs, taking three hours for the effort. He commented, "For once we worked harder than the dogs."

The Inuit had warned that, as they moved higher, they would encounter vicious winds. They said that Pangnirtung Pass and Kingnait Pass were the windiest places they had ever been. Their description had obviously not adequately prepared Dewey for the reality. Where the river widened into a narrow but distinct tarn, they were hit suddenly and with great force: "At times the stronger squalls bowled them [the dogs] over completely while they struggled, with mournful howls, to keep on an even keel."

On one occasion the wind upset a loaded sled. Dewey reported stones weighing from ten to fifteen pounds being whipped from the slopes and tossed onto the frozen tarn. The wind swept the snow away so that, when it came time to camp for the night, Akatuga and Kilabuk had difficulty in finding suitable snow with which to build their shelter.

As they climbed higher, they came upon more icefalls, high and steep. Once again they cut steps, but at these two barriers the dogs were sent up without the sleds. Dewey, Akatuga, and Kilabuk man-hauled the empty sleds using bridles. They then went up and down the steps for hours carrying the food and supplies. It was exhausting work but the end of the climb was in sight. Dewey calculated that the average gradient from sea level at the head of the fjord to the summit of the pass was in the order of sixty-five feet to a mile. With the worst of the uphill climb over, Kilabuk's work ended. He turned downhill alone, except for his dogs and a few supplies on his otherwise empty sled. Dewey was extremely complimentary about his temporary assistant, describing Kilabuk as, "Always cheerful, and a hard worker always exercising good judgement and having plenty of 'know-how.'"

Dewey and Akatuga, with the remaining fourteen dogs and a heavy load, reached 1,300 feet, the highest point of the pass, later that day. A long, narrow lake that Dewey marked on his survey map as Summit Lake stretches five miles toward the north. The two tired men wanted to reach the far end of the lake before stopping for the night. The lake ice was thick and smooth from wind abrasion, but it undulated, making it hard work for their equally tired dogs. Dewey tried running ahead in the hope of inspiring the team to greater effort. It didn't work. The dogs had enough energy to pull the sled at walking pace, but no more. Still, Dewey and Akatuga kept them moving to reach their objective for that day. They finally stopped for the night, long after dark, in the shadow of another large moraine: the rubble from the Turner Glacier.

In daylight, after a night's sleep, they portaged the sled and contents piece by piece to the top of the moraine, giving the dogs an extra couple of hours to rest. They now followed a frozen creek under the granite stare of Mount Asgard (6,598 feet), Tête Blanche (7,073 feet), Mount Battle (4,420 feet), and others as yet unnamed.

"Everywhere one looked were nameless mysterious peaks, canyons, icecaps and glaciers. It was an unforgettable polar panorama, the vast Penny Icecap lying a short distance away to the northwest."[10]

Gale-force winds and wind-chill temperatures down to eighty below zero blasted them again. Dewey wrote in his daily journal:

> This monster of a pass has some torment in store for us every day in the way of various difficulties, hardship and suffering. The top of the Turner moraine is a wide, rugged waste of boulders, hummocks, and depressions interlarded with ice patches and mounds of snow; frequently there was not enough snow for proper sledging. Under such circumstances it was then necessary to cross naked rocks and gravel with exertion at the lash ropes, or else unload and carry through piecemeal. After a long session of sweaty toil we made it over.[11]

Dewey was well aware that the route they were following to the east coast was considerably more arduous and difficult than the alternate route through the Kingnait Pass. The Inuit from Pangnirtung Fjord had told him they would always use the Kingnait route for their own winter journeys to east coast settlements. Dewey's purpose in crossing the Pangnirtung was to make a proper survey of the route to update government maps. He admitted in one publication that "Anyone who succeeded in accomplishing it once [in winter] would hesitate to repeat the experience ..."[12]

In addition to surveying the land, Dewey was constantly on the lookout for wildlife. In this he was mostly disappointed. On the six-day crossing, the only signs of life were tracks of a small herd of caribou at Summit Lake, and the trail of a lone wolf in the same area. They also saw a raven near the mouth of the Weasel River early in the crossing. Other than that, Pangnirtung Pass was devoid of wildlife.

Now that they were over the pass and on a downhill slope, their progress improved. A tailwind, hitting them square in the back, helped them along the few miles of Glacier Lake, with Dewey wishing the lake was much longer, so easy was the travelling. The descent of the upper limits of the Owl River slowed them again: "In short order we found ourselves on a winding course through a snarl of boulders in a gloomy ravine."[13]

They angle of descent was steep, and both men were wary of making a false step. An accident up there, with no hope of rescue, would almost certainly have proved fatal. At the halfway point they released the dogs to make their own way down, and carefully lowered the sled on ropes, often taking up the strain by wrapping the restraining ropes around boulders to keep the sled from getting away from them. It was, Dewey wrote, "Truly brutal terrain."

Once off the steep incline and back on reasonably flat land, they harnessed the dogs to the sled again. The Owl River continued as a crystal-clear frozen stream of ice, averaging five feet in thickness and sometimes rafted and broken to twice that amount. The ice, when it was level, was beneficial to travel on in that the men, the dogs, and the sled could move at a fast pace, providing the weather conditions stayed calm. A sudden gale, however, powered down from the heights and drove into them with malicious intent.

"A vicious wind struck that went right through our heavy caribou skin clothing.… Our dogs were repeatedly bowled over and over on the glassy ice, and sometimes the heavy sledge surged sideways out of control."[14]

Inevitably, with the dogs out of position after being knocked off their feet by the wind, and the sled at the wrong angle, the dogs' traces became tangled. Straightening out that mess in a howling gale was no easy task. Dewey said the winds "sapped the vitality of men and dogs alike."[15]

The tempest blew itself out as suddenly as it had started, although a wind continued to blast them with fine sand. Darkness fell but the men and dogs pushed forward under the light of the moon. They had to keep going along the windswept Owl River valley until they reached the north end. There they found snow enough to build an igloo and rest for the night. They fed the dogs some seal meat but were too tired to cook for themselves. Instead they wrapped their sleeping bags around them and both fell into an exhausted sleep. Dewey wrote of that night: "Merciful is the relative joy and comfort of a snowhouse after the wind, sinister cold, toil, and fatigue."

The following day was not much better. They did make progress, but only with great care as the ice-covered stream was littered with large boulders that protruded above the surface. That night, February 10, 1925, Dewey calculated they had travelled a mere sixty-three miles from Pangnirtung at an average daily run of marginally more than twelve miles. Under the circumstances, he felt they had made quite good time.

They came down to the sea just before noon on February 12. North Pangnirtung Fjord was frozen solid. Some distance from where they stopped, an iceberg, estimated to be about eighty feet in height, was frozen into the fjord, more than fifty miles from the open sea of Davis Strait. Dewey and Akatuga camped early that day, to rest themselves and to rest the dogs that had suffered so much on the gruelling crossing of Pangnirtung Pass.

Under normal conditions, Kivitoo, their destination, should have been no more than a hard day's run. The winter refused to cooperate. Accumulations of loose snow and sometimes insurmountable obstacles of rafted pressure ice slowed them down. Despite the hard going, Dewey did not fail to notice the many tracks of the caribou that had crossed the fjord and climbed the snow slopes.

They arrived at Kivitoo in two days instead of one, in a blinding snowstorm, having followed vague signs of sled trails leading toward the small settlement run by a trading company. Once there, they built an igloo and stayed for two days to dry their clothes and sleeping bags. Both Dewey and Akatuga were suffering from patches of frostbite on their faces, in addition to general fatigue. The extended stop gave them time to attend to their own well-being as well as to that of the dogs.

On the trail again, in the general direction of home, they travelled on sea ice to Kekertukdjuak, a Native village on Broughton Island. There they had to shoot two of the dogs, which had come down with an illness resembling distemper. At that time the disease was incurable. Dewey traded tobacco and ammunition to purchase two fresh dogs from the locals. Continuing southeast on the sea ice paralleling the coast, they made Merchant's Bay after a hard-fought two days. Along the route the shore was just about as inhospitable as it could be, with cliffs in some places rising sheer to great heights. Soft, drifting snow and rafted ice impeded progress and kept them well offshore. They camped at night about a mile out to sea, off the entrance to Merchant's Bay.

Getting into Merchant's Bay from the open sea meant dragging the sled across a series of pressure ridges and rafted ice — always a slow and potentially dangerous task. They made it without accident and at once found the sled ran smoothly as they raced past Cape Searle toward the mouth of Padle Fjord, where there was a Native village. Twelve miles into Merchant's Bay they made camp out on the ice. The journey continued to be a daily challenge.

By morning the weather had turned against them once more. Drifting snow and squally winds reduced visibility. Neither Dewey nor Akatuga knew the exact location of the Native village, and the weather made finding it difficult. They eventually discovered sled tracks leading to the southeast and followed them to the shore of an island where a group of igloos were just discernable.

Dewey had been told that the men of the village, appropriately named Padle (for the adjacent fjord), were excellent hunters. That gave him confidence that they would be able to buy enough seal meat to keep his dogs fed for the overland crossing of Kingnait Pass back to Pangnirtung. Their unexpected arrival at Padle was greeted with enormous pleasure by the inhabitants. Strangers were always welcome, especially in the depths of winter. Dewey and Akatuga received an invitation to stay with the head man and his family, which included three attractive daughters. He described the rather unusual dwelling:

> The big lodge in which they lived was made of seal skins heavily banked with snow, measuring about 12 by 18 feet. Surprisingly enough, it was furnished with a board floor. Out of the ordinary, too, was a total of four large seal-oil lamps, which they used for heating, cooking, and lighting, and two good-sized sleeping platforms thickly covered with caribou and polar bear skins. The home was cosily warm, tidy, and clean.[16]

Dewey had planned to stay for two days to rest and prepare for another rough crossing of the mountain pass, but again the weather interfered. A warming spell took the temperature above zero on February 27 as dark clouds gathered overhead and in all directions: clear signs of an imminent blizzard. When the snow came soon after, it fell to a depth higher than a man's knees. Dewey said the lodge in which they stayed was almost buried under a huge snowdrift. There was no way the dogs could pull a laden sled under those conditions. For two days Dewey waited impatiently. On March 1, he and Akatuga tried to break out and start south, hoping to find the snow had crusted enough to bear the weight of the dogs, men, and sled.

They managed to travel a mere three miles in four hours before the soft snow forced them to give up the struggle. After making a cache of the dog feed and some equipment, they turned back to Padle. Until the snow hardened, there was nothing more to be done.

On March 6, with a marginal improvement in the weather, Dewey decided to try for the pass. The village headman, Kingodlik, volunteered to help for two days, as did his brother Kopik. They would carry part of the load on their own sled to make it easier on the dogs, and help break the trail. Averaging two miles per hour, the party pushed through thick snow and deep into Padle Fjord, making camp on the west side after eight hours of hard going. The next day, with lower temperatures and hard-packed snow, they reached the head of the fjord and continued up the Padle River to a natural campsite the Natives called Kangiana. There Kingodlik and Kopik prepared to return home.

Dewey was impressed that neither of the two Native men had asked for payment of any kind for their services. In thanks for their unselfish help, he gave them all of his remaining trade goods: "Files, ammunition, tobacco, matches, and two pocket knives which they received with undisguised delight." He was sad to say goodbye to his new friends and admitted he would have enjoyed their company for longer had they not turned back for Padle. On the morning of March 8 the four men said their goodbyes. Two went back down the fjord; two began the climb up to the pass. Dewey's main reason for taking the Kingnait Pass route home was to undertake a careful survey in order to update maps of the time.

The weather, which had caused them so much delay, turned once again. The clouds drifted away and the sun shone down to bring the temperature above zero. Dewey and Akatuga removed their caribou-skin outer clothes, took off their hats, and enjoyed the warmth. Around midday they saw a herd of fourteen caribou, and soon after, another five. Ravens appeared and croaked at them with their coarse voices. A couple of hours later they came upon a caribou herd Dewey numbered at seventy animals. The sight and smell of fresh meat on the hoof drove the dogs wild, causing Dewey and Akatuga to tie the sled to a large boulder to prevent the dogs running away with it.

Akatuga took out his rifle and brought down a caribou. Now they had fresh meat for themselves and for the dogs, and Dewey had another good

Courtesy of University of Saskatchewan and Roland Soper.

Sketch of barren ground caribou with antlers in the velvet phase, by J. Dewey Soper.

specimen for the museum. Working together, it took the two men only an hour to measure, skin, cut up the meat, and load it; then they were on the move again. As the afternoon wore on they passed more caribou herds, the abundance of which was a definite surprise to Dewey. He had expected to see a few, but not nearly so many.

The mountains bordering Kingnait Pass are less rugged than those at Pangnirtung Pass. They are not as high and they lack the glaciers and moraines that determine the course of the latter cross-country route. Even so, the Kingnait Pass is no less formidable. The winds blow just as strong up there as on the more northeasterly route. On Dewey's crossing, those winds created havoc anew for the dogs and for the men, who often had to walk doubled over to avoid being blown off their feet.

A lake straddles the Arctic Circle about halfway over the pass. In view of its geographical position, Dewey named it Circle Lake. They stopped there for a brief lunch break and to gather their strength for a steep climb. Dewey described what lay ahead: "Immediately south of Circle Lake is a rocky ridge nearly 200 feet high and approximately 600 feet above sea level. This crest totally obstructs the valley and constitutes the height of land between north and south drainages of Kingnait Pass."[17]

Good snow and a manageable slope meant they could reach the top without backtracking with loads. The men still had to help the dogs by hauling the loaded sled with them, taking occasional rest stops on the way up. At the top, another lake led away to the south before the trail dropped off again. Unlike the approach on the north side of the pass, the south side was a steep drop in two distinct sections that required them to cut steps in the hard snow and lower the sled by hand, the dogs having been taken down first.

From the ridge the trail runs down a river of ice littered with a dreadful collection of jagged rocks and rounded boulders for a couple of miles. At times the obstructions were so numerous and so close together that the dogs and sled had to run over the smoothest ones: hard on the sled runners and rough on the dogs' feet. The men found the going just as difficult as the dogs, and rested regularly, sometimes stopping for a mug of hot tea and a smoke. Dewey said that they were sweating, even without their caribou-skin clothes, though the temperature sat at −20°.

They had hoped to reach the head of Kingnait Fjord by nightfall but the frozen rubble down the river held them back. After eleven hours of abysmal travelling, men and dogs had had enough. The sea could wait until the next day. They found good snow with which to build a house and were settled in by mid-evening.

The last day of their crossing began early, and by about 10:00 a.m. they were almost at the sea, but their way ahead was barred by a final few hundred yards of turmoil. That penultimate stretch runs through a river gorge. The river was frozen, but the twice-daily high and turbulent tides had created a jigsaw puzzle of broken ice and pools of salt water. Threading their way through to the safety of the shoreline took skill and care, not to mention a certain amount of luck.

When they came out onto the level surface of the fjord, Dewey noted that they had completed the land crossing from north to south in two and a half days. In 1884 the German-American anthropologist Franz Boas[18] had taken eleven days to cross from south to north. Dewey's surveying measurements would be used to update the map that Boas had drawn forty-one years earlier.

Racing down the smooth fjord to the ice of Cumberland Sound, they surprised a white fox, the first they had seen. Akatuga aimed a couple of shots at it but missed. With ninety miles to go and no further land obstructions to slow them down, they covered the distance to Pangnirtung in two long days. They had travelled over five hundred miles of incredibly difficult terrain in thirty-four days. More important, Dewey had taken precise readings en route for the new maps he would draw.

As was his custom, Dewey immediately set to work typing his notes and official reports of the expedition, as well as preserving the few specimens he had collected. With those tasks completed, he began preparations for his next, much longer expedition.

9

The Nettilling Lake Expedition

On April 22, Dewey set off again, this time on a planned four-month expedition. The objective was to make a detailed survey of Nettilling Lake to update current maps, to investigate the wildlife of the region, and to return with as many specimens from nearly all departments of natural history. This time he was nominal head of a large party that included Constable Tom Tredgold, as well as nine Inuit — six men, two of their wives, and one child.

None of the Inuit in the group had ever travelled to the lake, so it was a new adventure for them, as well. Tredgold went along, with the blessings of his superior, as an assistant/companion to Dewey, and to make his own report on the interior, as little was known about it at the time.

Between the ten adults they managed several sleds and about seventy dogs. Twenty of the dogs were there just to haul a sled that had been specially built to carry a surf boat (*The Fly*) that was to be used as an exploration vessel on Nettilling Lake. The boat, which weighed about eight hundred pounds, was also loaded with over a thousand pounds of supplies. Equipped with sails and a centre-board keel, the boat was on loan from the RCMP. An eighteen-foot canvas canoe had already been shipped to Kangertukdjuak Bay, on Nettilling Fjord, the previous autumn.

They had planned to spend the first night on the trail at the Inuit village on Imigen Island, some forty miles away to the southwest across Cumberland

Sound. Rafted ice along the shore of the sound combined with high, rounded snowbanks out on the sea ice slowed them down. The dogs had trouble pulling the big sled with the boat over the hummocks, so the Inuit team drivers took a few from the other sleds and added them to the original twenty. The rolling terrain created another problem, and, concerned by the lateral swaying of the boat, four men had to trot beside it to keep it steady. Instead of forty miles, they covered only twenty-eight — still a good distance considering the conditions on the sea ice — before they stopped and built snow houses for the night. The next day was no better, although they did reach Imigen in late afternoon.

Having the boat on Nettilling Lake obviously was to be a distinct advantage when it came to surveying the lake's coastline in the short summer, but getting it there in late winter proved to be a daily challenge. Fifteen miles west of Imigen, as they turned into the mouth of Nettilling Fjord, patches of open water along the coast and across the fjord and the thin ice around them forced the group to detour over a rocky ridge. Getting the boat over that obstacle required the best efforts of forty dogs and everyone in the party. The problems continued as they moved up the narrow fjord. Dewey wrote, "A few miles beyond … we encountered much water under the snow.… The slush and water were fully a foot deep, and deceptively crusted over with a layer of dry hard snow."[1]

Such conditions are a nightmare for travel by dog team or on foot. If the snow crust is strong enough to carry significant weight without cracking or breaking, it is possible to keep moving. Dogs can usually cross without difficulty. The weight of a man, however, can break through. A heavily loaded sled becomes a distinct liability. The expedition's sleds broke through the hard snow and sunk up to their crossbars. Often they had to employ two dog teams in tandem to pull a sled free. The large sled and boat (still loaded) caused almost insurmountable grief. When that weight broke through in one location, it took the might of sixty dogs, plus all the manpower, to get it moving again and onto more solid ground. Dewey described the hardships and the triumphs:

> Just when the morale of the exhausted party was at a low ebb — when darkness was near at hand and the cold slush was freezing our legs and the sledges — we emerged from another bog of slush and reached hard snow beyond.[2]

The Nettilling Lake Expedition

They were on firm ground again, but their trials were far from over. In the morning a southeast wind blew up the fjord. The temperature rose to 16°, the wind strength increased to gale force, and snow began to fall. Soon the land was barely visible and even the dogs up ahead were often lost in the swirling snow. There was no alternative but to make a halt, build snow houses, and get under cover as fast as possible. The blizzard lasted throughout that day and night and into mid-afternoon of the next day. With so many people, and all with wet clothes, there was no possibility of getting anything dry. They crawled into their sleeping bags as they were and tried to sleep.

When the wind and snow had died away, and the convoy started moving again, they ran into more water under the snow crust. As soon as they found a large enough dry section, Dewey called a halt for the rest of the day. He detailed the men to go seal hunting to feed the dogs, while the women worked on drying the clothes.

As they moved up the fjord, the slush and water persisted. The day after their rest they covered only six miles. Progress was now blocked by open water, where a tide rip spanned the fjord from shore to shore. Now the boat became useful, no longer a heavy and awkward hindrance. They launched it during slack water at low tide and spent the next two hours ferrying everything — dogs, people, freight, and sleds — across to the solid ice beyond the gap.

There is another, far more dangerous tidal rip called Sarbukdjuak farther up the fjord. Said to be the most dangerous in the region, it was to be avoided at all costs. That meant taking an inland detour and making two trips to carry all the freight. To allow time to get everything together beyond the tide rip, to repair a sled and dog harnesses, and to hunt seals, Dewey called for a two-night stop.

His writings to this point on the expedition, after ten days on the move, are completely devoid of wildlife notations. At the location of the two-night stop he explained the lack and at last added some sightings: "Tredgold and I explored the locality on snowshoes, took bearings for a new exploratory map and kept our eyes peeled for wildlife. As yet, the latter was scarce, but here and there were signs of hare, fox, wolf, weasel, and caribou. This day the first male snow bunting appeared, though still without song."[3]

That day, too, a huge flock of an estimated one thousand king eiders (*Somateria spectabilis*) flew over, heading northwest. Later, dozens more landed on the open water of the nearby tide hole in the ice. Such sightings were guaranteed to brighten even the hardest days for Dewey.

When they were ready to trek again, he moved part of the outfit close to Kangia, at the head of Nettilling Fjord, leaving the main camp by the tide hole while the seal hunt continued. By this time temperatures during the day were rising as high as 45°.

On May 4 the party teamed up again at the cache near Kangia, leaving some freight still at the camp by the tide pool. From this point a chain of small lakes linked by streams are scattered west for close to twenty miles, to the eastern extremity of Nettilling Lake. Dewey broke it down thus:

> The first lake along the route is 2 miles long and lies between two steep, broken ridges about 500 feet high. At the northwest end of the lake the land rises brokenly and a stream 840 yards long enters from the second lake to the west. This lake lies 130 feet above the sea. A small stream with a waterfall enters on the north shore from a series of lakes in that quarter. The second lake is half a mile long. A portage of 495 yards separates it from the third lake, which is 1¾ miles long and lies at an elevation of 200 feet. A narrow, rocky stream connects the two. The surrounding hills are bold and broken, with an average height of about 400 feet. The next and largest lake of the route is Amittok, which is 8 miles long and lies at 180 feet above sea level. The drainage of the first three lakes is to Nettilling Fjord.[4]

On the evening of May 5, Dewey's thirty-second birthday, they set up base camp at Isoa, on the mouth of the Takuirbing River at the eastern tip of Nettilling Lake. This was the end of the line for most of the dogs and for four of the Inuit. Relieved of their burden of the boat, they returned at once to Pangnirtung with the large sled. Akatuga and Kungesinil, their wives, and the child remained with Dewey and Tredgold, along with seven of the dogs. While Dewey waited for the weather to improve, the two Inuit collected the remaining stores from the tide pool camp and brought them up to base.

The Nettilling Lake Expedition

Dewey in early spring garb while snowshoeing at Nettilling Lake, Baffin Island, late May or early June 1925, when temperatures were above zero.

The base camp, which would be a semi-permanent home for a few months, consisted of a canvas tent for the Inuit families and a double silk polar tent for the two white men. They surrounded both with a windbreak of a high snow wall.

The site had some historic importance. German scientist Bernard Hantzsch had camped there with his Inuit assistants in 1910 while exploring across the southwest foot of Baffin Island. The Inuit, too, had often camped at Isoa because the site offered fresh water and food, including caribou, hare, ptarmigan, ringed seal, and Arctic char.

Dewey was anxious to get in *The Fly* and sail around the lake to explore and chart its bays and inlets. With ice covering it as far as the eye could see, he had to exercise patience. He was well aware that Crawford Noble Jr.,[5] son of the Scottish owner of the Blacklead and Kekerten Island whaling stations, had sailed all the way around the lake in 1902, sketching a rather rough map from compass bearings alone. Despite that amateurish survey, Noble's map was the first rendition of the estimated outline of the lake. As soon as possible, Dewey wanted to survey and draw the first professional map of Nettilling Lake — or Netchilik, the "Lake of seals."

The May weather proved intractable. Blizzard after blizzard pounded the camp, leaving the men little choice but to take to their sleeping bags: there to rest, converse with one another, or read until the winds dropped and the snow ceased. One storm, with winds up to eighty miles per hour, lasted a noisy eight days. When the weather eventually relented, the initial migration of snow buntings arrived. Scores of the males entertained the camp and surrounding tundra with their songs, which Dewey referred to as, "A real musical treat that I was now hearing for the first time."

While he waited for the ice to break up and dissipate, Dewey worked long hours, usually sixteen hours each day, hunting, collecting, preserving, pressing, and cataloguing specimens. Caribou sightings became more frequent and they were able to shoot a few for meat and for Dewey to preserve the hides and antlers for the museum. Akatuga harpooned a few ringed seals through the ice on the edge of the lake: meat for the dogs and additional specimens for the museum. When the specimens were later examined in Ottawa by Dr. R.M. Anderson, he discovered they were a new subspecies that he subsequently named the Nettilling ringed seal and gave the Latin name of *Phoca hispida soperi*, in Dewey's honour.

Dewey ready for a late spring hunting trip.

Roland Soper Collection.

The midnight sun lasts an all too short three weeks in June at that latitude. Dewey took advantage of the constant daylight to work increasingly long hours. "Despite our fatigue, it somehow seemed a sacrilege to go to bed at midnight when the sun was shining brightly and the birds were rapturous with song."[6]

As the weather improved with the advent of summer, the long-awaited Baffin Island wildlife reappeared. "Caribou appeared in increasing numbers.... We saw wolves and Arctic foxes with greater frequency and new bird arrivals were now daily events."[7]

His list of birds sighted and specimens taken over those few weeks included horned larks (among the first to arrive), Lapland longspurs, loons, pipits, plovers, red phalaropes, purple sandpipers, gulls, loons, and old squaw ducks. Beside the birds, which he loved to listen to, he thrilled at the mournful sound of wolves howling from the sanctuary of the nearby rocky hills. Flocks of Canada geese, lesser snow geese, and blue geese circled over the lake ice, landing occasionally to feed on the tundra.

Dewey bringing in a caribou specimen by canoe for the National Museum of Canada. East end of Nettilling Lake, Baffin Island, August 1925.

Dewey hoped the geese would settle close by, or in adjacent meadowlands, and nest. At that time, no one in the scientific world knew where the blue geese had their breeding grounds, so he was disappointed when they all soon flew away. Neither he nor any member of his party saw any indication of geese nesting in the vicinity of Nettilling Lake in the summer of 1925. As the birds and mammals returned, so, too, did the Arctic plant life. Purple saxifrage (*Saxifraga oppositifolia*) soon carpeted the snow-free slopes of the neighbouring hills. Tufts of grass and heather peaked through the snow at the lower levels. In late June and early July, later flowers bloomed, among them white heather (*Cassiope tetragona*), mountain avens (*Dryas integrifolia*), Arctic blueberry (*Vaccinium uliginosum*), and Labrador tea (*Ledum palustre*). In July and August an abundance of other plants added their beauty to the landscape.

August arrived but the ice on the lake stayed put. A north-pointing arm, however — one connected to the lake by three very narrow channels — was open. Dewey paddled the canvas canoe on part of it without seeing much, apart from some old Inuit campsites. As the weather improved, Akatuga and Kungesinil caulked the seams of the surf boat where necessary and prepared it for use. Earlier on the expedition, Dewey had shown his Inuit helpers how to properly skin, preserve, and pack large mammals and birds. That left him with more time for the smaller, more delicate specimens and for writing his notes, while waiting for the ice to retreat.

Dewey in his voluminous tent preparing bird specimens for the National Museum of Canada at his camp beside Nettilling Lake, Baffin Island, summer 1925.

In the middle of the month the lake was open enough to launch the sailboat. Once loaded, and with the canvas canoe in tow, they set course to find the mouth of the Amadjuak River on the south side of the lake. A strong north wind kept the gaff sails filled the first day and all onboard, whites and Inuit alike, enjoyed being out on the water. The second day was more of a trial. The wind dropped and the surface of the lake became glassy smooth. The sails hung like limp rags. There was no alternative but to break out the oars and row the heavy boat. That night, after rowing for hours, they suffered aching backs and blistered hands. The total distance from base camp to the Amadjuak River, on the most direct route, would have been approximately 88 statute miles; however, Dewey would have explored all the bays and inlets, taking survey measurements wherever possible, in order to create an accurate map of the southern side of Nettilling Lake. Consequently, *The Fly*'s course would have been much longer.

Contrary winds and choppy waves slowed the boat's progress. Two gales forced them ashore. As soon as the weather marginally improved, they went back on the lake. Nettilling's shores are heavily indented on the north, south, and east sides, and littered with islands and islets. The land decreases in altitude toward the west until it is little higher than the lake. Finding the mouth of a river, hidden as it was by "a screen of overlapping islands and points" proved difficult, but not impossible. The Amadjuak flows out of the eponymous lake and runs at considerable speed for its forty-mile journey to Nettilling Lake. Dewey and his party walked upstream for a few miles, noting the power of the many rapids. He acknowledged that the river could be navigated by canoe but would require many portages to bypass the worst rapids. The season was too far advanced to go farther up the river in 1925. That exploration would have to wait for a future visit, as Dewey wanted to study the western and northern shores of the lake and complete a circumnavigation.

They spent days cruising slowly along the swampy west in mixed weather: sometimes under sail; sometimes rowing hard. The Koukdjuak River connects Nettilling Lake with Foxe Basin. It is a wide river (varying from half a mile to two miles) and roughly forty miles in length. Its depth close to Nettilling Lake is no more than two or three feet with a fast current, although the surface is deceptively smooth. Dewey had intended following it to the sea at Foxe Basin. Once again, the weather intervened. Although they managed to cover an estimated ten miles, a succession of gales forced them ashore and kept the party in camp on soft tundra for four days.[8] Dewey made the sensible decision to retreat to base camp, more than one hundred miles to the east, if the winds would allow it. They managed to get out of the river on September 5, after taking one and a half days to cover the short distance upstream. Four and a half days later they arrived back at the camp.

In less than ten days the RCMP boat *Lady Borden* was due to meet them in Nettilling Fjord. They stored the surf boat on land at the southeast corner of Amittok Lake, between the Takuirbing River and Nettilling Fjord. There it would stay until required again the next summer. The heavy load of specimens collected over the past months also had to be considered. Dewey cached that immensely valuable cargo, with a quantity of food supplies, in a cave not far from base camp. Covered in a waterproof tarpaulin and, one assumes, protected by a thick wall of stones, they would be safe from scavengers until winter snows made it possible to retrieve them by dogsled. After paddling up the Takuirbing River and through the chain of lakes in the canoe, the expedition party arrived at Nettilling Fjord in time for their reunion with the *Lady Borden*. Unfortunately for Dewey and his team, the boat was delayed, so they spent a wet, windy, and uncomfortable week in their tents waiting for it to arrive. They eventually reached Pangnirtung in late September, after an absence of five months.

Between the end of September and early January there was little opportunity for travel by land and virtually none by water, the weather making journeys impractical. Dewey spent that time writing his reports, updating maps, and preparing for a winter return to the west coast.

10

A Winter Traverse

Dewey left Pangnirtung to attempt the overland crossing to Foxe Basin on January 9, 1926, with four Natives — Akatuga, Newkeguak,[1] Poojut, and Attaguyuk — and three dog teams and sleds. Two of the Natives and one dog team would retrieve the specimens cached in the cave the previous September and take them back to Pangnirtung. Dewey, with the remaining two Natives and dog teams, would continue to the west coast at Foxe Basin, if possible. If successful, it would make him only the second white man to accomplish the feat.[2]

Following an extremely arduous journey in temperatures varying from −30° to −42°, Dewey and his men reached the approximate site of the cache on January 26. En route they had stopped for nine days on Nettilling Fjord to hunt seals for dog food — needing, by Dewey's estimate, approximately one ton to feed the animals for the overland crossing. A full day of searching for the cache proved ineffective, hidden as it was by heavy snowfalls. Frustrated, but determined to complete his expedition as planned, despite only having just enough dog feed for the purpose, Dewey sent two Natives and one dog team and the empty sled back to Pangnirtung. He and Akatuga, along with one other companion, spent two days crossing the frozen length of Nettilling Lake, reaching the western shore north of the Koukdjuak River. From there they struck out on January 31 on a course of 290°. In

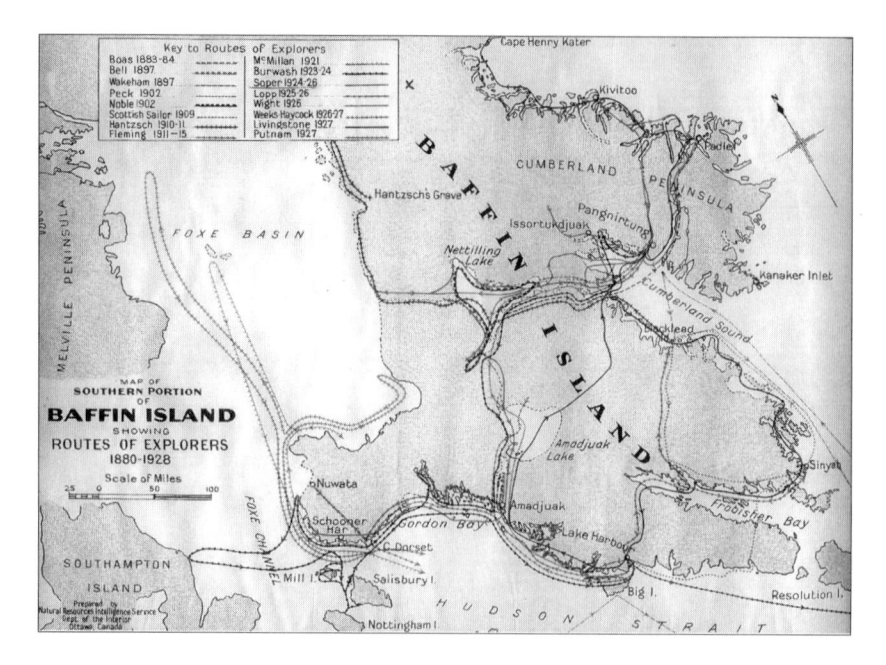

Map of Southern Baffin Island, showing routes of explorers, 1880–1928. **Source:** Library and Archives Canada/*Southern Baffin Island: An Account of Exploration, Investigation and Settlement During the Past Fifty Years* /AMICUS 4379308/Map between pages 102–03).

the distance they could see a range of low-lying hills, which Dewey had observed from the Koukdjuak River in September. When they reached them, the rounded hills were found to be no more than thirty feet high and swept clean of snow by the wind.

Planning on making a lightweight dash to the coast, Dewey camped on the frozen tundra for a night in a quickly built igloo and cached all of their supplies except those needed to sustain them for five days. They camped the next night close to the seashore. Dewey was almost certainly excited to be there but his notes betray no emotion. On the morning of February 2 he began his survey. Describing the scene, he wrote, "The coast was found to run northeast in one direction and southeast in the other. It was bordered by a wide tidal flat packed with broken ice resting on mud. To the south and southeast a line of vapour extended inland, probably indicating the course of the lower part of the Koukdjuak River.... Back from the shore the land rises very slowly."[3]

Along the shore, thick-broken ice was rafted into pressure ridges between ten and twenty feet high. His observations showed that the Foxe Basin coast of Baffin Island was actually 2° of longitude east of that marked on existing maps of the time. At the same time he noted that Nettilling Lake was, in fact, only about half as big as originally believed. Dewey followed the shoreline of the Foxe Basin northeast for about five miles until he could again see low hills. Those, he assumed, were a continuation of the ones they had crossed on the journey from the west end of the lake. Having achieved his goal and taken his measurements, Dewey and the Natives retraced their route to the lake, collecting the supplies cached a few days earlier.

On the north side of the lake, where caribou traditionally are to be found during some seasons, Dewey had intended shooting a few for dog food before making a second crossing to Foxe Basin at a more southerly point. In this they were disappointed. There were no caribou to be found. Even worse, one of the dogs, which had run off a couple of weeks before, had broken into the dog feed cache and eaten everything, including a couple of good caribou skins. With his dogs starving, Dewey had little choice but to turn in the direction of Pangnirtung. Now began a tough journey in extremely low temperatures. All three men suffered facial frostbite and the dogs found it hard going in the cold. Dewey recorded his thoughts about that first day heading east:

> The whole day has been an unceasing battle with the cold. It is positively forbidding, savage and sinister in its intensity — quite unlike the more moderate cold of the eastern seaboard. The dog harness is frozen stiff even in use, while the rawhide traces are hard and brittle and rather easily broken. The like of this had never come into my life before. The hours seemed interminable with the tramp, tramp, tramp of many feet and the endless fight to keep warm. Freezing was a serious factor. Eskimo faces appeared to freeze as readily as my own. Last night we treated our faces with carron oil which seemed to give some relief.[4]

Following the north shore, and recording each inlet and bay and details of the terrain behind, including seeing regular mirages and leaving a cairn with a brief record of the journey, it took five days to reach a point where they intersected their westbound trail. Nearly sixty years later, in August 1984, an expedition team discovered two, possibly three, of the cairns that Dewey Soper built on the shores of the lake. In two, at least, he had left brief, signed, handwritten records of his journey. One, in the Karmang cairn at the top of Mirage Bay, on the north shore, is dated February 1926. Strangely, included with Dewey's message is another note written in syllabics, dated July (but, apparently, no year given), and signed by Nungusuittuq. There is no record in Dewey's notes, published or otherwise, to suggest anyone named Nungusuittuq had worked with him on the expedition; therefore, it is most likely that the Inuit had opened the cairn sometime after the Soper party departed in April 1926 and left his own note.[5]

Dewey's note reads:

> Record deposited by J. Dewey Soper, Naturalist, of the Geological Survey of Canada, February 6th, 1926. Left Pangnirtung Fiord, Cumberland Gulf, with four natives, Akatuga, Newkega, Pasjoon and Koonalooso[6] on January 9th to make a traverse to Fox[e] Channel via Nettilling Lake. The two latter natives were engaged as extras to freight dog feed to the east side of Nettilling Lake, from which point they were sent back on the morning of January 28. I successfully reached Fox[e] Channel at a point approx. magnetic north from the exit of the Koukdjuak [River], in the forenoon of February 2nd. The coast there is many miles farther east than is shown on the latest maps. Leaving Fox[e] Channel the following day I adopted a course southeast, then east, true, until Nettilling Lake was reached, after which its west coast was followed and mapped to this point. Today I start back for Pangnirtung, following and mapping the north coast of Nettilling Lake en route. Dog feed low and no game. All well. J. Dewey Soper, Northern extremity of Nettilling Lake, Baffin Island, February 6, 1926.

A week after reaching the head of Nettilling Fjord, they stopped off for a night to visit with William Duval and his family at American Harbour. On the final leg home they met Sergeant Wright and Constable Tom Tredgold of the RCMP heading out on patrol. The policemen gave Akatuga the sad news that his wife, Unga, had died during his absence. It was, therefore, a much saddened party of three who returned to Pangnirtung. They were home, having covered 650 miles in thirty-seven days, but there was still a large cache of important specimens somewhere to the west between the head of Nettilling Fjord and the lake.

Three weeks after getting home, Dewey set out once more to find his missing collection. Once again he left with the same four Natives and three dog teams. As with all winter journeys that crossed water, frozen over though it was, the Natives sought out blowholes in the ice and took as many seals as possible for dog food. The weather played rough, keeping the group in their tents for a few days as a typical Arctic storm swept through. On March 19, two weeks out from Pangnirtung, they reached Amittok Lake, where *The Fly* rested onshore.

Dewey and Newkeguak then took a sled-load of dog food and cached it just east of the mouth of the Amadjuak River on the south side of Nettilling Lake.

Pen-and-ink sketch of *The Fly* under sail on Nettilling Lake, by J. Dewey Soper.

The remaining three Natives and dog teams, with Akatuga in charge, stayed behind to dig through the deep snow in search of the collections cache. To Dewey's relief, this time they were successful. *The Fly* was also well covered with snow, requiring hours of digging to free her. The five men then somehow hauled not only the scientific collection but also the heavy surfboat down to Nettilling Fjord and partway along its length toward Cumberland Sound. Before long the sea ice became too rough for the small party to move the sleds with the boat. There is an air of resignation in Dewey's words about the latest problem: "With much difficulty, the boat was hauled to the shore and left there above the high tide mark."[7] Without that heavy burden, they covered the final miles across the sound to Pangnirtung by the evening of April 1.

Dewey spent the next week or so working long hours on his specimens from the summer expedition and preparing them for shipment to Ottawa when the SS *Beothic* arrived in the summer. He also was getting ready to leave Pangnirtung for the last time. For his final months of this two-year Baffin Island expedition, Dewey planned to base himself at Cape Dorset in order to find out as much as possible about the flora, fauna, and geography of the Foxe Peninsula over the summer. He needed to leave as early as possible to ensure that his two Native companions would be able to return from Cape Dorset before the ice began its annual melt and prevented them from travelling. Consequently, a scant ten days after his return to base he said goodbye to the Mounties he had lived with since the summer of 1924, and to the village of Pangnirtung. Although he travelled extensively over southern Baffin Island in the next few years, he never returned to the windy fjord.

11

Cape Dorset Summer

With Akatuga and Newkeguak, and with two sleds and twenty-seven dogs, Dewey started back to Nettilling Lake on April 11, 1926. The initial goal on this part of the journey was the HBC post at Amadjuak Bay on Hudson Strait. Travelling fast, perhaps due to the number of dogs with them, they reached the Amadjuak River in eight days, despite having been stormbound for one full day. There they retrieved the cache of dog food left a few weeks earlier. Dewey also took a side trip of a few miles with one sled and team to take a close look at the Pingua Hills, which, he believed, had never been visited by a white man. Rising some four hundred feet above the surrounding terrain, and easily visible for many miles, Dewey noted there was a "good view from the top, in all directions."

From the mouth of the Amadjuak River to Hudson Strait they were in virtually uncharted territory.[1] Neither of the two Inuit had been there. Dewey certainly hadn't either. All they had to guide them was what Dewey referred to as "an old, inaccurate map" and his skills as a navigator.

Following the river as much as possible in deep snow, they reached Amadjuak Lake, fifty miles away, in three days. They camped[2] on the north shore for one night, then set course almost due south to where the lake meets the short Mingo River. They made the crossing in one day, having covered an impressive forty miles.

ARCTIC NATURALIST

From there, after a fast run across Mingo Lake, the flat land gave way to a coastal mountain range. Dewey had been told of a gap in the range and, after some searching, found it and two small lakes partway up. Getting their supplies up the incline required two trips with all dogs hitched to one sled. It was a difficult route but, once over the divide, they had a relatively trouble-free run downhill to the HBC post, which they reached in mid-afternoon of April 26. They had covered an estimated 385 miles in difficult wintry conditions at an average speed of twenty-four miles per day. David Wark, the local HBC manager, was pleased to see them. New faces were always welcome at remote outposts.

As soon as possible, Akatuga and Newkeguak went seal hunting with local Inuit to collect enough seals to feed their dog teams for the long journey back to Pangnirtung. Meanwhile, Dewey found considerable frustration in trying to persuade the Inuit who would travel with him to Cape Dorset to get out and hunt seals for *their* dog teams. He was anxious because the sea ice was already beginning to rot and lose its stability. Two weeks went by before sufficient seal meat had been accumulated to ensure the dogs' survival on the journey. Dewey wrote, "The delays and frustrations here were not easily forgotten. [David] Wark intervened on my behalf on several occasions, but apparently got little or no results." For the first time, Dewey showed a semblance of anger at the Inuit: "I began to see that these natives seemed to lack the reliability and drive of the Pangnirtung Eskimos."[3]

Hudson Strait is noted for its high tides, its ice, and for the strength of its currents. Along the north shoreline, from the vicinity of Lake Harbour — where the highest tide is over forty feet — to the longitude of Cape Dorset — where the tidal level reaches sixteen feet — the ice can be in motion even in the coldest months of January and February. By the time Dewey was able to leave on May 14, the sea ice was already showing signs of weakening. Sea water covered it in many places for the first fifty miles, although the travelling otherwise was reasonably good. Twenty five miles farther on, off Chorkbak Inlet, they found open water with no ice where it was needed most.

Fortunately for Dewey there was a large Inuit whaleboat, known as a Peterhead boat, and a driver at a Native settlement on the nearby Tikoot Islands. He was able to hire the boat and its owner, plus another Tikoot Islander, to transport his complete outfit of men, dogs, sleds, and provisions some forty miles along the coast. On the west side of Andrew Gordon Bay, with Cape Dorset less than fifty miles away, they found land-fast ice again. One advantage to the unexpected open water was that they were able to shoot a couple of swimming seals for the dogs on the way. Throughout the Soper party's trek along the coast by ice and by sea they suffered many falls of wet snow and sleet with freezing nights. By the time they reached Cape Dorset they were, Dewey said, in wretched condition with all clothing soaked. He was relieved to arrive at the HBC post, where manager Jim Aitken and his assistant (McBride) greeted them. There the Inuit with the dog teams left Dewey and hurried back to Amadjuak before the ice made coastal travel too hazardous.

Jim Aitken gave Dewey a comfortable room big enough to live and work in when necessary. After his tough 525-mile journey from Pangnirtung, he was comfortable again and able to dry his clothes and sleeping bag in readiness for his next journey: "Now I could settle down to full-time zoological and geographical investigations for the entire spring and summer. In this region at that time very little was known scientifically about the country and its inhabitants. I brought my field notes up-to-date, mapped the Pangnirtung–Dorset traverse, and unpacked taxidermy instruments and materials in readiness for the specimens I was soon to collect."[4]

June carried spring weather to the region, bringing warmer air. The snow began to melt and the rivers and streams filled to overflowing. Dewey had not been able to collect any specimens of note over the winter, but now he happily recorded taking "weasels, some brown and collared lemmings, and ringed and bearded seals." The birds, always his greatest pleasure, started to arrive with the warmer conditions. He took specimens of Lapland longspurs, snow buntings, semipalmated plovers (*Charadrius semipalmatus*), water pipits, horned larks, a rough-legged hawk (*Buteo lagopus*), and a purple sandpiper.

In open water on the sea and on local ponds he saw old squaw ducks (*Clangula hyemalis*) and red-throated loons (*Gavia stellata*). Hundreds of snow and blue geese[5] flew over, honking all the way to their breeding grounds somewhere north of the Dorset Mountains. Discovering the breeding grounds of the blue goose was, at that time, one of Dewey's greatest passions. He watched the arrowhead formations flying high overhead and pondered the whereabouts of their eventual landing and nesting sites — perhaps, he hoped, somewhere not too far away, in the upper part of the Foxe Peninsula or maybe a little farther northeast, close to Bowman Bay.

Spring, especially the Arctic spring, excited Dewey. His notes are rich with colourful reactions to the new season: "What a thrill to witness and feel once again the various manifestations of awakening spring, especially after a long Arctic winter!"[6] He even quotes Thoreau on the subject: "Spring is a natural resurrection, an experience in immortality."[7]

Much of Dewey's two and a half months based at Cape Dorset was spent studying and collecting specimens of sea birds. On June 19 he sailed to the Foxe Islands,[8] on the west side of Andrew Gordon Bay, in a rented HBC whaleboat with two Inuit companions and their wives. On leaving Dorset, the boat had to be dragged over sea ice for more than a mile to open water.

Once there, he stayed on the island group for the rest of that month with the Inuit, collecting skins and eggs, and studying the breeding colonies of eiders, old squaw ducks, and herring gulls: "In some places the nests were so close together that real care was required not to tread on the eggs. While the females incubated [the eggs], multitudes of handsome males gathered in sociable 'rafts' on the surrounding waters."[9]

While on one of the islands, Dewey met an old, and apparently well-respected, Inuit hunter who, he said, "claimed he knew the exact location of the nesting grounds of the blue goose." Another Inuit confirmed the old man's story. For Dewey, knowing he did not have time to embark on a journey to prove the claim that summer, it was a bittersweet revelation. He knew he could not get there until at the earliest the next summer, and before that he would have to convince the authorities in Ottawa that the expedition would be a worthwhile expense.

Having the sailboat and knowledgeable Natives with him at the island group helped Dewey immensely. With their assistance, in addition to the birds, he was able to collect a few mammals, marine invertebrates, and plants. He noted, "Many new records highlighted the day's activities. The entire period proved to be a time of especially stimulating discoveries and zoological rewards."

Cape Dorset stands on an island which is separate from the mainland at most, but not all, stages of the tide. Soon after Dewey returned to Cape Dorset from the islands, he went to the mainland and explored a series of small lakes a few miles inland. The lakes drain into the Elik River, which

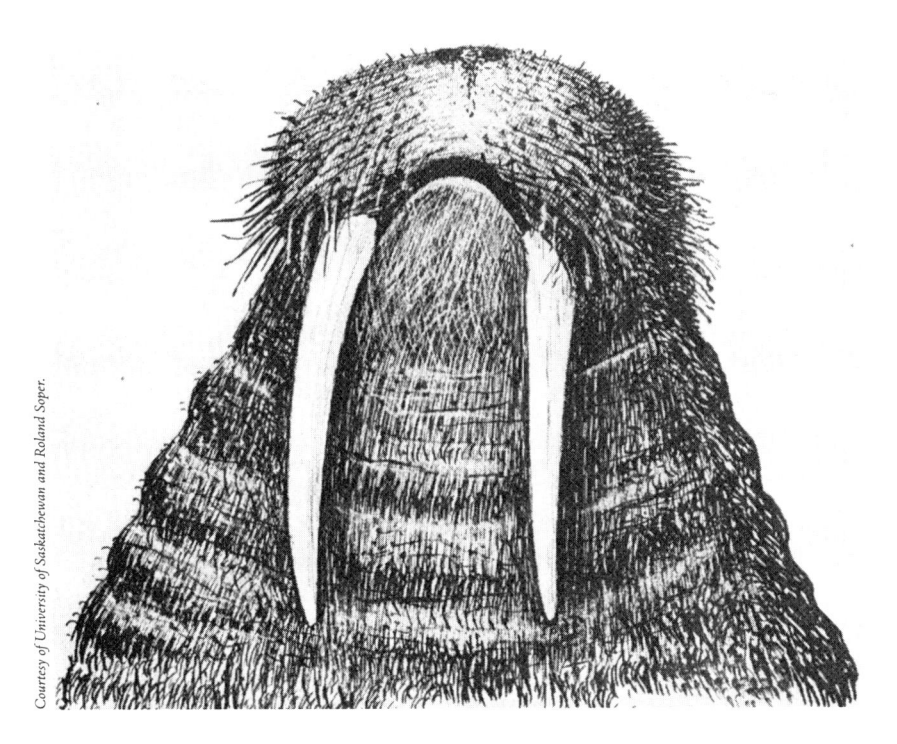

Sketch of a walrus head and tusks, by J. Dewey Soper.

drops thirty feet[10] to the sea in its short length of half a mile. Dewey was up at the lakes for three days and nights. He had people with him, but does not specify who they were. It's possible that Jim Aitken was among them, as Dewey named the lakes after the HBC post manager.

They collected a large number of birds during their brief stay, including red-breasted merganser (*Mergus serrator*), common eider, Arctic (*Gavia arctica*) and red-throated loons (*Gavia stellata*), old squaw ducks, non-breeding blue and lesser snow geese, Hutchins's geese (*Branta canadensis hutchinsii*), snowy owl, rock ptarmigan, herring gull, and white-rumped sandpiper (*Calidris fuscicollis*). On a coastal cliff, during the same excursion, Dewey collected eggs and specimens from black guillemots (*Cepphus grylle*), plus what he called "some strange plants."

On July 24, Jim Aitken took Dewey with him on a coastal voyage to Bowdoin Harbour in the HBC schooner *Metik*. The 140-mile return voyage took them past King Charles Cape into Foxe Channel and almost as far as the Trinity Islands. Aitken was there to buy furs from the local Inuit, probably from the coastal village of Nuwata, halfway up the Foxe Peninsula, and stayed two days at Bowdoin, allowing Dewey many hours in which to explore the surrounding high terrain[11] on foot and to collect specimens. It was only a short time away but an important episode for Dewey's work. The time for his departure was near and it was with regret that he said his good-byes at Cape Dorset.

Courtesy of the HBC, Jim Aitken sent Dewey back to Amadjuak in a power launch with an Inuit crew. This time, with the summer season far advanced, there was little or no ice on Hudson Strait and the sea remained smooth. East of Chorkbak Inlet there were so many birds on and around the many islands that Dewey regretted not having a week to spare to explore them at his leisure. They did stop at Chamberlain Island for one night, where the abundant birdlife prompted Dewey to report, "Sometimes the din of the birds' incessant, querulous voices was almost overpowering." The following noon, on another beautiful Arctic summer day, they arrived at the HBC post at Amadjuak. There Dewey would wait for the imminent arrival of the HBC steamer *Nascopie* for the next stage of his journey home.

As often happens in the Arctic and subarctic, the annual supply ship was late in arriving. Never one to sit idle and wait, that delay gave Dewey an extra twelve days to add to his collection of birds, especially during a side trip of about fifty miles, east to Markham Bay. There he took a peregrine falcon (*Falco peregrinus*), a white gyrfalcon (*Falco rusticolus*), snowy owl, and additional examples of the Hutchins's goose. He noted that Markham Bay held a much richer sampling of avifauna than at Amadjuak. For most of the time he spent waiting for the ship, Dewey collected close enough to base that if the ship arrived suddenly he would have time to complete his packing for departure.

He went inland on foot to Boas and McGee lakes, which he had crossed by dog team in winter. Finding the geography and the scientific study possibilities far more interesting than on the winter journey, he expressed the wish that he could stay longer and explore as far north as the much larger Mingo Lake. Near McGee Lake he caught brown and collared lemmings and again added to his bird collection. He also found that "both flowering and non-blooming vegetation were relatively rich in various niches, and were represented by several dozen species. In all I preserved 57 sheets of the local flora."

RMS *Nascopie* showed her funnel on the horizon on August 11, and soon after steamed slowly into Amadjuak Bay. She discharged her cargo, took Dewey and his crates of specimens onboard, and departed for Fort Chimo, in northern Quebec, far up the Koksoak River at the foot of Ungava Bay. Dewey took advantage of the brief stop to go ashore and collect a few more plants before the ship left again for Port Burwell, on Killinek Island, off the northern tip of the mainland shared by Quebec and Labrador. *Nascopie* was headed far to the north on her annual voyage to supply remote settlements with provisions — coal and other merchandise — so Dewey disembarked at Port Burwell. There he had to wait for another HBC ship, the SS *Bayrupert*,[12] for the continuation of his voyage south.

For the next twenty days, Dewey was billeted with the local RCMP detachment, thoroughly enjoying the company of Corporal H. Nichols and Constable Sydney Montague. In 1939 Montague wrote about his experiences in the subarctic in *North to Adventure*,[13] in which he briefly mentions Dewey Soper. There wasn't much in the way of wildlife on the barren island but Dewey enjoyed a few excursions by whaleboat along the rugged coastlines in search of seals to feed the police dog teams. They also jigged for cod on Ungava Bay, both for themselves and as a supplement to the dogs' diet.

SS *Bayrupert* arrived at Port Burwell on September 12, and departed two days later with Dewey and his collections onboard. Just over two weeks after that, following an uneventful voyage down the Labrador coast, the ship docked in the almost landlocked harbour of St. John's, Newfoundland. From there, Dewey and his considerable amount of baggage took the train — known as "The Newfie Bullet"[14] — to Port aux Basques. He then crossed to North Sydney on Cape Breton Island by steamer before continuing his long journey to Ottawa by train. Dewey's two exciting years exploring southern Baffin Island were over, but there was much work still to be done. He had collected close to four thousand scientific specimens and added much data to maps of southern Baffin Island, all of which had to be catalogued.

Within days of his return to Ottawa he attended the annual convention of the American Ornithologists Union — the first time it had been held in Canada. There he was finally able to meet E.T. Seton, as well as notable ornithologists such as Edward Preble[15] and Arthur Bent,[16] among others. Meetings with museum authorities to report on his two-year expedition took up more time.

He was happy to be in Ontario again but, once he had seen his family and friends, he desperately wanted to return to Baffin Island as soon as possible to search for the breeding grounds of the blue goose, as well as to explore hitherto unknown regions. First, though, during a six-week leave, he made the round of visits to relatives in Ontario before taking the train west to Alberta. He spent some of that time in the west with his sister Edith and her family, now living in Wetaskiwin, Alberta.

Edith, a nurse, had just given birth to a daughter, Patricia. In consequence of that happening, Dewey met Carolyn (Carrie) Freeman, a graduate nurse eleven years his junior, and fell in love. He was then thirty-three years old. His relationship with Carolyn is the first indication we have of any girlfriend in his life, most of which, since his school days, had been spent in the company of wildlife or other men. The attraction must have been immediate, and was obviously mutual. When Dewey returned to Ottawa, he and Carrie continued their friendship by letter. The naturalist was in love and he was not about to let Carrie get away. With his usual single-minded determination, he purchased an engagement ring and proposed to her by mail. She accepted. When he wasn't wooing Carrie by mail, he spent the winter alone, writing of his Arctic experiences and his collections, some of which was later to be published by the federal government as *A Faunal Investigation of Southern Baffin Island*.

12

A Brief Prairie Interlude

Carolyn joined Dewey in Ottawa in March 1927, and they were married in Percy and Ida Taverner's home on March 17. Taverner, himself a native of Guelph, was at that time the ornithologist at the National Museum of Natural Sciences in Ottawa. In addition to members of the museum's faculty, the wedding was attended by a group of Dewey's RCMP friends, all attired in full dress uniforms.

In March, Dewey was still expecting to be sent back to the Arctic in the summer. One month after he and Carrie were married he received the news that he would not be returning to Baffin Island after all. Instead, as far as the museum authorities were concerned, there was a more important job that required his attention. He was given the assignment of undertaking a survey of wildlife along the International Boundary, from the Rocky Mountains in Alberta to Lake-of-the-Woods on the Manitoba-Ontario border. This was the first time such a survey had been conducted. Dewey's disappointment at not going north was ameliorated by the fact that his employers gave permission for his new bride to accompany him on the far-ranging prairie wildlife survey.

Once Dewey had gathered together all the necessary equipment for preserving wildlife specimens and camping for months on the road, he and Carrie travelled cross-country, probably to Calgary, by train. Dewey had to collect a government-owned Model T Ford pickup truck from Munson, near Drumheller. The truck had been left there by palaeontologist Charles Sternberg the previous autumn.[1] That vehicle was to be the newlyweds' transport for the summer, and a tent was to be their home. "Thus," wrote Dewey, "[began] my introduction to the strange, semi-arid and virtually 'exotic' environment existing in the southern prairie West. Much of this territory lies in the Missouri drainage and harbours many species of birds, mammals and plants not found elsewhere in Canada — consequently a region of extraordinary interest."[2] It was also Carrie's introduction to her husband's nomadic way of life and, perhaps, a warning for the future, when he would be away from her for months at a time.

Nurse Carolyn K. Freeman at Wetaskiwin, Alberta, 1926. She married Dewey in March 1927 and in 1930 she became the first nurse to spend a winter in the eastern Canadian Arctic.

Roland Soper Collection.

Working from a series of tent camps located between forty and fifty miles apart, Dewey explored the landscape and collected mammals and birds in a band of Canadian territory forty to sixty miles wide, due north of Montana, North Dakota, and Minnesota. Accompanied by Carrie for much of the time, he spent five months gradually working his way across the prairies from the mountain foothills to Manitoba.

In Alberta he started at the foothills of the Rockies, north of what is now the Waterton Lakes National Park, and ended at the Elkwater area on

A Brief Prairie Interlude

the Alberta side of the Cypress Hills. His first camp in Saskatchewan was at Battle Creek, also in the Cypress Hills, and his last at Glen Ewen on the Souris River.

As a late honeymoon, the trek across the prairies would have had its limitations. Not many brides spend the early months of married life living in a tent and moving every few days so that her husband can occupy most of his waking hours chasing wild creatures. To Dewey Soper it was perfectly normal behaviour. He was a naturalist and he had a job to do. And he did it well. Carrie, strong-willed and extremely capable, proved she was his equal by fitting in, apparently without complaint.

Close to Eagle Butte on July 22, 1927, Soper found a subspecies of shrew, the prairie dusky shrew[3] (*Sorex vagrans soperi*), never before collected in Alberta. On August 6, from his camp at Lodge Creek, south of Elkwater, Alberta, he made the first positive Canadian sighting of a pallid sagebrush vole[4] (*Lagurtus curtatus pallidus*). And again, three weeks on, at Val Marie, Saskatchewan, on the banks of Frenchman's River, he made the first Canadian record of a black-tailed prairie dog[5] (*Cynomys ludovicianus ludovicianus*).

Dewey and Carrie's campsite beside the Milk River, Alberta, during a summer-long investigation of prairie wildlife in the first summer of their marriage, 1927.

He wasn't always successful. One of the small mammals he was keenly interested in collecting was the Maximillian pocket mouse (*Perognathus fasciatus fasciatus*). Although he counted hundreds of trap-nights during his search for the creature in Alberta, he came up empty-handed. Many years later he would estimate that, during that survey and subsequent attempts, he had spent eight thousand trap-nights on that particular quest in Alberta, without taking a single specimen.[6]

Even though the summer of investigations across the Prairie provinces was generally successful, Dewey obviously felt that too little time had been allocated for the task. A few years later he wrote of the limitations of the work he had been assigned:

> It may be said that in addition to the mammal work, notes were drawn up on all species of birds sighted in each working locality in what limited time was available. When opportunity permitted numbers of birds were also collected from time to time. For the most part these were distinctly valuable acquisitions, for in numerous tracts of country no natural history collecting had previously been done. Because of prevailing circumstances, of course, most of the avian results were based simply on binocular observations and spontaneous identification of living birds. Needless to say, for some forms collecting is essential for later identification.[7]

In September, as the nights began to get colder, a by now pregnant Carolyn returned to her family in Wetaskiwin while Dewey continued on alone as far as Max Lake, in the Turtle Mountain area of southwestern Manitoba. Due to ice on the lakes and ponds and snow on the ground, the fieldwork came to an end on November 3. Dewey reported in September that extending the survey to Lake of the Woods "was out of the question in relation to the desired frequency of working localities; the prevailing handicaps of car travel in those days; and the time available before the onset of winter."[8] In other words, the original assignment instructions expected him to do too much work over too large an area in too little time.

A Brief Prairie Interlude

From Max Lake, Dewey drove north on another assignment for the National Museum. In October, Dr. Anderson had asked him to go to a wilderness area northeast of Prince Albert, Saskatchewan, to collect specimens of big game animals, particularly the elk. On the seven-week late autumn/early winter hunt in the Birchbark and Harper lakes area, he managed to supply the National Museum with two moose skins, plus four elk and two mule deer, to add to the 646 mammals and 103 birds he had collected along the international boundary. The long stay in the north Saskatchewan bush, he explained, was because he wanted to obtain the best possible specimen of a big bull wapiti (elk). With that accomplished, he hurried away from the cold outdoors and headed for Alberta, arriving at his in-laws' home in Wetaskiwin just in time to welcome his son, Roland, into the world on December 22.

At that time Dewey regretfully resigned from the National Museum due to a disagreement about not being given a permanent appointment and the increase in salary he felt he was due, particularly after his stellar work on the two-year Baffin Island expedition. He was still classed as a "junior zoologist," only earning one hundred dollars per month, plus a small clothing allowance, and knew he was worth far more. Without a job, he spent the rest of the winter writing articles for magazines and newspapers and preparing a manuscript of his Arctic experiences.

13

Baffin Island, 1928–29

At the end of February 1928, Dewey was approached by Mr. O.S. Finnie, director of the Northwest Territories and Yukon Branch of the Department of the Interior, to join his staff for further Arctic exploration. Dewey, not surprisingly, was delighted at the invitation and accepted immediately. The conditions of employment gave him double the salary he had received from the National Museum and would include appointment to the permanent staff at the end of the first year.

Dewey's first assignment for his new employers would be the expedition he had been waiting for: to return to Baffin Island for a year and search for the breeding grounds of the blue goose. Another dream was about to come true. The only downside was that he would have to leave Carrie and his infant son, Roly, in Alberta for the duration of his assignment. During the months he was on Baffin Island, there would be no opportunity of contacting Carrie and no way for her to contact him.[1] They both had to have faith and believe each would be safe in their far different worlds until Dewey returned in the summer of 1929. Such has always been the lot of explorers and their life partners.

At the beginning of June, Dewey said goodbye to his family and went to Ottawa to make final preparations for the expedition. He was scheduled to sail from Montreal on the RMS *Nascopie* in the middle of July and to arrive at Cape Dorset on approximately August 4. The by now familiar voyage up the Labrador Sea and the Davis Strait passed without incident. On arrival at Dorset, Dewey was greeted by his old HBC acquaintance David Wark, who had been transferred in from Amadjuak to replace Jim Aitken, who had also been transferred. As before, Dewey would be based at the HBC post, although he did not anticipate spending much time there: "Among the first chores I had to attend to was to establish an astronomic station near the [Dorset] post to tie in surveys, and to serve as a reference point in the true meridian in order to make magnetic declination observations and for other surveying purposes."[2]

Having travelled west to Bowdoin Harbour with Aitken in 1926, and knowing the rugged coastline held many opportunities for collecting, Dewey's first journey was by sea to complete a survey of the coast up the Foxe Channel as far as Cape Dorchester. Leaving on August 15, in "a big motor-powered freighter canoe" with two Inuit — Shappa and Eliak — they made camp in the shelter of almost landlocked Bowdoin Harbour a few hours later. Thick fog and gales kept them there for over a day as "Foxe Channel was whipped into an awesome fury of high seas and foam."

Once the seas subsided and the fog cleared they pushed on toward Nuwata, halfway up the west coast of the Foxe Peninsula. In the 1920s Nuwata was the only permanent Inuit village on the west coast of Baffin Island between Cape Dorset and Fury and Hecla Strait at the extreme northwest of Foxe Basin. They reached the village on August 19 and were promptly stormbound again. The unpredictable weather patterns coming off Foxe Basin and down Foxe Channel brought a succession of gales to the peninsula. Rain, sleet, and fog combined to keep the three on land with little to do until August 23. Then, taking advantage of a brief break in the storms, they ran for the north, making headway almost to Cape Weston before a northeast gale drove them into a bay that Dewey named "Storm Cove." High winds and big seas kept them on a sandy shore, sheltered to an extent by a headland, for another three days, during which the tent was battered unmercifully.

The storm passed as suddenly as it had begun. A few hours later the freight canoe came in sight of Cape Dorchester. There Dewey went ashore and tied his survey in to the geographical cairn erected by members of the Putnam Expedition from the summer of 1927.[3]

Baffin Island, 1928–29

Sketch of walrus on ice in Foxe Basin near Nuwata, by J. Dewey Soper.

Dewey's brief was to conduct a disciplined search for the nesting grounds of the blue goose, in addition to surveying[4] much of the Foxe Peninsula. His coastal voyage was part of the mapping survey, yet, knowing that the geese he sought almost certainly nested on the lowlands of the interior south and east of Bowman Bay, it must have been extremely tempting for him to continue east from Cape Dorchester. The distance in a straight line to the coast of Bowman Bay was only about one hundred statute miles. The dreadful weather, combined with the knowledge that the breeding season was probably over for that year, no doubt held him back.

The frequent storms and overcast skies made surveying difficult, but Dewey persevered and succeeded. His determination did the same for recording and collecting birdlife. The Inuit from Nuwata made their own contributions by helping him with walrus skins. He extended his mammal collection with skins from polar bear and caribou, and added a variety of waterfowl. In total, he collected seventy specimens — mostly birds — on the journey. He mentioned that the Inuit from Nuwata, many of whom were away on a walrus hunt when he first arrived, lived mostly on a diet of walrus meat. He did not say that he had tried it.

The return journey to Cape Dorset was a miserable experience of squalls and drizzling rain. A couple of hours away from base they ran into trouble. A squall blasted off the hills to the north as they were crossing the mouth of an inlet. Within minutes the waves built up into whitecaps and threatened the stability of the canoe. They immediately turned for shore, trying to outrun the increasingly wild seas. Before they could get to safety, a comber broke over the gunwales and flooded the boat. It also stopped the outboard motor. With the wind howling offshore, the canoe was swept out to sea while the crew fought desperately to restart the engine. For a while the situation was dangerous in the extreme. The nearest land to the south was Salisbury Island, and that was at least thirty nautical miles away. In stormy seas, and without a motor, they would have been unlikely to survive the crossing.

Starting a waterlogged outboard motor in smooth conditions is difficult. With the canoe rolling wildly in concert with breaking waves, and spindrift cutting visibility to zero, the task is almost impossible.[5] While they worked on the motor the canoe continued to be blown farther and farther from shore. Fortunately, desperation often produces unheralded skills: "Just when we began to fear the worst the motor roared into action and we were thankful to get safely into calmer water beneath an overhanging cliff."[6]

The weather, inclement even for this harsh region, played havoc with Dewey's journeys on sea and on land, but he rarely allowed it to slow him down or stop him for long. Less than two weeks after his return to Dorset he set off again, this time with Shappa and a new Native helper, Kavivau. The objective was to explore a series of lakes extending inland from the head of Andrew Gordon Bay and, if weather permitted, reach a river the Inuit knew as Kommanik, and follow it to its mouth on Foxe Basin. Shappa and Kavivau had both hunted caribou in the region of the lakes, so each had some knowledge of the terrain.

Dewey recognized that he was starting this new endeavour late in the season, but was determined to see it through as far as possible. Using the same freight canoe and outboard motor as on the previous survey, they followed the coast to Andrew Gordon Bay and started up the chain of eight lakes. Between each one they portaged the boat and supplies. Dewey measured the distance as best he could and recorded it as approximately 1,190 yards from the beginning of the first lake to the eastern end of the largest, Tessikdjuak Lake. Two days out from Dorset they made camp beside Tessikdjuak in a bay Dewey named Hare Harbour after seeing three Arctic hares there. He measured the lake's altitude at 125 feet above sea level.

Foul weather in the shape of gusting high winds, sleet, and rain kept them in camp at Hare Harbour for three days. When that storm passed, and with reasonably stable conditions for a while, they loaded the canoe and started out for the western end of the lake, following the north shore while Dewey conducted his surveying. The Kommanik River flows out of the north side of the lake. The first three and a half miles of the river runs over rapids before flowing into another lake — this one known to the Inuit as Angmaluk. At the end of this section they portaged the canoe and outfit eight hundred yards to set up camp on the west side of the lake. There Dewey left a cache of basic provisions for use the next summer. Shappa told Dewey he was the first white man to have been to that region.

From their camp the Kommanik River runs northwest for twenty-five miles to Foxe Basin. The series of lakes and rivers Dewey had navigated on this journey to date, combined with the Kommanik River, show a highly feasible canoe route across the Foxe Peninsula from Hudson Strait to Foxe Basin. Although he longed to descend the Kommanik and complete the crossing himself, the weather delays, lateness of the season, and dwindling food and fuel demanded that they turn around and get off the lakes before freeze-up, which would happen much sooner for fresh water than on the sea. If the lakes froze before they got out, they would be in trouble again. There were no caribou for food and few other creatures crossed their path. Most of the migratory birds had also already left the peninsula. En route a mix of heavy rain and snow kept them in camp for yet another three days, while the food supplies continued to dwindle. Once they reached the coast at Andrew Gordon Bay, more storms over the sea slowed their progress along the coast to Dorset, so they took four days to get home instead of the expected two.

Dewey's remarkable resilience shows through in the contrast between his words and the work he managed to achieve that fall. He wrote of the problems created by the weather: "The autumn of 1928 in the region appeared to be unusual, not so much because of the severity of the temperature but rather with respect to the violence and persistence of gales, and the frequent incidence of gloomy days that consisted of rain, sleet, and snow. The majority of days were of this character, posing a formidable problem for geographical and other work."[7]

He estimated the total distance for the lakes journey to have been 244 miles. Along that route, under mostly impossible surveying conditions, he had taken over three hundred bearings to update his maps. In spite of the often atrocious October weather, he continued his survey of the coastlines adjacent to Cape Dorset, and he climbed the eight-hundred-foot-high Cairn Mountain near the HBC post to take bearings on geographical features in all land directions. Somehow he also found time to continue to secure wildlife specimens for his collection.

Throughout November and December Dewey wrote his reports and drafted maps of his two recent journeys. Each day when at base, and when possible on the trail, he recorded air and sea temperatures and took regular readings for magnetic declination by day and by night. At the same time he started preparations for a short winter exploration of the so far unknown regions of the Foxe Peninsula. Once the sea ice formed along the coast and snow covered the hinterland, conditions would be ideal for the sledging journey he had in mind. His plan was to travel on shore-bound sea ice as far as Andrew Gordon Bay. From there he and his Inuit companions would turn northwest and follow an unnamed river deep into the interior and eventually cross the middle of the peninsula to Nuwata. The return would be made on a different route. Wherever possible he would measure the altitude and take bearings on any geographical points of significance.

He, Shappa, and Kavivau left Dorset on January 10, 1929, with one sled and a dog team. They made good time along the coast to Andrew Gordon Bay but then had to build an igloo and sit out a two-day blizzard before they could continue. The river, when in flow, runs twenty miles from a lake at 140 feet above sea level. On its rush to the sea its course takes it over rapids and falls. Dewey's expedition followed its frozen length uphill on rocky ground, passing the mouth of a small stream that enters it from the north halfway up. Dewey named the main river Saunders in honour of his naturalist friend W.E. Saunders from London, Ontario.[8]

Hard-packed snow underfoot meant the dogs and men could move fast, with the hissing of the sled runners for musical accompaniment. They

Baffin Island, 1928–29

Courtesy of University of Saskatchewan and Roland Soper.

Sled dog sketch, by J. Dewey Soper.

continued uphill beyond the lake to another lake situated beside an escarpment at about 250 feet above sea level. Dewey guessed that the escarpment would run all the way to Cape Weston, some distance north of their destination. The downhill slope toward Nuwata was gradual, made up of "gentle slopes, terraces, and monotonous lowlands." A few Inuksuit[9] showed that occasional parties of Inuit caribou hunters sometimes crossed this barren region. Ten days after they left Cape Dorset, they pulled in to the Inuit village at midday on January 20, having covered 150 miles according to the sledge meter, or basic odometer (a wheel with a known diameter attached to the rear of the sled, to count the number of revolutions and thereby measure distances). Dewey said it worked well.

At Nuwata, Dewey received an unexpected gift. An old local named Saila drew him a rough map of the location of the breeding grounds of the blue goose. That information confirmed what he had been told by the Tikoot Islander earlier.

The Nuwata village chief invited Dewey, Shappa, and Kavivau to stay with him in his igloo. Good manners required that they did so, plus it saved them the effort of building their own snow house. It was a reasonable arrangement that almost cost Dewey the contents of his stomach: "A considerable amount of putrid walrus meat … was piled inside the igloo.… The penetrating fetid odour, *tepealuk* (the big stink!), nearly caused me to be sick and no doubt I would have been had I not repeatedly fled into the fresh 40 degree below air outside each time I was overcome with nausea until it passed."[10]

The walrus meat had gone off after unseasonably warm weather in late summer. Dewey somehow found the fortitude to sleep in the igloo, but turned his bed so that his head was as far from the meat as possible. They left the village, apparently without regret, on January 22. With them they took three hundred pounds of fresh walrus meat Dewey had purchased for the dogs.

Their return course took them due east for fifteen miles to the Weston Escarpment. On top, at an average altitude of 260 feet above sea level, they found a slightly rolling plain with occasional old marine terraces, and glacial boulders scattered over the landscape. Harsh gusts of wind and drifting snow slowed them as they made their way across the highlands to the edge of the plateau. From there they descended gradually about seventy-five feet, passing more old marine beaches on the way down. After crossing three lakes, one unnamed and the other two with Inuit names only (Nukvuk and Unggenuk), they turned southeast and camped at Hare Harbour, where they had camped the previous autumn. Two nights later they made their final camp for that expedition at Catherine Bay, on Hudson Strait, having covered just over fifty miles from Hare Harbour. The following day, January 28, after a trouble-free coastal run of twenty-one miles, they arrived back at the Cape Dorset HBC post.

Prior to 1929 the coastline of west Baffin Island, from Bowman Bay as far as the eastern access to Murray Maxwell Bay at the northernmost end of Foxe Basin, was basically unknown. Maps of that era show the coast as a dotted line, a clear indication that no surveying had been done.[11] Today's maps and nautical charts show islands in Foxe Basin, such as Prince Charles, Air Force, Foley, Bray, Rowley, as well as the prominent Baird Peninsula jutting into the sea off the Baffin coast. None of these land masses were known in the late 1920s. Dewey explained his theory for the lack of earlier surveying work: "Some of the reasons that this coast was neglected for so long were due to its relative inaccessibility from the east, the total lack of native inhabitants, and the heavy ice-glutted, dangerous state of Foxe Basin through which ships usually could make no headway whatever."[14]

Bernard Hantzsch had followed the coast north of the Koukdjuak River in 1910, crossing an unnamed river approximately fifty statute miles north of the Koukdjuak. He turned back while probably in the region of what is now known as Straits Bay. Dewey planned to go at least as far north as the unnamed river, which he intended recommending to the Geographic Board of Canada as the Hantzsch River. Once at the river, he would follow it inland and survey its course.

Dewey put together an impressive expedition to fill in some of the blanks on current maps. Cognizant of the fact that few if any game animals would be seen on land and that there was little chance of open water along the coast to find seals, he had to be prepared with sufficient dog feed and provisions for himself and his Inuit helpers to last them for a return journey he estimated at nine hundred miles, perhaps more, and taking at least four or five weeks. Shappa and Kavivau would again play important roles in the expedition: "On the outbound trip we planned to establish well-spaced depots of supplies for the future from which men and dog teams, in succession, would depart for home at specified times, meanwhile picking up their share of depot supplies en route."[13]

The logistics of feeding the men and dogs alone were quite staggering. The expedition team would consist of Dewey plus five Inuit dog-team drivers, five sleds, and fifty-six dogs. Considering that each dog required approximately three pounds of seal or walrus meat per day, and the men had to be fed as well, each sled had to carry close to a thousand pounds at the start from Cape Dorset — an extremely heavy load. Each day, of course, en route to the site of the first supply depot, the loads would become marginally lighter by the amount of food eaten — at least 170–180 pounds. But that only amounted to a lessening of the load by, at most, thirty-six pounds per sled, per day. Departure was set for March 11, 1929.

The route Dewey mapped out to reach Bowman Bay would follow a previously used route for much of the way: east along the coast of Hudson Strait to Andrew Gordon Bay and up the river route to Tessikdjuak Lake, where they established the first food depot. The depots were built in the form of snow houses, or igloos, with a small flag flying from the apex of each to aid in finding them again on the return journey, in case of blizzard or whiteout conditions. Dewey was leaving little or nothing to chance when it came to survival in the coldest months of the year.

They positioned the second depot on the south side of Bowman Bay on March 17. Kavivau and his team of eleven dogs left the following morning to return to Cape Dorset. They had hauled a significant weight of provisions over the Foxe Peninsula to supply the main party on their way home. Their job was now done. Dewey and Shappa led the others north along the coast on the tundra between the Great Plain of the Koukdjuak and Foxe Basin. The flat land of tundra on sedimentary bedrock stretches 150 miles north to the vicinity of the Hantzsch River. For three days they trekked northwest with great sculptures of rafted ice on the seaward side and mostly flat, snow-covered land to the right. This was more uncharted land; Dewey took bearings wherever he could: "From the south end of Bowman Bay the somewhat irregular coastline trends in a northwesterly direction for sixty-seven miles to approximate latitude 66° 10′ N and about longitude 74° 35′ W. Here the striking deflection of the coast forms a wide flat headland that I named Cape Dominion. The true nature of this [geographical] feature was previously unknown."[14]

From Cape Dominion the coast turns northeast, across the Arctic Circle and beyond the Koukdjuak River for eighty-five miles. Eighteen miles along the coast beyond the cape they built the third supply depot. At that point it was the second member of the support team's turn to retrace his sled tracks.

Travelling alone, with only his dog team for company, Powlusee had more than two hundred miles of harsh white wilderness to cross before getting home to Cape Dorset.

On March 20 the depleted party camped on the Arctic Circle. Dewey found his surroundings somewhat disturbing: "The lowlands present a depressed and featureless aspect everywhere. At times silvery shimmering images altered the landscape with weird and shifting distortions. The miles could scarcely have been more monotonous — a feature which linked with the eternal silence and solitude is singularly impressive."[15]

They reached the Koukdjuak River on the afternoon of March 21.[16] Dewey was quite surprised to find the river mouth was a fraction over two miles wide, as measured by the sled odometer. Along the shore, rafted ice reached ten to fifteen feet high, with no open water in sight, therefore no possibility of hunting for seals to replenish the dog food supplies. North of the river they stopped at the place where he and Akatuga had reached the west coast in February 1926. On taking survey readings he was delighted to find that they were only two statute miles different from those made on the 1926 survey: "A gratifying result which was surprising considering that the two route surveys of approximations had originated at points about 360 miles apart."[17]

The continuation of the lowland plain narrows and comes to a halt at Taverner Bay. There it is bordered by a low-lying limestone escarpment that curves north to an as yet undefined limit for Dewey. In the opposite direction it stands south toward the Koukdjuak River before turning east in the direction of Nettilling Lake. Since 1929 this escarpment has been known as the Soper Highlands in recognition of Dewey's work in the region.[18]

Dewey cached the final load of provisions at Depot 5, on the shores of Taverner Bay, on March 24. With that accomplished, two more of the Inuit — Patagook and Nunasweeto — left with their dogs and sleds for Cape Dorset, now about three hundred miles to the south. For the final push to the Hantzsch River, and possibly beyond, Dewey and Shappa retained one sled and the remaining dog team.

It is rare in Dewey's writings to find long tracts of text without mention of wildlife sightings. On the expedition to Hantzsch River, in the depths of winter, wildlife was significant by its almost complete absence. There were no

Drawing of the Soper camp at Taverner Bay, Foxe Basin, in March 1929, by J. Dewey Soper. The original was a watercolour, now held in the archives of the Arctic Institute of North America. Copyright remains with the Soper family.

large mammals, such as polar bears, wolves, or caribou. Among the smaller species they saw only spoors of a few Arctic foxes, as well as some lemming tracks. The stark emptiness of the region is exemplified by this comment from Dewey: "For a distance of about sixty miles on either side of the Arctic Circle not a single trail of any animal was seen by the party."[19]

As Dewey and Shappa worked their way north from Taverner Bay their progress was slowed by rocky outcrops and granite ridges. Also, the dogs were getting tired, as were the two men. Dewey didn't help matters when he slipped while taking photographs of the rafted shore ice and sprained his ankle. Weather, too, created problems; repeated blizzards kept them igloo-bound, sometimes for a few hours, at other times for a day or more. The only advantage to the enforced halts was that both men and dogs could rest, and Dewey's ankle had a chance to heal. In the dreadfully low temperatures, frostbite became another hazard.

As stated earlier, Dewey was only the second white man to travel on this part of the west coast of Baffin Island, the first being the ill-fated Bernard Hantzsch eighteen years earlier. He was, therefore, determined to see as much as possible and to map the coastline and the rivers and lakes as he met them. On March 28 they reached the frozen mouth of the Hantzsch River, which they found to be 150 yards wide. The expedition chronometer was not working properly, so Dewey was unable to calculate the longitude accurately, which was disappointing. He did take readings for latitude and for magnetic declination.

The next morning they started upstream. After only a short distance they entered a gorge about forty yards wide with granite cliffs up to fifty feet high. In summer the river would be powerful, racing through the confined space, tumbling over rapids and small waterfalls. Eleven miles inland they came to an area where the river drops sixty-five feet "in a wild series of low falls and rapids interrupted by a chain of three lake-like extensions."

Once above the rapids the land flattened; the going was easier and the dogs and sled ran more smoothly. They camped for the night about twenty-five miles inland. By noon the next day, following and charting the river's course, they reached latitude 67° 32′ at a point thirty miles from Foxe Basin. Moving quite fast, considering the necessary stops to take bearings, Dewey forged on toward the northern rim of the highlands, naming Granite Lake en route and setting up their most northerly camp forty-five miles upriver from the sea. At this time, with no game animals to hunt, dog food was running low, and a return to Depot 5 became imperative. Before leaving the highlands, Dewey was surprised to find another Inukshuk, hundreds of miles from any known Native villages.

Travelling through a blizzard, they cut across the highlands in a south-westerly direction toward Taverner Bay. By April 2, with the dogs well-fed again, they had loaded the cached supplies at Depot 5 and were moving south at all possible speed. That sense of urgency did not prevent Dewey from taking time to explore partway up the Koukdjuak River. They collected more supplies from Camp 2 on Bowman Bay on April 7. With more than adequate provisions to sustain them for the remainder of the journey to Cape Dorset, they made a detour of thirty miles to the windswept Putnam Highlands, where there was little snow, to collect a selection of fossils from the talus, or natural rock debris. Dewey was pleased with the find: "Among these were corals, bryozoans, and numerous gastropods and cephalopods. Had our time not been so limited perhaps more species would have been found."

They left Camp 2 on April 9 with the width of the eastern boundary of Foxe Peninsula, via Tessikdjuak Lake, still to cross. Camping each night in snow houses, they reached the Cape Dorset base in the afternoon of April 15. The sled odometer recorded that the expedition had covered 819 miles in thirty-five days — an exceptional achievement by any standards. As a result of this and his earlier surveys, Dewey was able to redraw government maps of southern Baffin Island. Most particularly, in the case of the most recent expedition, he now had an accurate map of the west coast as far north as the Hantzsch River. He also established that the west coast of Baffin Island was actually some distance farther east than previously thought.

14

In Search of the Blue Goose

As the spring of 1929 approached, Dewey began making concrete plans for the expedition to find the breeding grounds of the blue goose.[1] Based on an old Inuk's report from a chance meeting on an island in Hudson Strait, and on the evidence of Saila's hand-drawn map, he was determined to have his team at the estimated location well in advance of the anticipated arrival of the annual migration from the south. For Dewey this was the most important expedition he had undertaken to date. He had been working toward this scientific adventure for many years. His enthusiasm is almost palpable as his words spill onto the page: "The closer the time approached to start out on this journey of discovery, the more eager I became to commit myself to it totally."[2]

The long-awaited day arrived. On May 17, Dewey left Cape Dorset with five Inuit, four heavily laden sleds, and forty-two dogs. As always, dog feed was a major part of the load. The balance consisted of provisions for the men for three months in the interior, camping equipment, Dewey's scientific paraphernalia, the freighter canoe and outboard motor, plus gasoline.

They followed the by now familiar route along Hudson Strait and Andrew Gordon Bay, thence into Chorkbak Inlet and up to its head. From there they crossed the Putnam Highlands to an ideal camping site on a low but flat granite ridge beside a river, which Dewey promptly named the Blue

Lesser snow goose (*Chen caerulescens*) in blue phase.

Goose River. The campsite set up on May 24 was dubbed "Camp Kungovik," this being the Inuit name for the blue goose. Three of the Inuit, the sleds, and all the dogs returned to Cape Dorset the following day, leaving Dewey, Kavivau, and Ashuna alone for the summer. They still had the freighter canoe for transport out by way of Bowman Bay and Foxe Basin when the time came. It was either use that or walk all the way across the tundra.

For the first time on this or any other expedition, Dewey showed signs of what could be interpreted as a bout of homesickness, although whether that was real — or imagined in retrospect — is not known. Either way, Dewey rarely commented on his personal feelings. Relating to the weeks waiting for the blue geese to arrive, he wrote, "There was such a feeling of isolation and contentment prevailing that I recognized this as a unique opportunity for the quiet expansion of my mind into unaccustomed channels of thought and comprehension. Beside this, I sometimes found myself speculating as to what was going on at home …"[3]

Now, with snow still on the ground and semi-winter conditions prevailing, Dewey had to maintain his faith in the location as the correct one. That meant waiting, day after day, waiting for the first flocks of geese to arrive, heralded by typical honking calls. At first Dewey and his men used snowshoes to get around. The temperatures started to rise in early June. Snow began to melt, only to be replaced by more snow as gales raged over the Foxe Peninsula and the temperature dropped again. At one point the tents were barricaded by snowdrifts three feet deep. The first geese arrived, too, on June 2; a mixed scouting party of white and blue flew over the camp, honking loudly. They circled a few times but did not land. To Dewey's disappointment, they flew south again.

Four days later his dream came true. The geese came back in large flocks, and some of them landed. Over the next few days thousands of the birds flew in to land on the soaking wet lowlands. The largest concentrations arrived in mid-month, and Dewey was ecstatic. His romantic nature dictated the event for posterity: "No more exciting experience befell us on the western tundra than the sight of the clamouring host of striking birds cleaving northward on their great annual pilgrimage, bravely breasting the howling 'nor-westers' and filling the air with a primeval symphony of eagerness and determination."[4]

Drawing of the Soper campsite at Blue Goose River, by J. Dewey Soper. The original was a watercolour, now held in the archives of the Arctic Institute of North America. Copyright remains with the Soper family.

Even though some of the flocks continued north, the majority settled on the lowlands adjacent to Camp Kungovik. Dewey found the first blue goose nest on June 20. It contained a single egg. As the days progressed, more and more nests appeared. The breeding season that Dewey had waited for was upon them. Soon the nests contained their clutches of eggs, sometimes only two; more often the nests cradled three or four eggs. The geese weren't the only birds to settle on the lowlands. There were also thousands of eider ducks and many other species. Dewey recorded their nesting and added a wry observation on the weather: "Nesting birds were everywhere, including geese, red phalaropes, white-rumped sandpipers, ruddy turnstones, jaegers, Sabine's gulls, snow buntings, Lapland longspurs, and horned larks. Here we have the paradox of prolific birdlife and lowly vegetation geared to one of the foulest summer climates in the world."[5]

The first week in July proved the truth of his assessment of the weather. A gale roared in and blasted the camp for four days and nights. Dewey and his helpers went out in the storm to work but, he said, "[the storm rendered] our investigations trying and unpleasant."

Dewey was often critical of Vilhjalmur Stefansson's overly optimistic view of "the friendly Arctic."[6] Much as he loved the north, he had no such illusions, openly describing the Arctic as having "altogether too much hardship, suffering, slow starvation and death …"[7]

With succinct style, he described the climate of the lowlands near Bowman Bay as "austere." Even many years later the weather for that summer stayed in his mind. In his eighties he wrote, "The entire summer in the blue goose country, up to the time of our departure near the end of July, was the bleakest, gloomiest, and most inclement season that I have ever experienced."[8]

Even he would have admitted though that the expedition to find and study the breeding grounds of the blue goose was one of the highlights of his life; one he would not have missed for anything. The cold and snow had advantages, anyway, and not only for ease of travel by dogsled. On the blue goose expedition, Kavivau and Ashuna dug a snow cave out of a large snowdrift for use as a natural refrigerator. They stored fresh meat in there, as well as the geese they had collected. Once the doorway was sealed with frozen blocks of snow, everything was preserved — until the snow eventually melted, but that was much later.

The Inuit helped Dewey in the preservation of wildlife specimens, too, once he had shown them how. While he took care of the more fragile small specimens, Kavivau and Ashuna skinned and salted the larger creatures, which included a caribou — hence the fresh meat. Strangely, given the enormous congregation of birds on the lowlands, predatory mammals were scarce. The only carnivores they saw that summer were a few foxes and one wolf. A few miles south of the camp they came across the den of an Arctic fox, complete with four pups. Aside from that, they found only a few lemmings and Arctic hares. Dewey probably didn't mind the lack of mammals. He was really only there to study the blue geese.

Throughout July, Dewey and his companions collected birds and eggs. He recorded the non-stop activity around and in the nesting sites. He had to be a man of all talents, from studying the birds and writing notes, to taking the photographs and making sketches. He was a surveyor, a cartographer, an ornithologist, a botanist, and a mammalogist, as well as an explorer.

Kavivau and Ashuna loading the freighter canoe for departure from Camp Kungovik at the Blue Goose River for Cape Dorset, July 20, 1929.

Using the freighter canoe, he led his team up the Blue Goose River to chart its course, study the geology of the river's banks, and look for its source. As a canoe route, it was not a long river. From where they launched the canoe, Dewey noted they travelled roughly five miles upstream to the northeast, working over riffles and a few rapids. The river then turned east across the tundra for a few miles before it separated into a series of small and shallow streams, where the canoe could not go. The geese were there, on either side of the river, and there were more blues than whites. Dewey made an observation about the number of blue geese in the immediate area: "One of the most interesting features of the breeding ground was the astonishing abundance of blue geese in relation to the number of [their] nests."[9]

On July 20, Dewey became the first white man to see blue goose chicks in the wild. Away from the formal scientific records, his popular description of the young supplies a colourful picture of new life venturing into the world:

> The goslings are covered with thick down of a dusky colour tinted with a very pale greenish cast, lighter below and buffy whitish on the throat. The bill, feet, and legs are black. They are precocious and leave the nest shortly after hatching when they have dried off. Within a day or two they become markedly active, running about the tundra with their parents. In ponds they can swim at once and dive with ease. When they take to the water they seem especially preoccupied and happy, bobbing about with all the joyous abandon of young ducks.[10]

Seeing a mature couple with five agile and active young while on the river, Dewey and his men gave chase. Callous as it may seem to some today, his objective was purely scientific. The National Museum did not have any specimens of goslings from the blue goose. Dewey was determined to correct that omission.

The adult geese did everything they could to keep their young out of harm's way. They led them up a steep clay bank, some three or four feet high, with the young struggling and some falling in their haste. Once on top, while the men found somewhere to safely tie up the canoe, the geese and goslings ran at full speed for safety. Dewey chased after them for nearly half a mile. The parents stayed with their young, who, Dewey said, "were far from being exhausted," until he was no more than twenty yards away. Then, obviously realizing there was nothing more they could do to defend their babies, the parents flapped their wings and took off, loudly expressing their concern. Dewey didn't say if he took all five goslings, although it is highly unlikely that he would do so. He did report that he collected nine very young geese over a two-day period.

The work at the breeding grounds was at an end, and Dewey had a ship to catch. Unable to carry all his equipment and all the collected specimens in the canoe, they built a weather- and animal-proof cache. After erecting a stone cairn and secreting a record of their work in it, they closed down Camp Kungovik on July 20 and started for the mouth of the Blue Goose River at Bowman Bay. That short distance took four days to cover, as Dewey continued his fieldwork on the way.

For the return journey to Cape Dorset, Dewey had planned to attempt to cross the Foxe Peninsula by canoe, using the rivers and lakes and portaging when necessary between. That route would take them across the eastern rim of Foxe Basin from Bowman Bay to Gibson Bay. From there he intended to ascend the Kommanik River to Tessikdjuak Lake, then to follow the chain of smaller lakes and streams down to Andrew Gordon Bay. The appeal was that no white man had ever traversed that route. The only alternative course with the canoe was to follow the wild coast of the Foxe Peninsula all the way to Cape Dorset, if sea and ice conditions permitted.

Their arrival at Bowman Bay caused some consternation. The bay was filled with ice, some of the floes as much as twelve to fifteen feet thick. A few leads, or open-water channels, showed. They followed one lead as far as Farley Point, at the western end of the bay, before being forced to take the canoe ashore and wait. Ice, even when packed into a bay, is constantly on the move. Leads can open and close quickly enough, and with enough pressure to crush most boats. Each time a lead opened in a rough westerly direction, they launched the canoe and motored as far as they could. At Cape Alberta, not much more than ten miles from Farley Point, the ice stopped them again: "We were now confronted by massive ice which was pushed right up to the rocks, forcing us ashore to make camp."[11] And there they stayed for nine frustrating days.

To add to their problems, food was running low. Day after day they listened to the ice groaning, complaining, screeching, thundering, and grinding together. Fortunately the weather, at last, treated them kindly, but the ice remained fast to the shore with no leads in sight. Dewey went out collecting to pass the time, and to hunt if game should be available, but they were all ready to leave at any time should a lead open up in the desired direction.

As they stepped out of their tents on the morning of August 3, they were excited to see a wide lead had opened up during the night. It ran parallel to the coast, quite close in, and it gave them a narrow highway to travel. Their initial euphoria did not last long. A few miles farther on the lead changed direction and headed out to sea. The tide worked against them, too; it was on the ebb, and soon the canoe settled on the rapidly drying seabed some two miles from shore. So, there they were, three men in a fragile canoe, surrounded by potentially deadly ice at least as thick as they were tall, sometimes twice that, and no water in sight. The tide would, of course, come back and it would move the ice. When it did, although it could offer an escape route, it could also kill them. Only time would tell which. With nothing else to do, they caught a few hours sleep with one of the trio always on watch. Ice was not the only problem. A sudden visit from a marauding polar bear could be just as deadly.

Dewey taking a sun shot for latitude. He is standing on the granite seabed of Foxe Basin near Cape Alberta while surrounded by stranded sea ice at low tide. August 11, 1929.

When the tide came in, it shuffled the ice around enough to afford a reasonably safe passage through veins of open water to the land. For eight days, travelling only when the tide was full, the grounded ice in motion again, and shore leads aiming west-southwest, they worked their way along the coast for more than seventy miles to the mouth of the Kommanik River. The sea was covered in pack ice in all directions. The only open water was at the river's mouth, where the action of tide and current kept it in motion and free of ice. Because of the natural turbulence, it was not a good place to be in a canoe.

At this juncture they had run out of food. There was little game available and the nearest cache, put down in the autumn of 1928, was on the west side of Angmaluk Lake — about thirty miles away, upriver. Until then they would have to exist on whatever they could shoot. Fortunately they did find a few hares and ptarmigan for the pot to keep them going. There were no caribou.

On the morning of August 12 they started up the Kommanik. Not having been there before, they really had no idea what to expect. The river proved to be shallow and stony in places, which necessitated long and tiring portages. Small lakes broke up the river's passage, giving the weary and often hungry travellers a break from the hard physical labour of the portages. Dewey named the lakes for his much-valued Inuit companions[11]: Ashuna, Kavivau, and Shappa.

When they reached the cache at Angmaluk Lake they made camp and ate a big meal. After a good night's sleep, they would continue. The cache also held gasoline. That, too, was needed to get them the rest of the way.

They finally came down to Andrew Gordon Bay on August 16. One day later they were back at Cape Dorset, but there Dewey experienced another disappointment. He had planned to leave on the RMS *Nascopie*. That ship had been into Cape Dorset, unloaded, and had left two weeks before, while Dewey was battling ice on Bowman Bay. No other ships would call at Cape Dorset until the following summer. Dewey had to find another way to get home to his family in Alberta.

With help from the local HBC manager he chartered an Inuit schooner to take him to Lake Harbour, nearly three hundred miles to the east, where the last ship to leave Baffin Island for the 1929 season would soon make its call. There wasn't just Dewey to carry. Boxes of specimens collected over the past year had to go with him. The items left in the cache at Camp Kungovik would be brought in over the winter by Natives and shipped on to Ottawa the next summer, where they did eventually arrive at the museum in good condition.

Getting to Lake Harbour was a rough trip, bucking headwinds coming up Hudson Strait all the way. Native schooners and their crews are tough and the boats are extremely seaworthy. The winds slowed them down but the schooner ploughed on through the waves. They arrived at Lake Harbour in the evening of August 24. They were just in time. Nine hours later the SS *Beothic* steamed into view.

Once the ship was underway for the south, her radio broadcast the news of Dewey's success with the blue geese to the museum. From there it was spread by newspaper and radio to the world. He wrote, "Ornithologists especially would be gladdened by the event. People had waited a long time to learn where the blue geese nested, and now the long mystery was solved."[12]

A couple of weeks later Dewey was home with Carrie and Roly. He had been away for just over thirteen months.

15

Lake Harbour, 1930–31

The 1928–29 series of expeditions out of Cape Dorset had realized an additional collection for museums of 512 specimens, consisting of mammals, birds, fish, and eggs. Over the winter of 1929–30 Dewey wrote an account of his field studies on the blue goose, which was soon published by the Department of the Interior as a sixty-four-page booklet.[1] The success of his previous year's work on Baffin Island convinced the government to commission an up-to-date survey of the coastal regions east and west of Lake Harbour. Not surprisingly, Dewey got the assignment. At that time the north coast of Hudson Strait had not been accurately surveyed, except, as Dewey noted, "in broad outline." There was still much detail missing.

    He returned to Baffin Island, on what would be his final expedition to the region, in the early summer of 1930, this time with Carolyn and their infant son, Roland. They sailed there, as Dewey had done in 1928, in the famed HBC steamship *Nascopie*. For Carrie the voyage gave her an opportunity to see more of Baffin Island than just Lake Harbour. The ship's itinerary took them first far up Davis Strait and Baffin Bay to Pond Inlet, which Dewey had visited in 1923, followed by Pangnirtung, where he lived in 1924. Onboard *Nascopie* that year was a sixteen-year-old English boy, Edward Beauclerk Maurice,[2] on his way to Pangnirtung as an apprentice to the HBC. Maurice went ashore with Dewey at Pond Inlet and was treated to a brief discourse on the birds of the region from an expert.

Based for the year at the small settlement of Lake Harbour, on Baffin Island's south shore facing Hudson Strait, the Soper family initially shared accommodation with the four HBC personnel in their building, until a comfortable scientific station/residence could be built. Dewey, the journeyman carpenter and experienced house-builder, was just the man for that job. All the construction materials had arrived on the supply ship with them, so he, along with Carrie and other local workers, helped build the house they would live in for the duration of their Lake Harbour sojourn.

There were twelve non-Natives at Lake Harbour in 1930. They were: three Mounties, four HBC employees, the three Sopers, plus an Anglican minister, Reverend Bailey, and his wife. Carrie and Mrs. Bailey were the only non-Native women on southern Baffin Island at that time, and they soon forged a strong friendship.

As on previous expeditions, Dewey's work encompassed exploring and surveying, collecting and studying wildlife, and photography. Carolyn, a registered nurse, became the first white female nurse to work on Baffin Island. Her presence proved to be a boon to the Inuit, although there were still tragedies. Soon after the family's arrival a deadly sickness broke out in Lake Harbour. Carolyn had no idea what the disease was but treated it as best she could. In spite of her efforts, five people were buried in one day. She wrote an account of the tragedy for *The Beaver*:[3] "The symptoms were a sore throat and difficulty swallowing, with very little rise in temperature, The onset was sudden with death occurring in about two days.... In spite of painstaking effort night and day, eight deaths occurred before the epidemic finally subsided."

When the annual steamship arrived the following year, the ship's doctor diagnosed the problem as respiratory polio. The Sopers and the other nine non-Natives were lucky that not one of them was touched by the deadly malady.

Having avoided polio, two-and-a-half-year-old Roland almost didn't survive his first Arctic winter anyway. There was a picket fence around the house and Roly was supposed to stay within its confines. However, snow had drifted into banks on either side of the fence, making a useful bridge for a toddler anxious to go exploring on his own. He climbed up one side of the drift, crossed the fence, and slid down the other side. Today Roly has no recollection of where he went, but we do know he was missing for a few hours. At some point the sea ice, not far away, caught his attention, so he wandered away from the house in that direction. Shore-bound or barrier ice is often badly cracked and rafted with clearly defined crevasses. Roly strayed onto the shore ice and fell into a deep crevasse. Fortunately, it being winter, he was well bundled up against the cold, so suffered no injury, but being a very small boy, he could not climb out and so was trapped for an unknown length of time. The HBC employees and the local RCMP officers joined Dewey and Carrie as they searched for him. Eventually the rescuers heard his cries, found where he was hidden, and pulled him out. Dewey commented, "He was a badly frightened little boy." Had there been an incoming tide while he was trapped, he would have drowned. Had the ice moved under tidal or any other pressure, he could have been crushed.

Carrie had warned Roly of the dangers of leaving the garden by crossing the fence because of polar bears, which occasionally wandered into or past the settlement. After his adventure in the sea ice, in what today would perhaps be considered a misguided attempt at Arctic safety

Roly Soper at Lake Harbour, winter 1930–31, age 2½.

Roland Soper Collection.

The Soper home at Lake Harbour, Baffin Island. The building was designed as a scientific station as well as a residence and was the property of the Department of the Interior, Ottawa.

education, she donned a polar bear skin, complete with head, and jumped out to frighten him. Roly commented that, later, his mother was contrite because she had scared him. The rough lesson did the trick, however, and Roly never again ventured away from the Lake Harbour home.

During the early part of the winter, Dewey spent a lot of time surveying in the immediate area and plotting the results on a new map. Looking to the northeast, he planned a January expedition to Frobisher Bay, Silliman Hill, and back to Lake Harbour by way of Amadjuak Lake with his new Inuit partner, Moosa. This time his plans came to naught. Not long before departure Dewey was out on the jigsaw puzzle of rafted ice along the shore and fell heavily. In doing so he wrecked his right knee. Unable to walk without pain, he had no choice but to cancel the journey and to rest from sled travel for a few weeks.

Lake Harbour, 1930–31

Left: Dewey, Carrie, and Roly Soper at Lake Harbour.

Above: White residents of Lake Harbour, 1930–31. (Left to right) Constable Lavoie (RCMP), Mr. MacKenzie and Abe Ford (both of the HBC), Carolyn Soper, Roly Soper, Corporal McKeller (RCMP), and Mr. Fraser (HBC). The only one missing is Dewey: he took the photograph.

While Dewey recuperated, one of the local Inuit hunters was lost with his entire dog team while seal hunting alone in White Strait, between the south shore of Baffin Island and nearby Big Island. Sled tracks at the edge of a wide lead told the story: the man, his dogs, and his sled had plunged into the water and been carried away under the sea ice by the current. It would have been a sobering discovery for all.[4]

Early in June, with Dewey's knee healed, he and Moosa, together with Carrie, Roly, and Moosa's wife, Neve, took a short camping trip to McKellar Bay. Only fourteen miles southeast of Lake Harbour, the journey by sled was on sea ice all the way. A significant level of water covered the ice due to the early summer melt, so they lashed the freighter canoe on the sled and placed all their belongings inside to keep dry.

Although it had all the appearances of a short family holiday, there was a serious side to the excursion. The migration of land birds was in full swing. From their campsite near the sea, Dewey could observe the various species of birds, collect the ones he needed, and he could continue his geographical survey of the coast.

Dinner at the Soper home in Lake Harbour, March 1931. The occasion was the Sopers' fourth wedding anniversary. (Left to right) RCMP Corporal McKeller, Dewey, Roly, Carrie, and RCMP Constable Lavoie.

On the return trip four days later, the water cover was even deeper. It was time to tie up the dogs and put the sled away for the rest of the season. Dewey's time was now divided between surveying and the collected specimens: "birds, mammals, fish, and insects, and adding more items to the plant press." As little of the interior of the Meta Incognita Peninsula had been explored, he also planned journeys inland to see and chart what he could before the end of his assigned year.

A river runs from the uplands of the Meta Incognita Peninsula of southern Baffin Island to a lake inland from Lake Harbour. No one knew the exact location of its source, but the Inuit claimed it was about forty miles south of the head of Frobisher Bay. They knew it as the Koukdjuak (Big River), the same name as the large river flowing into Foxe Basin from Nettilling Lake. To them it was just a big river. In 1931 the Geographic Board of Canada officially named it the Soper River. At the same time the board also named the lake after Soper.

Lake Harbour, 1930–31

At the end of June, Dewey and two Inuit companions, Moosa and Mutuse, set off to explore the lake and the river in the freighter canoe. The lake was calm. While one of the Inuit handled the boat, Dewey plotted bearings and made notes. The mouth of the river, where it disgorges into the lake, was a wild rapid that forced them to make a portage of more than six hundred yards along the east bank. For the next few miles the river was wide, deep, and slow-moving, making that part of the ascent easy for the canoe. High, rugged hills, some towering up to a thousand feet, shadowed the river. At midday they reached another rapid, too turbulent to navigate. After a lunch break they hand-lined, or tracked, the canoe up the rapid to avoid unloading and portaging; it was still heavy and often difficult work. As they progressed, the rapids frequently held them back. When the current proved too strong for the outboard motor, they either hand-lined the canoe or portaged everything. They almost lost the canoe and all their supplies in the middle of that first afternoon. The power of one rapid proved too much for them and turned the canoe so it came close to rolling. Swamped with water, they made it to shore safely and spent the rest of the day drying out.

Dewey painted a powerful word-picture of the scenery as they moved on upstream: "The mountainous walls of the valley are wildly spectacular and mostly barren. Here and there thick talus slides occupy the lower slopes. Numerous streams roar down steep tributary valleys in a long series of snow-white cascades and rapids, or plunge in showy falls to the valley below."[5]

The fast-flowing and unnavigable Livingstone River races into the Soper River from the northwest, about a mile north of where the canoe mishap occurred. Dewey passed it and kept moving slowly onward. The temperature climbed to a high of 75°, creating some discomfort for the Inuit. Even Dewey admitted he would have preferred cooler conditions. At latitude 63° 50′ N, on July 1, they came to a temporary halt. The river had become too shallow and too difficult to navigate farther with the load they were carrying. Dewey used that interruption for valuable scientific work: "We spent the rest of the day here collecting plants, getting magnetic values, adding to the stock of survey data, and taking photographs. I also climbed to the top of the valley to get altitude figures which proved to be around 1,500 feet above sea level."[6]

Many willows grew near the river at that latitude and to Dewey's surprise they were big ones by Baffin Island standards. He described many clumps that were between four and six feet in height. The largest tree of the species he measured in that vicinity was twelve and a half feet high and had a trunk of more than three inches in diameter. Most Arctic willows tend to be little more than ankle to knee high. Dewey collected a few samples of these large examples for the National Herbarium in Ottawa.

Leaving the supplies and specimens on the riverbank, the three men slowly ascended the river, often taking to the banks to hand-line the canoe past rapids. After a few miles of slow going they came to another stream, this one flowing in from the east. Leaving the canoe beside the Soper River, they walked along the tributary's banks to see where it led. It was definitely not a canoeist's river. In three miles they passed "rapids, cascades and falls." About two-thirds of the way up, they reached a waterfall with a ninety-five-foot drop, the highest on that stretch of river. Dewey named the busy tributary the Cascade River.

Back on the Soper they soon came to an impasse. The current was too strong for the outboard motor and the terrain too high and steep for a portage. Beaching the canoe again, they continued on foot. Ahead was a prominent peak close to the river known to the Inuit as Kenowaya Mountain. Dewey arbitrarily renamed it Mount Joy in honour of Inspector A.H. Joy[7] of the RCMP. He continued his survey for another mile or two before accepting that they could not go any farther upriver by canoe. The only way to explore the upper reaches effectively would be on foot in the summer or by dogsled in winter when the rivers were frozen over, and he did not have enough time left for either.

With the snows melting, the Soper River was full and flowing faster than it had been a few days before. That made the descent an exhilarating, if nerve-racking, ride. From Dewey's writings it is probable that they ran the river all the way to the lake without having to resort to hand-lining or portaging. They certainly ran the last stretch of rapids that they had portaged around for hundreds of yards on the way upstream. A disappointing aspect of the river exploration was the scarcity of wildlife. Dewey wrote that "only a few individuals of the following species were recorded: Canada goose, common eider, red-breasted merganser, rock ptarmigan, semi-palmated plover, glaucous gull, horned lark, wheatear, water pipit, Lapland longspur, snow bunting."

He also saw signs of weasels, Arctic foxes, wolves, and lemmings, but failed to collect any specimens of the mammals. The Inuit told him that caribou frequent the highlands beyond the river, but none were seen.

More than seventy years after Dewey explored the Soper River, noted Canadian wilderness canoeing expert Max Finkelstein described it thus: "Although it is navigable for only 50 [kilometres] (by canoe), the Soper is a major river by Baffin Island standards. It is a Canadian Heritage River,[8] one of a select group of Canada's most outstanding rivers. The land it flows through is protected as Katannilik Territorial Park, meaning 'Place of Waterfalls,' and everywhere water tumbles down the steep valley walls."[9]

Time for exploring and collecting was running out. It was now July 4. The annual supply ship was due to arrive late in the month, and the Sopers were supposed to be onboard when it left. There were just enough days left for one more surveying expedition.

The loaded freighter canoe left Lake Harbour again on July 8 to survey the coast for a relatively short distance to the east. The weather, which had been so warm and calm on the river journey, was fair on departure, but it soon played false. Dewey, however, wrote of the coastal survey in a matter-of-fact style that belies the dangers and difficulties inherent in such a voyage: "Not long after setting out strong, choppy winds, high waves, and a misty rain developed forcing us ashore on Copeland Island in Westbourne Bay [to wait for an improvement]." When it came, they made a hurried crossing to the mainland and set up camp, just in time to be targeted by a violent gale, including thunder and lightning.

The next few days were not much improved, but the survey party kept moving, except when forced ashore by contrary winds. The coastline between Lake Harbour and Shaftesbury Inlet, the eastern extent of the planned survey, is carved in intricate patterns like a random jigsaw puzzle. Few of the inlets and bays had been properly charted before Dewey went to work that July.

Tides in Hudson Strait are notoriously high.[10] Lake Harbour, for instance, experiences a tidal change of up to 41 feet. The combination of racing tides and strong currents (the latter coming in from Davis Strait) flowing west often creates rough seas. Adding to that hazard are sheer cliffs of granite, rising straight out of the sea to heights up to a thousand feet. Taking a large canoe close to that coast for long distances, as Dewey and his Inuit companions did, would require exceptional boating skills.

In spite of the often dreadful weather, Dewey enjoyed the voyage. He wrote of camping beside the mouths of roaring rivers and passing towering waterfalls, all of which he viewed through the eyes of an experienced wilderness traveller and scientist. Evidence of summer fishing campsites told him the rivers of the coast were well-known to the Inuit for their Arctic char.[11]

On January 12, Dewey completed his survey, the final stretches being the east side of Shaftesbury Inlet and Ayde Bay as far as Ayde Point. From there they took the most direct route back to Lake Harbour, checking their outbound bearings en route. They made it home in one long and tiring day. The round trip had covered 140 miles. It was Dewey's last Baffin Island surveying expedition.

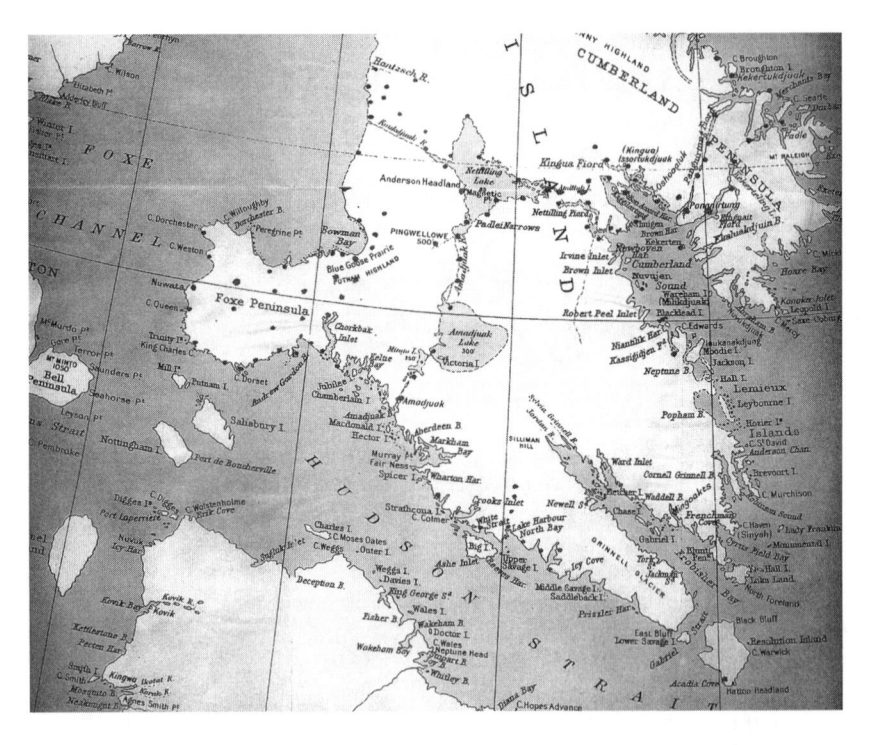

Map of Southern Baffin Island, showing Dewey Soper's campsites as black dots from 1923 to 1931. From: A Map To Illustrate Report on Exploration in Southern Baffin Island, 1929 **Source:** Library and Archives Canada/*Southern Baffin Island : An Account of Exploration, Investigation and Settlement During the Past Fifty Years* / AMICUS 4379308/ Map on page 130.

Lake Harbour, 1930–31

He and Carrie spent the next two weeks packing his specimens and scientific equipment, as well as their personal effects. Just before the ship came in, Dewey inspected the buildings to make sure everything was as it should be for the next resident, a doctor this time. The HBC steamship *Ungava*[12] dropped anchor at the end of July and the Soper family went aboard with Dewey's considerable amount of baggage. Instead of the long haul south down the Labrador Sea to the North Atlantic and up the St. Lawrence to Quebec City or Montreal, Dewey and his family went home by a westerly route. The steamship sailed across Hudson Strait to call at West Sugluk and Wolstenholme, both in northern Quebec, before crossing Hudson Bay to Churchill, Manitoba. From there the Sopers went by train on the newly completed 1,062-mile railway line[13] to Winnipeg and on to Ottawa. Dewey never returned to the eastern Arctic.

16

Two Decades of Stellar Service

After a year away from civilization, moving from the tiny subarctic settlement of Lake Harbour to the bustling capital city of Ottawa was a large step in geographical terms and a monumental cultural change. Dewey seemed to take such enormous adjustments in stride and there is no indication that Carolyn and Roly were unduly affected by the transition either. Once back in Ontario, Dewey took a few weeks' leave to take a rest, and for the three of them to visit family. Then, as always after a long, remote assignment, he started work on a long list of detailed reports of all aspects of his year at and around Lake Harbour. Among many reports, two major papers arose from that work, both published by the government as slim paperback books: *The Mammals of Southern Baffin Island, Northwest Territories, Canada*[1] and *Ornithological Results of the Baffin Island Expeditions of 1928–29 and 1930–31, Together with Recent Records*.[2] He also had maps to complete by plotting hundreds of bearings and redrawing coastlines and inland features, particularly the course of the Soper River.

Although Dewey wanted to spend more time in the eastern Arctic, knowing there was much more surveying work to be done along the coasts and in the interior — and, of course, many more wildlife studies to be made — the lack of available government funds in the Depression years negated that possibility. Instead, R.A. Gibson, deputy commissioner of the Northwest

Territories, and O.S. Finnie, director of the Northwest Territories and Yukon Branch of the Department of the Interior, offered him a two-year position investigating wildlife in Wood Buffalo National Park. As it was a region of Canada in which he had never travelled, and bordered on part of the Northwest Territories he had not visited, Dewey accepted. An additional carrot was that, as with the Lake Harbour posting, Carrie and Roly would be able to go with him. Accordingly, in May 1932, he moved his family out of the city again and took them west into a new wilderness.

In a remote corner of northeast Alberta, Carrie was once more far from home, family, and friends, yet she apparently accepted the new posting with equanimity. Home now was a large, comfortable, and properly furnished log house in the park headquarters beside the Slave River, about twenty-five miles south of the hamlet of Fitzgerald. With only a handful of Native residents in Fitzgerald, and with Fort Smith, the nearest town of any size, another fifteen miles farther north, the Sopers were quite isolated. However, there was usually some form of traffic on the river; therefore there were other people reasonably close by. Since the early days of the Hudson's Bay Company in the region, Fort Fitzgerald and Fort Smith had been the way stations bracketing the deadly rapids that required all boats to be portaged between the two settlements.[3]

The Soper log house at Government Hay Camp near the Slave River in Wood Buffalo National Park, where they lived from 1932 to 1934. Roly Soper is on the porch.

At the time of Dewey's appointment, no wildlife investigations of any kind had taken place since the park was established in 1922.[4] For Soper, it was a wonderful opportunity to roam at will and make a real study of the fauna and avifauna. At 17,300 square miles in area, it was then and still is Canada's largest national park and, even in the twenty-first century, it is one of the largest in the world. Within its extensive borders are large, uncut areas of boreal wilderness, unique salt plains, and excellent examples of gypsum karst landforms. Three major rivers flow into and north across the park: the Peace and Athabasca combine to form the Slave, which runs north into Great Slave Lake.

Dewey's major research for the two-year study was to be centred on the northern (wood) bison (*Bison bison athabascae*). He noted that there were ten thousand head in the park[5] — a vast, free-roaming, and self-regulating herd. In addition to studying the bison herd, he was to carry out an overall survey of the park's fauna, make observations on magnetic declination, study the physical geography, and report on the state of park cabins, fire towers, roads, and trails. Over the next two years he estimated he travelled some eight thousand miles by aircraft, powerboat, and canoe, on horseback, and by dog team. One dogsled journey alone took him over six hundred miles on little-known trails through the park. During his travels in Wood Buffalo he collected more than a thousand specimens of birds and mammals, which he preserved, crated, and shipped to the National Museum.

Wood Buffalo National Park held ten thousand bison when Dewey Soper was there in the early 1930s.

Dewey driving his dog team through a forest in Wood Buffalo National Park on April 22, 1934. He was out making a tally of the winter bison herds.

He wrote of taking two immature specimens of the Mackenzie varying hare (*Lepus americanus macfarlani*): "[They] came from a litter of six that was found in a shallow nest, under some shrubbery, in a woods of mixed spruce and aspen poplar.... They were evidently still being nursed as they were obviously occupying the original nest from which they made no effort to escape. When picked up and released in the tent, however, all were capable of vigorous activity."[6]

One of the smaller mammals he studied in the park was the boreal white-footed mouse[7] (*Peromyscus maniculatus borealis*). He estimated there were as many as 46,600 individuals per square mile in the summer of 1932. He obviously enjoyed watching them because he wrote, "While basically terrestrial, they do not hesitate to scramble up bushes and trees; in fact, their nervous energy lures them into all sorts of situations; withal, they are highly sensitive, timorous, alert and overcurious."[8]

Another tiny creature that shared Wood Buffalo National Park with the mice in large numbers was the Athabasca red-backed vole[9] (*Clethrionomys gapperi athabascae*). Not as numerous, having populations of up to 16,500 individuals per square mile, he collected specimens of young males and gravid females.

Northwestern coyotes (*Canis latrans incolatus*), red foxes (*Vulpes fulva abietorum*), and northern timber wolves (*Canis lupus occidentalis*) also lived in the park. Dewey said the red foxes were especially plentiful the second winter he was there. It appears though that the wolves excited him more. He recorded packs of anywhere from four to sixteen running together. And he commented on their vocal styling, as he had done before on Baffin Island, no doubt inspired by his nights out on the trail in winter:

Roly with a favourite sled dog in the early spring of 1933. Wood Buffalo National Park.

> The howling of wolf packs is one of the most thrilling sounds of the northern wilderness. The sensational choristers often perform with maximum effect on clear and bitterly cold nights. If trekking by dog-team, the latter animals reciprocate by adding mightily to the pandemonium. On one occasion a howling pack periodically raised the echoes all evening near our forest camp; the next morning it was discovered that the wolves had bedded down for the night in tall meadow grass not over 200 yards from camp; the pack of 16 members fled wildly when the area was approached.[10]

On one wildlife surveying journey while in the park, Dewey paddled his canoe silently down the Little Buffalo River, which meanders more or less

Sketch of a bison head, by J. Dewey Soper.

due north into the Northwest Territories from the northeast sector. Seeing a typical mudslide used by otters, he stopped to watch for a while in late afternoon. A family of four Mackenzie otters (*Lutra Canadensis preblei*) came out to entertain him. The otters made repeated runs, sliding on their bellies down the wide groove in the mudbank to the river. He wrote, "Their happy enthusiasm was enchanting to watch."[11]

The two years in Wood Buffalo National Park might have generally lacked the excitement or the danger of exploring new and uncharted land as he had in the Arctic, especially during the winter months, and there is no doubt that survival on a day-to-day basis, too, was much simpler in the vast park than on Baffin Island. But despite those elemental drawbacks, Dewey made the most of his two years there.

A great part of Dewey's success as a naturalist and explorer was due to the large amount of time he spent in the field. Rather than limiting his scientific study travels to a few weeks, he took his time to explore often difficult terrain alone, and he studied his subjects in their natural habitat in great depth. He was always a prolific collector of wildlife specimens and plants. If a particular species of mammal, for example, was abundant at a selected site, he would collect an intelligently considered series of them. Consequently, for any one species, he would collect different sexes and ages, thereby providing the basis for later comparative studies. Although Wood Buffalo National Park offered few opportunities for exploring previously unknown tracts of land — Dewey would have followed all known trails, anyway, and some new ones that he blazed himself — he never lost his passion for the study of geography. That passion was exemplified by the detailed mapping work he had done on Baffin Island between 1923 and 1931.

A few weeks before Christmas 1933, Carrie and Roly flew south to Edmonton, where Carolyn gave birth to a daughter, Mary Lou, on January 7, 1934, at her parents' farm near Wetaskiwin. Alone, but probably not lonely, Dewey kept to a rigorous schedule of work for the three months his wife and son were away, much of that time spent out on the park's trails.

At the end of his tenure in the park, Dewey went to Ottawa in June 1934 to prepare and present his reports. As a direct result of his two years in Wood Buffalo National Park, he wrote and had published a series of scientific papers about various species of fauna he had studied there. Unlike

A Soper camp in the foothills of western Alberta about forty miles east of Banff in the late summer of 1935. Dewey is cutting wood for the fire.

Dewey on a summer holiday trip with Mary Lou and Roly, 1935.

Two Decades of Stellar Service

Dewey Soper and a young plains coyote he captured at Johnston Lake, Saskatchewan, June 19, 1936.

his expeditions on Baffin Island, which he wrote about in great detail for a popular readership, his writings on the two years beside the Slave River are mostly in the form of scientific papers and reports for the government.

While in Ottawa, on July 1 he was transferred to the Canadian Wildlife Service with the title and position of Chief Wildlife Officer for the Prairie Provinces. This new position required that Dewey undergo several weeks of special training in relation to the legal aspects of the Migratory Birds Convention Act and its enforcement. He then moved to Winnipeg, where the family lived for the next fourteen years. They lived in a rented house on Telfer Street for the first two years, then, at the beginning of May 1936, they bought a house on Riverwood Avenue in Fort Garry, just south of the Winnipeg city limits. They lived there for the next twelve years: a long period of residential stability that Dewey had never before experienced.

The newly appointed Chief Wildlife Officer for the Prairies had an enormous expanse of land to cover, spread over three provinces, each of which is larger than many countries. To put the size of the territory into a different context, the combined areas of Alberta, Saskatchewan, and Manitoba total 758,100 square miles. That is an area equal to Alaska plus Montana and West Virginia or, in European terms, a similar size to Belgium, France, Germany, Netherlands, Poland, Portugal, and Spain added together.[12] This incredible spread required Dewey to travel extensively, which was nothing new to his family. His fieldwork was carried out in hundreds of locations, from the Rocky Mountains to Winnipeg and far to the north in the coniferous zone. Most years he travelled between fifteen and twenty thousand miles, often staying away from home for months at a time, although anywhere from two weeks to a month was the norm. His brief covered investigations on waterfowl species, and writing and preparing departmental reports for head office as well as scientific reports for publication. He was also expected to attend wildlife conferences in addition to delivering lectures and radio talks. With typical understatement, he wrote, "The programme of activities was quite demanding.... In fact, much overtime was required to even keep partially abreast of the demands."[13]

He wrote that, in the course of his Winnipeg years, he accumulated so much data on birds and mammals in his enormous domain that, "For lack of time a high percentage of this could not be written up for publication or otherwise." This admission explains the scarcity of narrative material that so highlighted his eastern Arctic experiences. His fieldwork during that long period took him as far west as the Rocky Mountains and north into the coniferous forests of the Canadian Life Zone.[14]

The study of migratory birdlife was intended to be the main focus of Dewey's work on the Prairies. Aside from that, he was often instructed to conduct surveys on mammals in the various national parks across the three provinces. Those additional assignments required more written reports. He noted that "Collecting was not mandatory.... Nevertheless, it was impossible to do accurate work in many instances without resorting to the capture and preservation of specimens. This was especially true with respect to the sub-specific identity of the smaller mammals."[15] Apart from the scientific necessity, knowing of Dewey's passion for collecting and preserving wildlife, it is not difficult to understand why he added those tasks to his already heavy workload. He explained his rationale thus: "Regardless of the situation, as a whole, I never relinquished the policy of collecting good specimens wherever the job called for it, or at any other opportunity when time and circumstances permitted and science would be served."[16]

Occasionally colleagues would join Dewey in the field for a few days. In August 1938, Dr. R.M. Anderson spent some time collecting with him in the Cameron Lake[17] and Akamina Pass areas of southwestern Alberta, north of Waterton Lakes. There they encountered an abundance of rufous-tailed chipmunks (*Eutamias ruficaudus ruficaudus*) gathering seeds for the winter. A few days later, just across the divide, they collected two more specimens, thereby establishing the first record of that chipmunk species in British Columbia.[18]

That same year, commenting on the Richardson red squirrel population of the Crowsnest Pass, Oldman River trench, he recalled that the species was rare when he collected there in the spring and summer of 1927. In 1938, working in the same area, he wrote in his field notes, "This race of dusky pelage [the Richardson red squirrel] is now a very common inhabitant of the spruce-pine-aspen woods of lower elevation (around 4,500–5,300 feet) where tree growth is more sturdy and rank.... At this mid-August time the animals were very vocal on fair days; their chattering calls and chipperings sounded almost constantly in the woods as they apparently answered each other from various distances."[19]

The securing and preservation built up into large collections of bird and mammal specimens over the Prairie years. In time the number became so great that Dewey had to spend some of his off-duty hours at home building more insect-proof cabinets to hold them, keeping birds and mammals separate.

The Second World War started in the summer of 1939 when Germany invaded Poland. That terrible conflict lasted for six long years, yet its effects on Dewey and his work appear to have been negligible. Dewey was always so focused on his wildlife studies that nowhere in his notes or personal reminiscences does he mention the war raging in Europe, North Africa, and Asia.

On winter weekends, usually on Sundays, Dewey and Mary Lou would go cross-country skiing or snowshoeing in the nearby woods or along the riverbanks. Mary Lou said of her father, "He was a wonderful man; very loving and caring." Sometimes, when Dewey was working reasonably close to home, he would take Mary Lou with him on short camping and collecting trips. Mary Lou learned to run her own trapline and, she said, became a good camp cook — after a few lessons from her father.

In May 1944 he was sent to the Grande Prairie–Peace River area of northwestern Alberta for a four-month assignment, primarily to study waterfowl distribution and numbers. In association with waterfowl, he was also expected to pay attention to other more general birdlife, as well as mammals. The waterfowl studies took him to thirty-two lakes between the Torrens River, in the Rocky Mountains close to the border with British Columbia southwest of Grande Prairie, and Cardinal Lake, a few miles west of the town of Peace River. Where possible, Dewey travelled by car to reach the study locations, then continued on foot. For the Torrens River area he rented a saddle horse and a pack horse from a local outfitter and went in alone, as was his preference and custom.

Little if any scientific wildlife study had taken place in the Grande Prairie–Peace River section of Alberta, so Dewey found the opportunity to be the first in many cases "exciting." From his teenage years Dewey had enjoyed trapping — an essential skill to catch small mammals. On the four-month expedition he collected 148 specimens in total, although he did not clarify the numbers of birds as opposed to mammals. His efforts over that summer resulted in publication of two official papers: *Mammal Notes from* the *Grande Prairie–Peace River Region, Alberta*[20] and *Birds Observed in the Grande Prairie–Peace River Region of North-Western Alberta, Canada.*[21]

Dewey fully enjoyed the long assignments in the outdoors. Each one gave him enormous scope for study and for adding to his by then massive collection of specimens in both museums and at home. By his own admission, he was rarely happier than when camping far from civilization and studying wildlife in all its forms. In March 1945 he was sent back to Wood Buffalo National Park for another four months, studying the life and population of the northern bison. Of course, Dewey could not possibly ignore other sightings of birds and mammals. Nor could he resist the opportunity of catching them and adding to his knowledge and collections. To that end, he returned with 112 specimens which, he noted, "were of distinct value."

From his Winnipeg base he went out on many short study and collecting trips, often accompanied by his friend Leonard Norris Elye,[22] at that time director of the Manitoba Museum and himself a keen and knowledgeable naturalist. Between them they added many specimens and their field notes to the museum's collections.

Each summer for many years while based in Winnipeg the Soper family would load themselves into Dewey's official car and travel west to spend a few weeks in Alberta. Always they stopped en route for a few days at the expansive Criddle Farm, sprawled across low, rolling hills near Brandon, Manitoba. It covered six thousand acres[23] and boasted five hundred head of beef cattle. Dewey and Stuart Criddle (1877–1971), a British-born

Mary Lou and Roland Soper in the garden of the Fort Garry house in the early 1940s.

gardener and amateur ornithologist, went birdwatching together whenever they could.

Inevitably, once at their Alberta destination, Dewey would go off on fieldwork. Occasionally Carrie would go with him, although she often stayed behind and visited with relatives. The two Soper children would be boarded out with other relatives, where they had plenty of playmates. As he got older, in his mid-teens, Roly managed to avoid the annual treks to Alberta by working for Stuart Criddle on his ranch for three summers. After that, Roly simply refused to go west with the family. He would have been seventeen or eighteen years old at the time and still considered too young to remain at home alone. As a result, Carrie and Mary Lou stayed behind with him while Dewey went off on his own combined vacation and collecting expedition. That summer separation did not make much difference to the family anyway. As Roly said, "From spring to autumn we didn't see much of Dad. Most years he was away for the whole summer." He added, "And in the winter he was at work; writing or painting."[24]

Talking about the normal day-to-day interaction between him and his father, Roly said, "We did not have the usual father-son relationship. Dad had no time for sports."

In some ways that is surprising, as Dewey had a slim but strong build, like his athletic son. As an outdoorsman, sports would seem to be a natural extension of his activities. He had the energy, and he had the requisite physical fitness. Time was almost certainly a major factor in keeping Dewey away from sports fields. He was usually away somewhere in search of wild creatures to study. Throughout Roly's school career, Dewey only attended one football match in which Roly played, and that because Carrie all but dragged him there. "I'm sure he had not a clue as to what was happening on the field," Roly remarked many years later.

Roly could not recall having much interaction with his father at all during his school years, mostly because Dewey never strayed far from his work. The naturalist's only friends were other ornithologists and mammalogists, both professional and amateur. The family, including Dewey, did, however, go to the movie theatre most Friday nights when Dewey was home. There they would sit together through two feature films, with a vaudeville-style concert at the intermission. That was, in effect, the extent of the family's activities together.

Reminiscing about their childhood, Roly mentioned that Mary Lou was Dewey's favourite. "She was a well-behaved little girl," he said. In contrast to Roly, who admitted to being a bit of a rebel, the compliment suggested that Mary Lou did as she was told without complaint. Mary Lou agreed. "Oh, yes. I was Dad's pet." Roly added that Dewey and Carrie were strict parents, but they were fair. Again Mary Lou agreed, saying of Carrie, "Mum was a strong-willed woman and quite opinionated."

Because of his work, Dewey always had guns of some kind in the house when he was home. They were among the tools of his trade. He favoured three: a pistol for small mammals, a .30-30 Winchester carbine, and a shotgun for birds. When Roly was in his mid-teens, most likely in 1942, he took his father's pistol, a single-shot over-and-under Marble "Game Getter," and went out for a wild evening with friends. The firearm had a .22 on the top and .410 shotgun shell on the bottom: "We went tearing around the [Fort Garry] neighbourhood in my friend's [Ford] Model T truck with me firing off this pistol into the air. It was the .410 option that [we] used. It made a helluva bang! I got paddled soundly that time."[25]

Dewey desperately wanted Roly to pick up his mantle and become a naturalist. Roly had other ideas. He said, "I quit university because I had been pushed into science but I didn't like it. I was not interested in ornithology as a profession." Although he was interested in most wildlife and retained that interest throughout his life, Roly did not see himself as another Dewey Soper. The two men, one little more than a boy of nineteen, had not really been close for many years, mainly due to Dewey's long absences on wildlife collecting expeditions. Roly's adamant refusal to follow in the family footsteps lit a fire in Dewey that exploded into a brief fist fight in the garden of the Fort Garry home. Roly, a lot younger and faster, and with a few years' boxing experience, was easily able to deflect or otherwise avoid his father's wildly swinging blows. Beyond that, most of the "fight" consisted of a few pushes from Roly, who did not attempt to throw punches at his father, and Carrie screaming at them to stop. She finally terminated the pointless engagement by placing herself between the assailants. Roly left home soon after that and rode a freight train west. On that journey he was arrested by railway police in Regina for trespassing and spent a night in jail before being fined seven dollars. Dewey, understandably, was not amused or impressed when he heard of

Dewey taking it easy in a zoological camp along Manitoba's Assiniboine River in the summer of 1945.

his son's transgression of the law. Roly put their reaction succinctly when he said, "My parents were horrified." Roly continued on to the west from Regina and spent the next two years in British Columbia working in a logging camp.

In the spring of 1948 the government recognized that the territory to be covered by one wildlife officer was too large. In consequence, the Ottawa powers divided the Prairie provinces into two divisions for wildlife studies. The Winnipeg office would take care of Manitoba and Saskatchewan, and a new regional office would be opened in Edmonton, with jurisdiction for Alberta, Yukon, and Northwest Territories. As a direct result of Dewey's Baffin Island and Arctic experience he was offered the Edmonton position, which he accepted willingly. Apart from the new and exciting possibilities offered by the Yukon and western Arctic lands, Dewey was pleased to be going home to Edmonton again.

Over the years, apart from supplying specimens to museums, Dewey's private collection of birds and mammals had increased enormously. When the time came to finally leave Winnipeg in 1948, the Manitoba Museum acquired his bird collection. Norris Elye had made it clear that, should Dewey considering disposing of them, the museum would like to have first opportunity of housing them. It's not clear whether Dewey sold the collection or donated them. Either way, the museum took ownership of 963 bird specimens. That collection encompassed species from the smallest passerines to the largest waterfowl.

Not surprisingly, considering the enormous number of hours he had lavished on his bird collection, Dewey was quite sentimental about the transfer to the museum. He justified it to himself by putting it in context with the move from Winnipeg to a distant city: "One thing in favour of this, at least, was the avoidance of much trouble in moving the cabinets to Edmonton."[26]

Dewey and Carrie sold the Fort Garry house and purchased anew on 75th Avenue in Edmonton, near Southside Park, a few blocks south of the Strathcona area where he had lived as a young man. They shipped the furniture and Dewey's office files by truck, while the family travelled by car, taking three days for the 850-mile journey in the first week of September 1948.

By the time the family was installed in the new home, and Dewey's two-room office in the Edmonton Post Office building had been set up to his exacting standards, winter had descended on Alberta and outdoor wildlife investigations ceased for the duration. He did not go out again until the end of winter. In the spring and early summer he travelled extensively by car and by light plane in southern Alberta to conduct counts of the waterfowl populations.

A new development at the beginning of summer was an assignment to locate potential sites and make recommendations on future bird sanctuaries in northern Alberta and the Northwest Territories. That was an exploration job tailor-made for Dewey Soper. First on the list was a search for breeding grounds of the whooping crane (*Grus americana*). He spent two weeks looking at areas from Edmonton to Hay River, via the Peace River, and along the southern sector of Great Slave Lake. From Hay River he flew on a five-hundred-mile circuit to the west and southwest, and then home by way of Fort Smith.

One week later he flew back to Fort Smith and embarked on a quite different type of journey, one he had not experienced in any way since he left Baffin

Island nearly two decades before. He and Federal Warden Frank McCall were instructed to take a motorboat, the *Caribou*, down the Slave River, across the southern part of Great Slave Lake, and almost the full length of the Mackenzie River to Aklavik on the Mackenzie Delta: a distance of some 1,500 miles.

Caribou was a large cabin cruiser; a much bigger and more powerful boat than either Dewey or McCall had driven at that point. Neither of them had had any experience with a river as vast as the Mackenzie either. Dewey wrote a brief account of the voyage:

> With good river charts and full of confidence in our combined abilities, we set out cheerfully on the long run. Taking turns in the wheelhouse, the days slipped by one by one without any trouble. Then, one morning shortly after casting off from the night's mooring, we ran smack into a sandbar somewhere between Wrigley and Norman. With the river current working strongly against us (and no help) two hours of exhausting work finally set us free. Curiously enough, this was the only mishap we had through that long voyage to the Mackenzie Delta.[27]

They spent the next two or three weeks investigating the waterfowl populations by flying over the myriad islands and streams that make up the delta, and along the Yukon coast as far as Herschel Island,[28] in the Beaufort Sea near the Alaskan border. The aircraft used was the redoubtable de Havilland Beaver, owned by a small aviation company in Fort Smith. The pilot was one Dewey would get to know well over the next few weeks. "Mush" Sharon was Chief Pilot for the company and an experienced bush pilot. That did not prevent them from getting into trouble occasionally. Dewey's first flight out of Aklavik took them northeast across the Mackenzie Delta and the Tuktoyaktuk Peninsula, and it almost caused them grief.

They had landed in the evening at the small settlement of Stanton,[29] on Wood Bay (itself at the southern end of the much larger Liverpool Bay), to spend the night. The sea from Stanton to far up the bay was completely free of ice, so setting the float plane down safely was not a problem. In order to save weight and, therefore, fuel, they left surplus gasoline, sleeping bags, and miscellaneous supplies, and took off with the bay still clear of ice. Their objective was to fly a coastal waterfowl transect to the north, toward Cape Bathurst, and east to Franklin Bay. After a few hours of flying, Arctic fog closed in and they were forced to retreat to Stanton for gas, and for safety. Dewey wrote of the experience:

> Meanwhile a north wind had blown the bay full of pack-ice making it impossible to land in the usual place. We had to come down somewhere in the locality, so we circled and circled and finally took a chance and landed in a small lake about a mile south of Stanton. A tight spot. Next morning after long heating of the motor we risked our necks in a short take-off. We were lucky; despite the short-run capability of the Beaver, the pontoons thrashed through the willows on the far side! This was a close one to be sure.[30]

Happy to be airborne again, they returned to Aklavik for fuel and a hot lunch. On the homeward flight to Fort Smith they set down at Fort McPherson, Arctic Red River, Fort Franklin on Great Bear Lake, Providence, and Fort Resolution, all in the cause of what Dewey referred to as "administrative purposes." They still had another route to follow. Refuelled and ready for waterfowl reconnaissance in the north again, they left Fort Smith and stopped at Fort Reliance at the far eastern tip of Great Slave Lake, then to Yellowknife and, after again refuelling, northeast across the barrenlands to Bathurst Inlet, on the mainland tucked away to the south of Coronation Gulf.

Neither Mush nor Dewey had ever been to Bathurst Inlet, so neither had any local knowledge of the water near the HBC post, or of its depth. Mush circled the Beaver over the bay in front of the trading post, checking possible landing sites for dangers. Satisfied it was clear of obstructions, he brought the plane down for a pontoon landing. Dewey was busy looking out the window at the time, watching a flock of eider ducks. He abruptly changed the focus of his attention when, "Suddenly the plane shot up almost vertically in a powerful ascent that nearly put me over the back of the seat." At the last moment before touching down Mush had seen a submerged sandbar, too close to the surface for comfort — one that had not been visible from the air. Dewey again: "Only the pilot's very fast reaction prevented a nasty smash-up. Had we hit the sandbar the plane would have performed a somersault or two without doubt!"[31]

Mush quickly recovered his professional composure, checked the area again, and made a safe landing a short distance away. At the end of Dewey's work they flew back to Fort Smith without incident.

Dewey managed almost four weeks at home base before leaving for another month. The job this time was a detailed survey of waterfowl in the Peace River–Athabasca Delta, including a part of southeastern Wood Buffalo National Park. An important aspect of his work in the area would be to learn more about the Ross's goose (*Chen rossii*). The delta was on the migration route and used by the geese as a stopover point. Part of Dewey's study was to consider ways to increase protection for the birds while in the delta. To get there he flew to Fort Chipewyan in a float plane, where he was met by Wood Buffalo National Park Warden Herb Spreu. They completed the journey on the Athabasca River in a motorboat to Spreu's workstation at the southeastern corner of the park. Dewey used that as his base for the next month.

He returned home for the winter at the beginning of October and, apart from occasional short field trips in the southern part of the province, he stayed close to home on administrative duties until the following summer.

The one large area of his assigned territory that Dewey had not been to as yet, apart from along its Arctic coast, was the Yukon. On June 5, 1950, he drove alone from Edmonton via Grande Prairie, Dawson Creek, and the Alaska-Canada Highway[33] to Whitehorse. From there, he and Them Kjar (director of the Game and Publicity Department of the Yukon Territory) and Assistant Director Gordon Cameron, embarked on an ambitious journey covering most of southern Yukon, from Whitehorse to Dawson City and the Klondike.[34] They travelled by car and motorboat, by canoe and by plane, and they employed saddle and pack horses when necessary.

There is a sense that this was more of a sightseeing excursion than a serious scientific study, although Dewey kept concise records of all ornithological sightings, not just waterfowl, and probably collected specimens, as well. The three visited the main points of interest to historians of the Klondike Gold Rush of 1898–99, and they took a trip by Jeep over a wilderness trail

Dewey with a fine catch of lake trout after completing his day's work on waterfowl observations. Kluane Lake, Yukon, summer 1950.

to the Yukon–Alaska border at Glacier Creek. Dewey enjoyed the southern Yukon and said so: "On the whole, this was a very agreeable season in the Yukon. I became deeply impressed with this charming and spectacular region in which many exciting activities had taken place."[35] Unfortunately, he failed to explain or describe what the "exciting activities" were. In September 1954 his scientific paper on the Yukon journey's results was published as *Waterfowl and Other Ornithological Investigations in Yukon Territory, Canada*.[36]

The Yukon experience was completed by the middle of August and the road home was a long one. Dewey arranged for Carrie to fly to Whitehorse and drive back to Edmonton with him. He had scheduled a business meeting with the U.S. game officials in Fairbanks, Alaska, which made a brief but interesting side trip for them both. In his memoirs he managed to dispense with the ten-day drive from Fairbanks to Edmonton in five lines: "This was a uniquely rewarding trip with considerable outstanding scenery and a good gravel road; since there was relatively little traffic, the dust problem was a minor one. Only one feature marred the entire trip — we ran into a fairly heavy snowstorm between 'The Summit' and points to the southeast as far as Grande Prairie."[37]

The spring of 1951 saw Dewey working closer to home, although often away for days at a time, as he studied waterfowl transects over a wide area around Edmonton. He followed that with a long period of research (forty days), also on waterfowl, in the Eastern Irrigation District of southern Alberta. For some of that time he based himself at Brooks, presumably in a hotel. For the rest, he put up a tent — always his preferred form of accommodation while in the field. He explained, "Camping out at various lakes was much more efficient for on-the-spot information for 10 to 14 hours a day." Among those bodies of water were Cowoki Reservoir, and Newell, Rolling Hills, Louisiana, and Barkhausen lakes.

That summer, Dewey had to go back to the Northwest Territories for additional waterfowl investigations and to further reconnoitre proposed bird sanctuaries along the Arctic coast east and west of the Mackenzie River delta. On July 17 he left home to drive due north to Hay River, on the south side of Great Slave Lake. He then roamed the southern half of the lake by motorboat with Warden Harry Camsell. Their studies took them east as far as Fort Resolution on the Slave River delta, west to Mills Lake (part of the Mackenzie River), and a substantial distance down the Mackenzie to Wrigley Harbour. Much of that, of course, was reasonably familiar territory for Dewey, having delivered the motorboat *Caribou* the full length of the river two years before with Frank McCall. On August 6, Dewey then left Harry Camsell at Hay River and took a commercial flight to Aklavik.

For a week he explored the Mackenzie delta by boat with another government official, Malcolm McNab. The fan-shaped delta is about fifty miles across and is a similar distance from the open sea to its beginning. In that vast area are large and small islands, many covered with trees, channels running north and south and east and west, and countless ponds. It is a complicated natural maze and, without McNab to drive the boat, or someone equally knowledgeable about the area, Dewey would have been lost regularly.

With the surface study behind him, Dewey took to the air again in another Beaver. After flying multiple surveys over the delta to complete that portion of his assignment, he flew to Stanton, site of the near mishap with a Beaver in 1949. As with the Mackenzie delta survey, this was a continuation of the 1949 work done by air. Employing local Inuit and their boat, he stayed a few days and completed a detailed waterfowl survey of the Anderson River delta. Once his work was over, Dewey flew back up the Mackenzie River from Aklavik to Hay River, again in a Beaver. En route they were caught in a violent electrical storm near Fort Providence. The plane, Dewey said, "Was tossed about like a leaf." Chain lightning crackled close past the windows. "It was the most elemental display of sinister power and commotion that I had ever experienced in the air. In one phase of the storm descending air currents dragged the little plane down to within about 200 feet of the spruce forest,"[38] he wrote. That terrifyingly memorable flight proved to be Dewey's final journey into the Arctic regions for the government. At Hay River he collected his car and drove the 687 miles home.

Soon after Dewey's return home in late August, Roland joined the Canadian Army. He said, "I volunteered for service in the Korean War in the fall of 1951 and was posted to the 3rd Battalion, Princess Patricia's Canadian Light Infantry (PPCLI) in Camp Ipperwash, Ontario."

It is unlikely that Dewey and Carrie were happy with this latest development, but there was nothing they could do about it. They had learned long before that their free-spirited son would live life his way.

Throughout the ensuing winter Dewey wrote reports and longed for spring when he could get out to watch his beloved birds again. When he did so, knowing his official working life was coming to an end, he was happy to do more work on waterfowl transects and to study the habitats of the Wilson snipe.

17

An Attempt at Retirement

The spring of 1952 brought news from Roly that would worry any parent, despite the fact that they knew why he had enlisted in the army: in March he was chosen to join "a 75-man reinforcement draft bound for [service with] the 1st Battalion PPCLI in Korea."[1]

Roly's long journey to the distant war took him from his base at Camp Ipperwash by troop train to Toronto, then across the country to Vancouver and south to Seattle. As the train was scheduled to make a stop in Calgary en route, Dewey, Carrie, and Mary Lou drove down from Edmonton to spend a few emotional minutes with their son and brother at the station. In Seattle he and the small Canadian force joined five thousand American soldiers on a U.S. troopship bound for Japan. Some of the Americans were detailed for occupation duties in Japan, others for the war in Korea. Roly recalled that voyage with distaste: "We lived in the lower decks of the ship which were crammed with bunks, four high in row after row of narrow passageways. On the fifth day of our three-week voyage we hit a violent storm and eventually everyone succumbed to seasickness. Water in the 'heads' sloshed back and forth like frothy green slime."[2]

Over the next few months, Roly, an NCO or non-commissioned officer, and his fellow Canadian soldiers went through battle indoctrination in Japan before being sent to Korea in a semi-reserve position. In August they moved into the fighting lines.

ARCTIC NATURALIST

The year 1952 was a busy one for the Soper family. Roly was at war in Korea, and Mary Lou married Michael Austdal, a serving officer in the RCAF, on June 14. Two weeks later Dewey Soper retired from government service. He calculated that during his years with the federal government services he had travelled approximately 350,000 miles. That exceptional distance had taken him almost from coast to coast across Canada and far north in the Arctic. In the course of his work and travels he had amassed an impressive collection of wildlife and other natural history specimens for museums, in addition to his written material:

> I was surprised to realize that since 1908 I had filled 21 volumes of field notes; 23 volumes of special 'day record' bird notebooks; and 21 yearly day journals. In addition there were eight major volumes of unpublished manuscripts; six volumes of specimen catalogues; and 23 manuscript reports on wildlife, the majority of which are illustrated with photographs and maps. Several thousand of the latter (chiefly on 4 x 5-in. Panchromatic film) were secured during the years on duty. As of November 1967 the number of personal publications had reached the total of 126 and the number of collected mammals and birds amounted to 9,560.[3]

Never one to remain idle for long, Dewey took a two-week rest, and then went back to work. Recalling his old building skills, he spent the summer months on house-building projects for friends. For him, used to spending long hours most days in the outdoors, it was, perhaps, the best possible way to ease into retirement. In the fall he took a month off from construction work so he and Carolyn could take a vacation in Mexico. Rather than travelling by commercial transport, though, they drove to Mexico City in their own car. The nine-thousand-mile round-trip journey took them through a total of ten U.S. states and three Canadian provinces.

Dewey spent part of the winter in Edmonton finishing interior woodwork on the houses he had helped build. He was also in negotiations with the University of Alberta regarding his private collection of mammal specimens. Dewey wrote,

> For several years approaches had been made by the Department of Zoology ... to acquire this collection, as it had a very poor representation of mammals of any kind. The matter was broached several times by my former professor in Zoology, Dr. William Rowan, who was then still on the staff. On many occasions members of the staff and advanced students came to the house to examine certain specimens to clarify questions.[4]

At the same time he was drafting plans to build a new home for himself and Carrie. In March 1953 he purchased a three-acre plot of land six miles east of the Edmonton city limits. That month, to Dewey and Carrie's immense relief, Roly completed his one-year tour of duty in Korea without injury and was shipped home. He noted that the eastbound voyage across the Pacific was smooth sailing compared to the outbound crossing.

While Roly was on the ocean his father spent almost three weeks working alone with axe and saw to clear a forest of aspen, balsam, and birch trees on the new property. With the land cleared, Dewey called in a bulldozer to scrape a long driveway and parking area, and a mechanical digger to excavate the basement. He then had the foundations cemented in. Once the concrete was set, Dewey began the serious work of building his new house.

Roly had a sixty-day leave due when he reached Canada, so he stopped off in Edmonton to stay with his parents for a week. Both Dewey and Carrie, of course, were delighted to have their only son back safely. There are powerful overtones of relief at Roly's survival in the war and a fierce pride evident in Dewey's subsequent fatherly actions. "He took me to meet his friends and he would introduce me with his arm around my shoulders," Roly said. But Roly, the restless warrior, could not stay. After just one week he headed south alone, hitchhiking to Mexico. Although he couldn't bring himself to stay longer with his parents, Roly marks that brief visit as the turning point in his relationship with Dewey: "After that, my father and I became very close friends." On his return from Mexico, with free time still available, he helped his father for a while on the new property. Roly still had about a year to serve in the army to complete the three years of his service, so, once his leave expired, he returned to base and resumed his duties. During that final year he qualified for his wings as a parachutist and, he said, "For a time I considered making the army my career, particularly since I was encouraged to seek commissioned rank." The possibility of a career in civilian business persuaded him against the idea of a military future. Most important, he and his father were close at last.

The forthcoming move helped Dewey make his decision about the sale of his prize collection of mammal specimens. Considering the weight of the cabinets for shipping and the amount of space they took up in the house, he decided to part with the 906 specimens, most of which, he noted, included the skulls. The fact that he would continue to have access to all of them at any time helped in his decision.

Having sold their house in the city, Dewey and Carrie came up with a novel temporary living arrangement that rather echoed his camping days. They arranged furniture and rugs in the garage of their new but unfinished house and lived quite comfortably in its confines for a while. Once the electrical wiring, plumbing, and septic tank installations had been completed they moved into the main house, now named "Hyla,"[5] even though the interior was still far from finished.

Dewey spent the winter completing and painting the interior, plus finishing the basement to add a den, workshop, laundry area, and a cold room. He and Carrie followed that indoor work by spending most of the spring and summer outdoors in the garden, landscaping the rest of the property, including putting up fences and laying pathways. By late summer 1954 they were tired and ready for a holiday. Dewey obviously enjoyed driving because they embarked on another long road trip, this time to Florida by way of Texas and Louisiana. At Mobile Bay, Louisiana, he saw and heard his first mockingbird (*Mimus polyglottus*), referring to its "joyous songs" in his notes. That was the only bird sighting he mentioned on the long journey.

At that time Mary Lou and Michael lived in Ottawa, Michael being based at RCAF Uplands.[6] On the return from Florida, Dewey and Carrie detoured via Ottawa to spend a couple of weeks with their daughter. While there, Dewey took the opportunity to visit his old friends from the government department he had once worked for and the National Museum, especially his now-retired former bosses, Dr. R.M. Anderson and Hoyes Lloyd.[7]

Dewey had been sketching with pen and ink since he was a teenager. In retirement he explored his undeniable artistic talents further by experimenting with watercolour paintings. Mostly landscapes, waterfowl (of course), and big game animals, he framed the paintings and gave them to friends and family members as gifts. Over the winter of 1954–55 he produced a series of watercolour paintings and gave most of those away, too.

The snow became a problem for him that winter, probably for the first time in his life. He wrote, "No small amount of time was also given to snow shovelling, but most of the time a small walking tractor with snow-blade could handle the driveway and parking area." Dewey was nearly sixty-two and winter in the country was not as easy to handle as it had been in his younger days. In a few years he and Carrie would have to think of moving again.

Mary Lou added spice to Dewey and Carrie's retirement when Michael Alexander Austdal, their first grandchild, was born on April 6, 1955. To add to that, Roly had left the army and started his own advertising and printing company, Soper Publications. He married Betty Neil on July 6, 1955, and the newlyweds settled in Calgary, her home city. Dewey was pleased they chose to live in Calgary because it was only a four-hour drive between the two Soper houses, so they could visit each other quite easily.

Dewey went back to the building business that summer, helping others with construction projects to keep himself busy and to increase his income. Mary Lou arrived at "Hyla" with baby Michael in mid-August and stayed until early November; it was a happy time for both the grandparents. The downside to that visit was that it ended too soon for Dewey and Carrie. There was an obvious void in the lives of the doting grandparents when the Austdals left, but Dewey filled that by keeping busy with a variety of projects. He spent time reorganizing his extensive reference library, and catalogued each book and pamphlet. He wrote wildlife articles for publication and began work on his autobiography.[8] He probably also did some local trapping and collecting because he mentioned preserving "a number of small mammals and birds." He also found time to paint, producing several more watercolours. He was definitely happy in his work and found the general tidying up of what he called his "loose ends" to be beneficial and satisfying. The winter was hard, though; heavy snowfalls and extreme cold made keeping clear the long driveway, parking area, and footpaths an onerous task. By the time spring arrived and the last of the snow melted, he knew they would have to move back into the city before the next winter set in.

To that end, Dewey purchased a building lot on 81st Street in Edmonton and put "Hyla" up for sale. Construction on the new house started in the third week of August. Once the excavating and concrete work for the basement walls had been completed, Dewey worked with a team of four carpenters, and the house went up quickly. He and Carrie were able to move in on November 30, even though, as with "Hyla" in the early days, the interior was far from ready. To Dewey that was a winter project that he could accomplish by himself, and he did so. He admitted that the living situation was far from ideal, but he and Carrie were no strangers to discomfort. Together they soldiered through and completed the interior by the end of April. While they were working hard in Edmonton, Mary Lou gave birth to a daughter, Brenda Lee, in Ottawa, on March 16, 1957.

When the snow cleared and the ground thawed out the supposedly retired Sopers continued their work on the new property by landscaping the garden, erecting fences, and building a garage. They spent the summer painting the house, and the garage, and the fences. July brought more exciting news for Dewey from Ottawa, but this time not from his family. The Honourable Douglas S. Harkness, then Conservative Minister of the Department of Northern Affairs and Natural Resources, wrote,

> It was my privilege recently to recommend to the Governor-in-Council that a newly established bird sanctuary, designed to protect the important blue goose breeding ground which you discovered between Bowman Bay and Koukdjuak River, on Baffin Island, be called the Dewey Soper Bird Sanctuary. I am pleased to inform you that this recommendation has been approved by the Governor-in-Council in the form of an amendment to the Migratory Bird Sanctuary Regulations. The Order-in-Council is P.C. 1957-862.

> Your efforts between 1922 [sic][9] and 1929 uncovered a great deal of valuable information on the physiography and fauna of Baffin Island. Major contributions to science resulted directly from your work. I feel, therefore, that the choice of name for this northerly bird sanctuary was appropriate and am delighted that the Government of Canada was able to give some lasting recognition to your work. To this tribute I should like to add my personal congratulations.[10]

The *Ottawa Citizen* picked up the story with a couple of complimentary paragraphs on August 27. The editorial refers to Dewey, justifiably, as "one of Canada's most distinguished biologists." Discussing his search for the breeding grounds of the blue goose, it also notes that "His report on that quest is a model of its kind, combining scientific precision with a graceful style and some fine descriptive passages."[11]

Although officially retired and sixty-four years old, as another winter began Dewey was getting ready to go back to work on a full-time basis — he just wasn't completely aware of the fact:

> In November of 1957 I commenced a project that I had dreamed about for the past 12 to 15 years; this was a book on "The Mammals of Alberta." My duties had been so strenuous in the Canadian Wildlife Service that it was out of the question to engage in such a major undertaking until after retirement. By this time I had accumulated an extensive mass of data on the mammals of the province dating back to 1912.[12]

As with all his projects, indoors or out, Dewey threw himself wholeheartedly into the preparation of the book. For eight hours a day, week after week, and month after month, he pored over his own notebooks, separating anything to do with Alberta mammals from the other information. He compiled an extensive bibliography of literature by other mammalogists that had any bearing on his planned book. To Dewey one of the most important results of his winter research was the discovery that there were still many areas of Alberta that had not been adequately covered by the science of mammalogy, especially in regard to small mammals. That knowledge galvanized him into action. He would go back into the field and rectify the omissions himself.

18

Researching the Mammals of Alberta

Dewey's reasons for returning to fieldwork in 1958 were twofold. In order for his book on the mammals of Alberta to be the best and most accurate publication possible, he needed to fill in the many gaps in current knowledge. And to accomplish that work, which would require extensive travel across the province for many weeks, he needed a sponsor of some kind.

Dewey knew exactly who to approach first. He contacted his longtime associates at the National Museum of Canada, and they stepped in to help. The museum's directors agreed to pay Dewey enough to at least cover expenses for the duration of his summer's investigations. In return, that institution would benefit enormously by receiving all the scientific specimens taken for the project, "and in due course provide me with all the subspecific determinations. This would do much to pin down geographical ranges."[1]

One can imagine the pleasure Dewey had in preparing the necessary camping equipment and scientific materials for his return to serious fieldwork. Starting on May 12, 1958, he spent just over four months roaming eighteen Albertan locations, "from Fort Assiniboine and Nestow to the Drumheller country and along the Forestry Road in the foothills from McLeod River to James and Little Red Deer Rivers and Racehorse Creek."

He noted that "the season's work resulted in the collection of 436 specimens that greatly extended our knowledge of regional occurrence, general

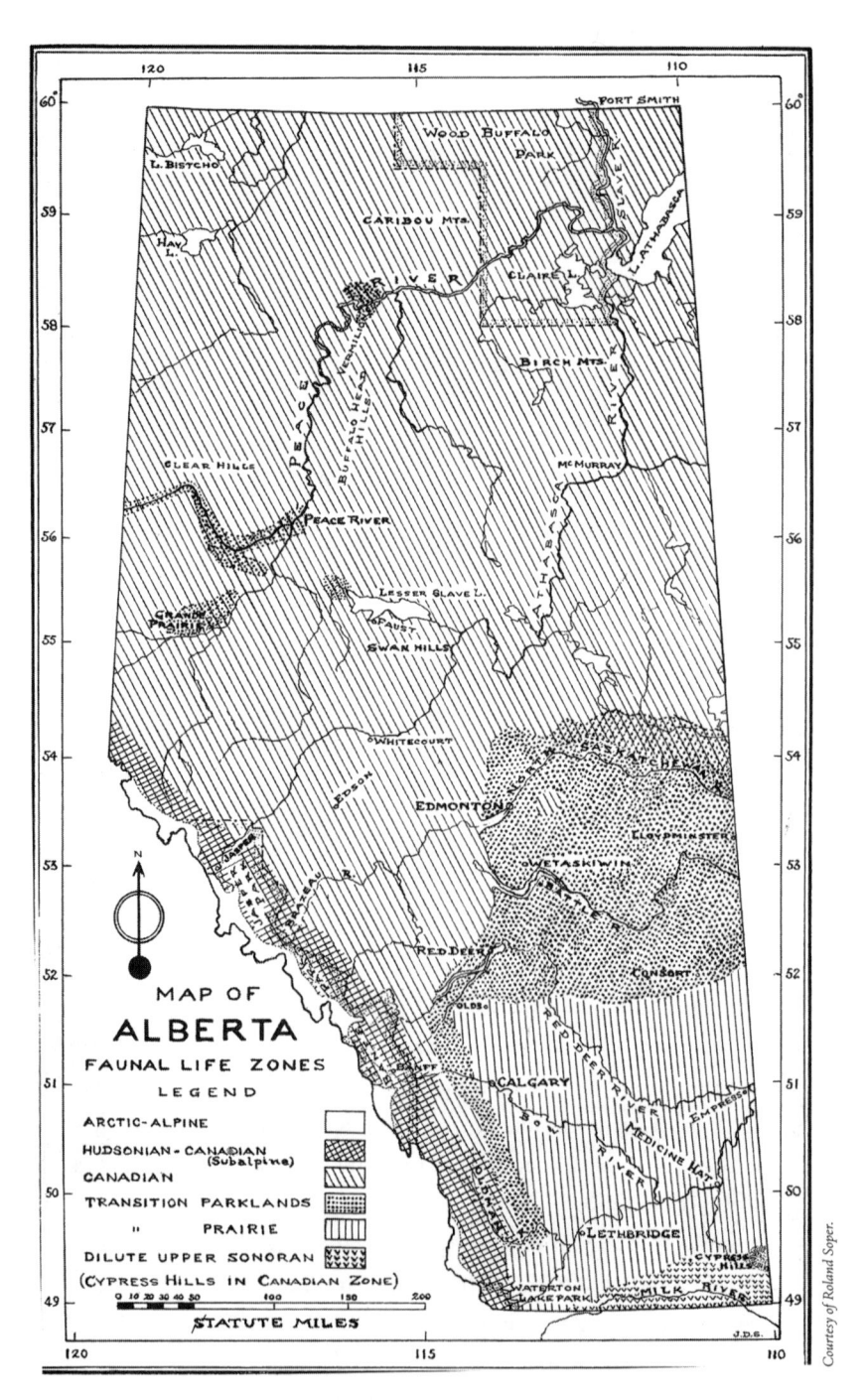

Map of Alberta's faunal life zones, by J. Dewey Soper.

distribution and subspecific identity. All information was new from previously unworked areas and for that reason was particularly valuable."[2]

The preserved specimens were duly shipped off to the National Museum, and Dewey spent another winter at home working on his book. There were still gaps in his knowledge, which was unacceptable to him as the value of his book as a scientific entity would be lessened by those deficiencies. Therefore, he decided to go back into the field the next summer to investigate other, as yet untouched, locations. Obviously pleased with his efforts of 1958, the National Museum again covered the expedition costs in return for the specimens he collected.

Pen-and-ink sketch of a raccoon in a tree, by J. Dewey Soper.

Courtesy of Roland Soper.

In the middle of May 1959, Dewey went out trapping and hunting small mammals for just over four months. That latest venture took him to fourteen more Alberta sites never before adequately studied by mammalogists: from Beaver River, Lac La Biche, and Fawcett Lake, to Travers Reservoir and Castle River, plus into the foothills to the Blackstone, Ram, and Oldman rivers, and along Dutch Creek. The fieldwork that summer resulted in 348 specimens being added to the National Museum's collection.

Despite his dedication to the task of researching Alberta's mammals, Dewey always had time in the autumn to go on a combined hunting, fishing, and collecting trip with Roly. They were special times for both men and they reflect the bond that had developed between them. Roly recalled a few wildlife sightings while they were camping together in the Castle River Valley of southwest Alberta:

> Near our camp were the remnants of an old logging operation: a clearing in the woods near a spring that created a small pond. In the evening moose and deer came to drink. While Dad did his fieldwork, I fished. At first I fly fished the main stream (the West Castle, I believe). One afternoon with my fly rod in a back swing I saw a bear a few hundred feet away on the same side of the shore crossing the river. I froze. Shortly behind the bear a large cub followed. The wind was in my favour and they never noticed me. A day or two later I explored a tributary that wound through heavy forest. Every once in a while the stream would open into a pool and I would gently drop a fly on the surface and frequently would take a cutthroat trout. I released most because Dad and I had had our fill of trout dinners. However, that day I kept two. We would be leaving the next morning and I wanted to take them home. Dad weighed them on his specimen scale: each weighed five pounds. It was on that same day of fishing deep in the wilderness that I saw my first (and only) bobcat in the wild. I had been standing statue-still watching my fly circling in a backwater when I glanced up and there it was, standing

on a log looking at me. I blinked and it was gone. Great memories, thanks to a great dad.

On another occasion, when Dewey had been asked to collect a series of pheasants — immatures, hens, and cocks — by the Department of Zoology, he and Roly and another friend, Tom Beck, went out together. Roly remembered the occasion this way:

> We drove east toward Brooks in an area that had always been productive. We parked the car and under the morning sun we walked in a skirmish line across a stubble field, our guns at the ready and three dogs (two of mine, one of Tom's) excitedly working back and forth in front of us.
> Although we hunted birds together many times, Dad never did get the hang of hunting behind a bird dog. To him, the Great Outdoors was more than a pheasant crouching in the stubble. If a flock of Canada Geese flew over he saw them, no doubt counted them, and if a vesper sparrow flitted by it did not escape the scrutiny of a man who had observed nature's creatures for a lifetime. His observations would be entered in his field notes. That morning, our first venture into pheasant territory, produced results very quickly. Thor, the son of a father-son dog combo, suddenly froze in a classic bird-dog point a few yards in front of Dad. Dad didn't notice, but it didn't matter. When he walked by Thor, a hen pheasant flushed skyward in a flurry of feathers. Dad calmly raised his double-barrelled .410, fired one shot, and the hen dropped. He picked up the bird and put it in his game bag.... Despite failing eyesight at that period of his life, he was an excellent shot. He seldom missed.

At this stage, as a joke, Roly had not told Tom that Dewey had a special permit that allowed him, as a scientist, to take whatever game he wished. Not surprisingly, Tom became upset because Dewey was shooting hen pheasants and that was illegal. Roly picks up the story again:

> I realized at that point that Tom probably had visions of court cases and jail time, so I decided to fess up. That afternoon, after Tom and I had our three-pheasant bag limit and Dad had a fine collection of immature birds, adult hens, and cock pheasants for the university, we headed for home. Along Highway 1 we came to a hunting check-stop manned by the RCMP and Alberta Fish and Wildlife officers. Tom and I looked at each other and without saying a word, mutually agreed to let the scene unfold. We stopped the car and, upon instructions of a wildlife officer, opened the trunk. At the same instant a wildlife department official who knew Dad came over to the car to have a visit. The officer at the back of the car couldn't believe what he saw. There, in the car trunk, neatly placed in rows, were hen pheasants of varying ages, not hidden, but displayed like trophies. He thought, no doubt, that he had hit the jackpot of bird-hunter prosecution. When the officer finally broke into the conversation, the wildlife official said to him, "I would like you to meet Dewey Soper. Dewey, do you have your permit with you?" Tom and I laughed all the way back to Calgary.[3]

Toward the end of the second winter of working on his manuscript, in late February, Dewey received news of a new honour. Dr. Walter Johns, president of the University of Alberta, phoned to ask if Dewey would accept an honorary Doctor of Laws degree. Dewey was surprised and deeply grateful. A few days later the official letter arrived:

> Dear Mr. Soper: I have great pleasure in conveying to you the invitation of the Senate of the University of Alberta to accept the degree of Doctor of Laws, *honoris causa*, at the

Researching the Mammals of Alberta

Spring Convocation schedule for Wednesday afternoon, May 18, 1960.[4]

Under normal circumstances Dewey would have taken off for the wilds on a collecting expedition by that date. In 1960 nothing could get him away from Edmonton until after the university convocation.

The Department of Zoology at the University of Alberta added to Dewey's pleasure by inviting him to take a staff position with the somewhat clumsy title of Honorary Associate Research Zoologist. This was a win-win situation for both Dewey and the Department of Zoology. At this stage in his manuscript Dewey could see that the information in his research files on small mammals in the Rocky Mountain areas was still lacking, particularly from the widely separated Jasper and Waterton Lakes national parks. He needed financial assistance for further fieldwork and the department wanted to build on its

Recipients of Honorary Doctor of Laws degrees at the University of Alberta, May 18, 1960. (Left to right) Dr. E. Sonet, Dr. J.D. Soper, Dr. S.W. Field. Photographer unknown.

collection of birds and mammals. To this end, the department gave Dewey a grant to cover his expenses. Again he planned a summer in the field.

May 18, 1960, was a proud day for Dewey and his family as he attended Spring Convocation at the university and accepted his honorary degree. The newly appointed Dr. Soper then returned to organizing his equipment and schedule for the summer's research in the field. He was late getting away, at least three weeks later, in fact, than he had anticipated. This inevitably had an impact on the later stages of the work, due to weather conditions.

Dewey drove the 194 miles to Jasper National Park on June 9 and made camp near the perhaps appropriately named village of Snaring, beside the Athabasca River. For the next four weeks he trapped and collected from the Snaring camp, as well as from subsequent camps at Derr Creek, Ranger Creek, Sunwapta River, and the mouth of Rocky River. He had planned to spend time collecting in the higher altitudes close to the upper limit of the treeline. His late start from Edmonton and the amount of snow higher up convinced him that "it would be better to defer the high altitude enquiries until another time." That meant the following summer.

Drawing of a Richardson's weasel. The original was a watercolour painted for use in *The Mammals of Alberta*, by J. Dewey Soper.

Having made that sensible decision (he was then sixty-seven years old and working in the outdoors alone), he moved south to Waterton Lakes National Park,[5] tucked into the southwestern corner of Alberta bordering British Columbia and Montana. He drove the 474 miles via Banff and Calgary and set up his first camp near Cameron Lake on July 18. He established later camps at Upper Bauerman Brook, Twin and Lost lakes, and Belly River, close to the international boundary. He left again on August 2 to drive back to Edmonton.

The Waterton Lakes study had been extremely valuable for him. He had his usual thick book of notes and an impressive eighty specimens for the university collection. After less than two weeks at home, he went to the Jasper area for another two weeks. This time he located his camps at "Geraldine Lookout; Whirlpool River near Moab Lake; Whirlpool River at the Sixth Meridian; and at Cottonwood Creek north of Jasper." The two mini expeditions into Jasper National Park netted 236 specimens to add to the eighty from Waterton Lakes, plus "a large number of bird records based chiefly on binocular observations."

Dewey's total driving for the summer expeditions amounted to well in excess of 1,250 miles. That was a mere outing for him. A few days after his return from the second Jasper trip he and Carrie drove across the country to southern Ontario to visit Mary Lou and her family, now living in Centralia — an additional round-trip distance of about 4,375 miles.

They returned to their Edmonton home on October 17 with Dewey suffering from influenza. That malady kept him out of action for over a week when he had expected to be out collecting prior to winter. He finally felt well enough to head out on October 27 for a few days. Working in a radius of forty miles from home, he managed to secure forty-one specimens from a variety of locations. That brought his total take for the summer and fall of 1960 up to 357 mammals and birds for the university's Museum of Zoology and, therefore, excellent additional resources for zoology students.

For the rest of November and throughout December he worked on his increasingly thick manuscript, revising, rewriting, and adding data. In his unpublished autobiography[6] he wrote, "The manuscript was finally completed in all details a few days before Christmas [1960]; naturally a profound relief! Three years had passed since the manuscript was begun."

He added that he immediately sent it off to the printers in Edmonton. It is most likely that Dewey had his dates mixed up because he continued his collecting research in the summers, and he worked on the manuscript for the next couple of winters. The book was not published until 1964. In it, while discussing the number of locations he worked while studying Alberta's mammals, he wrote that the studies were made from 1958 to 1963. Those dates fall more in line with the book's eventual publication date, and with later comments in his unpublished autobiography about the months spent working on the manuscript. Therefore, it is probable that he spent part of the winter of 1960–61 completing the sections on the species collected and studied the previous summer and making notes on the gaps still evident in the manuscript.

In February 1961 Dewey took a break from his manuscript while he and Carrie drove to Arizona to visit his youngest brother, Roy, who was seriously ill in hospital. Although the primary reason for the visit was to spend time with Roy, they took scenic routes in each direction to see as many famous natural sites as possible. Dewey logged the drive as covering 5,138 miles from start to finish. Roy passed away a few months later.

There is an indication of new vigour in Dewey's life at this rather late stage (he was now sixty-eight years old). Immediately upon his return from Arizona, he pulled his camping and specimen-collecting equipment out of storage, purchased a couple of hundred rounds of .410 shotgun shells (loaded with No. 12 shot), and planned his current summer of fieldwork, almost certainly still researching for his book on Alberta's mammals. After consultation with other staff members at the Department of Zoology, he had elected to return to the general vicinities of Jasper and Waterton Lakes national parks for the season. He noted that his principal colleagues in the department at that time were Dr. Victor Lewin, Dr. William Fuller, and Mr. Robert Lister. They occasionally joined him on field trips, but for the most part, away from the university, he worked alone.

For the first three weeks in May he worked close to Edmonton, enabling him to be out all day and home with Carrie in the evenings. When he set off alone to the west on May 30 he was a man on a mission. He made camp at Little Smoky River, over one hundred miles (as the crow flies) northeast of the entrance to Jasper National Park.[7] His drive that day would have been about 180 miles. He found a convenient spot in late afternoon, made camp, then walked an unspecified distance (probably a few miles) to set seventy snap-traps[8] before darkness fell.

Dewey held very strong opinions on the best bait to use in a snap-trap: "The most efficient is a handy combination bait made by heating together a mixture of about equal parts of Roman, or fine oatmeal, peanut butter, beef suet (or bacon fat) and finely ground raisins. When cool, the result is a paste of soft, putty-like consistency that keeps indefinitely." He added that, "A little oil of anise may be applied for rodents, and oil of valerian for shrews." His lesson continues with the advice that "apples, dry rolled oats, crisp bacon, smoked fish and raw meat" work well for the "larger rodents and carnivores."[9]

As he had in his youth, Dewey worked long hours on his traplines. He worked the Little Smoky River sets until June 3 and then moved his camp about thirty miles southeast to Iosegun Lake. He trapped in the new locality for a further three days. His efforts at those first two locations secured him thirty-nine specimens. Although he didn't say so, he probably went home to Edmonton for a few days en route to Jasper because his report stated that his next camp was at Sunwapta Pass in Jasper National Park on June 14. He maintained that site until June 21, when he moved to Shale Banks on the Snake Indian River for close to a week. His final work site in the Jasper region was at the timberline on Signal Mountain. There he did not need to camp, as Chief Warden Mickey Ryan had offered him the use of a log cabin, formerly for use by fire-watchers. He stayed there until July 6. The three weeks in Jasper National Park enabled him to collect 106 scientific specimens, mammals and birds, and added again to his wildlife data. He went home from Jasper and spent three weeks on paperwork. Waterton Lakes was next on his exhausting schedule.

He stopped off for one night en route to visit Roly and Betty in Calgary and completed his outbound road trip the following day. First camp was at Blakiston Brook and used for close to a week. He followed that with another six days at Belly River near Indian Creek, southeast of the Blakiston Brook site. That was his last collecting trip away from home for 1961, although he went out on a few day trips in August. As a result of the two weeks at Waterton Lakes National Park that summer, he preserved eighty-eight specimens of birds and mammals.

After taking care of his vegetable garden, Dewey went out collecting again in late October. By the end of the season he had taken 360 specimens of mammals and birds, which he said "[made] a major addition to the collections of the U of A Department of Zoology. This was particularly to the point, as I was the only one doing any serious and extended collecting for the Museum."[10]

Over the winter the National Parks Branch in Ottawa asked him to write a brochure: "The Mammals of Canada's National Parks in the Rocky Mountains." It took him over a month, but the end result was a 22,000-word manuscript that earned him a fee of $1,100. That work seemed to inspire Dewey to continue writing. He spent the rest of the winter collating his field notes, and produced a 66,000-word manuscript he titled, "Unpublished Records of Alberta Birds for the Years 1922 to 1961."[11] He sent copies to the University of Alberta's Department of Zoology and to the Edmonton Bird Club.

Dewey's spring and summer collecting season started with a few days at Cooking Lake, a short drive southeast of Edmonton. He, who usually worked alone, then went on a rare field study with other naturalists — all from the University of Alberta's Department of Zoology. They were Dr. Vic Lewin, Bob Walker, and John Ryder. Their appointed study site was at the Milk River Valley of southeast Alberta, close to the Montana border. Each of the scientists had particular assignments, although they worked in close proximity to one another. Dewey's role was to study and collect small mammals. He also added "a fair number of birds" to the collection.

Being in semi-arid terrain covered in mixed grasses, they had to be constantly aware of what was at their feet. Dewey and Vic Lewin both had close calls with prairie rattlesnakes (*Crotalus viridis*) in the Milk River area. Dewey noted that "a fair number inhabited the valley and tributary coulees." He added with studied understatement, "Such experiences cannot be called pleasant!"[12]

At Milk River they took two examples of the painted turtle (*Chrysemys picta*) and established the first scientific record of the species in Alberta.[13] The joint mini expedition was a resounding success, as Dewey wrote: "In total, the party collected several hundred specimens from this previously unworked district, which thus greatly enriched the collections of the Museum of Zoology. My personal 'take' was 93 specimens of mammals and birds. The others collected birds, reptiles, amphibians, fish and a number of plants." There was no further mention of rattlesnakes, but it is unlikely that four professional zoologists, working more or less together in one area, would pass up the opportunity of acquiring at least one specimen between them.

Dewey completed his work at the Milk River site in mid-June and drove to Calgary to spend a day or two with Roly, Betty, and the grandchildren — Philip, Trent, and Elizabeth. While there he loaded up with fresh food supplies before taking another look at Waterton Lakes National Park. The first week there was a typical week for Dewey. Camped close to Waterton River on the northern fringe of the park, he collected birds and mammals without any problems. Then he moved camp to Blakiston Brook, to the north of Ruby Ridge, and the unexpected happened: "I had planned on working there until later in the month, but one day black bears ripped up my silk tent so seriously that I could no longer carry on without extensive repairs. As this was locally impractical, I returned to Edmonton."[14]

His version of this to Roly and Trent was a little less formal. He told them he was camping alone at Waterton Lakes National Park when a black bear, or bears, ripped the back of his tent open. Dewey grabbed his shotgun and, he said, "[I] peppered [the bear's] backside with shot."[15] The bear, or bears, did not return.

For the next few weeks Dewey and Carrie stayed with Mary Lou and family at the Austdal's unfinished summer cottage on Lake Winnipeg. Dewey, of course, could not just relax and enjoy the lake view. He set to work with carpentry tools and built kitchen countertops as well as cabinets, and completed other interior work.

That summer was also the final season of roaming Alberta to document its mammals. At home he spruced up his flower garden and harvested some fruit before returning to work. On August 9 he drove to Jasper National Park again. This time he camped just inside the park's eastern boundary, beside the confluence of Fiddle River and the Athabasca River, for the first of his four weeks in the field. He did not specify which creatures he studied and or collected, but he did say he worked long hours each day in pursuit of wildlife and was happy with the results. When he moved, he travelled deeper into the park, beyond the Jasper town site to where the Astoria River flows into the Athabasca. There he worked for another week or more of long hours with similar results. His final stop was at Celestine Lake, between the Athabasca

River and the Snake Indian River. For this period he was able to dispense with the tent, as a cabin had been left available for his use. At the end of his stay in the park he had, he said, "a wealth of field notes and a total of 130 mammal and bird specimens." They were all destined for the University of Alberta, and the results of his studies would be included in *The Mammals of Alberta*.

Dewey went straight home from Jasper, but only stayed a few days. He and Carrie then set off by car for Seattle to visit the World's Fair, taking two weeks of leisurely driving to cover the 3,514 miles round trip.

He had already decided that he would not go camping that autumn. That didn't mean he stayed at home. For the last week of September and all of October he was out almost every day, collecting and studying at eight different locations, each one of which was close enough for him to return home to his own bed at night. Those locales were: Cooking Lake Highlands, Lindbrook, Tawatinaw, Calmar, Fort Assiniboine, Battle Lake, Breton, and Lindale. For those weeks alone he secured eighty-five specimens, including, he said, "a beautiful series of 22 ruffed and sharp-tailed grouse."

Dewey's mental and physical energy at the age of sixty-nine was phenomenal. As soon as he had preserved his latest specimens and deposited them at the university, he typed a catalogue to go with them. He followed that with a series of individual reports on the mammals and birds collected the previous summer at Jasper and at Waterton Lakes. Copies of those went to the university and to the National Parks Branch. Both would eventually find their way into print as small books: the eighty-page *The Mammals of Jasper National Park*, published in 1970, and the fifty-seven-page *The Mammals of Waterton Lakes National Park, Alberta*, published in 1973.

With the holiday season fast approaching, he and Carrie left Edmonton by train on December 18 for Christmas with the Austdals in Winnipeg, taking Roly and Betty's young daughter, Elizabeth, with them. Then back they went to Calgary in time to celebrate New Year's Eve with Roly and Betty and family, before taking another train home on January 1, 1963.

Whereas other men of his age might have taken an understandable long break, Dewey immediately went back to his manuscript on mammals and made the final additions and corrections. There was still more work to be done: "I also had to do a further number of line drawings for the book, together with five water-colour plates having to do with the varying hare, pocket and harvest mice, and Richardson and least weasels [as] no colour photographs were available for these species. This, along with much other office work, kept me very busy until the early days of spring."[16]

The Mammals of Alberta contains informative references to the description and habitats of hundreds of species and subspecies. It also contains sixty-six photographs, colour and black and white, plus seventy range maps and forty-one pen-and-ink drawings by Dewey Soper. In addition, he included a section on approximate latitude and longitude references for each of the place names mentioned in the text, a bibliography, and an index. Dewey Soper was nothing if not thorough. In addition to the excellent cataloguing of Alberta's mammals, he took the time and space to discuss the best traps to use and trapping methods,[17] plus the correct procedures for preparing and preserving specimens in the field and at home base.[18] He went further and added his advice on the firearms and ammunition required for successful collecting of species great and small.[19]

The book had taken a few years of long hours and extremely concentrated work, both in the field and at home. Sponsored by the Alberta Department of Industry and Development, today the four-hundred-page *The Mammals of Alberta* is considered a classic and a necessary resource for all students of zoology, especially those studying the title subject matter.

In his prologue to the book, Dewey proudly describes Alberta as a habitat for mammals:

> For its size and position, Alberta possesses an unusual diversity of mammal life.... The total number of known species and subspecies within the province amounts to 153, represented by 58 distinct genera. Species range in size from the tiny pygmy shrew (the smallest known quadruped at 2.8 grams), up to the massive wood bison, which weighs about 440,000 times as much, and ranks as the largest land mammal in North America. Between these extremes are scores of different species and races varying greatly in size, appearance, behaviour and general habitats. As to the daily lives of many of these, scarcely anything is known — an interesting challenge to the student of natural history.[20]

A few paragraphs later he acknowledges that the most recent years of concentrated study were preceded by the many volumes of field notes he had written, and the hundreds of specimens he had collected in the province since 1912. They had all contributed to the content of his latest book. In those five decades he had studied mammals and collected specimens in more than one hundred Alberta locations across the province. Sixty of those locations were explored between 1958 and 1963; the major years were spent researching material for *The Mammals of Alberta*.

That winter he also found time to add to his earlier reports on the Arctic expeditions of 1923 to 1931, some of which were, more than thirty years later, still in his own handwriting.

19

A Second Retirement

A man like Dewey Soper, with a passion for birds and mammals, as well as almost all other wild creatures, would have been a fascinating character for young people to be with. Philip Soper, Roly's eldest son, spoke of his grandfather with evident pride mixed with elements of humour. He recalled going on a combined camping and collecting trip with Dewey to the Sheep River area southwest of Calgary when he was ten years old. Philip's description of the amount of gear that his grandfather carried with him on these trips is the first indication that Dewey's wilderness camps were set up in a fashion vaguely reminiscent of the great white hunters in Africa and India during the early years of the twentieth century. Although there were no Native servants and no gun-bearers, Dewey camped in a certain enviable style. He had a large house-like tent, with standing headroom, complete with a small pot-bellied stove for cooking and heating. The wood-burning stove had its own smokestack, or chimney, which protruded through the tent's roof. Inside the tent Dewey set up a folding table and chairs, plus two sleeping cots complete with sleeping bags.[1]

Of their meals, Philip said, "Grandpa had a licence to shoot out of season, so we ate pretty well." "Pretty well" in this case meant, for example, stews of grouse and vegetables, or rabbit and vegetables. Dewey helped Philip set up his own small trapline before taking care of his own, more professional needs.

When he showed Philip how to bait them, the youngster was fascinated by the knowledge that wild creatures would enjoy peanut butter.[2] For a ten-year-old, running a trapline was an exciting experience. Philip obviously wanted to do well and please his grandfather, but it didn't quite work out that way.

One of Philip's traps held a kangaroo mouse[3] (family *Zapodidae*) by its toes only. The boy felt sorry for the struggling creature so he opened the trap and let it go. "I still remember it hopping down the trail to safety," he said. His other traps held small mammals, such as shrews, which he proudly took back to camp. When he told Dewey about setting the kangaroo mouse free, the old naturalist became quite angry at him for not keeping it. Philip remembered that he "felt badly about disappointing him."

Midway through the camping trip, on a Saturday afternoon, Roly and Betty arrived with Philip's younger brother and sister (Trent and Elizabeth) in their camper trailer. They stayed for a family get-together until Sunday evening when they returned to Calgary. Dewey and Philip went back to collecting the next morning. Philip said of those few days with his grandpa, "It was an absolutely wild adventure."

After dropping Philip off in Calgary, Dewey made one more trapping stop en route to home, this time at Medicine Lake where, he said, "an excellent collection of birds and mammals materialized, together with scads of valuable notes."

Brenda Lee, Mary Lou's daughter, remembered being bitterly disappointed that she was not allowed to go camping and collecting with her grandpa. Part of that emotion possibly stems from an element of jealousy, as her brother Michael had been allowed to travel alone by train from Winnipeg to Alberta when he was about nine in order to join Dewey in the wild.

Trent Soper, Philip's younger brother, loved going on long nature walks with his grandfather. "[Grandpa] had a great sense of humour," he said, a warm smile spreading across his face. "On one walk he hid from me behind a large tree. I thought I was alone and suddenly I heard this loud growling coming from the tree. I thought it was a black bear. Then Grandpa jumped out at me, still growling."

Trent's story echoed his father's tale of Carrie dressing up in a polar bear skin to frighten the infant Roly when they lived on Baffin Island. By today's careful standards, the actions of both Dewey and Carrie seem quite bizarre.

A Second Attempt at Retirement

Whereas Dewey, the hard-working and long-distance travelling naturalist in the 1930s, 40s, and 50s, rarely had time for social chats with his own son, Trent recalled many conversations with Dewey about politics, sport — particularly football — and, of course, wildlife. "Grandpa could talk about anything," he said. Philip concurred: "He was quite a talker."

Most of all Trent loved being in the basement of Dewey and Carrie's house in Edmonton. His enjoyment of that part of the house was shared by Brenda Lee. She said, "It smelled down there, but I loved being there."

"Down there" was a veritable museum of Dewey's world. It was part library, part den, part archive of wildlife; to some, perhaps, it was a horror museum in miniature. There, Dewey worked at his preservation and cataloguing of wild creatures, and young Trent (aged about nine or ten at the time) was fascinated by the skins stretched out on display boards and the tiny skulls standing on shelves. There were many shallow drawers in cabinets where Dewey kept the smaller specimens in his collection. Trent and Dewey worked on them together for hours, with the elderly naturalist explaining the finer points of his craft and the creatures to his attentive audience of one. Completely unfazed by the macabre skins and skeletons in the main room, Trent liked to sleep on a cot in Dewey's office right next door, where, he recalled, he wrapped himself up in a warm but scratchy HBC blanket, just as his grandfather had done on so many cold nights in provinces and territories across Canada.

It's not surprising, therefore, that Trent followed in his illustrious grandfather's footsteps. He eventually attended the University of Montana, where he took his degree in wildlife biology. He admitted to quickly becoming something of a "teacher's pet" because he was already extremely knowledgeable about the subject when he arrived for the first semester and soon commanded the attention of his tutors, one of whom — Professor Leslie Pengelly[4] — counted Dewey Soper among his friends.

By contrast, Philip studied computer science at the University of Alberta. For the five years he was there, away from his immediate family, he visited Dewey and Carrie often. Adding to Trent's comments about Dewey's love of talking, Philip said, "Grandpa was a storyteller, but mostly he just wanted to talk about the good old days in the Arctic."

Dewey's eldest grandson, Michael Austdal (Mary Lou's son), enjoyed the collecting field trips with his grandfather as much as Roly's boys. Long after Dewey passed away, Michael told his mother that it was those collecting trips that he remembered most about his grandfather. Echoing her sentiments about having Dewey as a "loving and caring father," Mary Lou said he was also a doting grandfather to all the grandchildren. Her daughter, Brenda Lee Swindells, agreed. She said Dewey was "a wonderful, warm Grandpa."

Dewey did not truly retire until late into his seventies. He'd stop working occasionally to go travelling with Carrie, or to visit his family in Calgary and Winnipeg. But all the while his health allowed he went on with collecting and studying wildlife. He wrote, "I continued my association with the U of A Department of Zoology. In this connection practically all activities were confined to field work and writing up the results. This involved many months of the year."

Ten days after his seventieth birthday, Dewey drove west again to Jasper National Park. The car was loaded with camping equipment and food, trapping and hunting supplies, and the necessary impedimenta for preserving wildlife specimens in the field. Camp number one was at Roche Miette Creek. There he set out his traplines, baited them, checked them, removed his catches, and preserved them, and generally kept himself physically busy for ten to twelve hours each day. He followed the same time-honoured procedures at The Pallisades and at Medicine Lake. Again, as with other recent collecting expeditions in the foothills of the Rockies, he left Jasper and spent the two weeks between June 21 and July 4 at two sites in Waterton Lakes National Park. Then he drove back to Jasper to see what creatures he could lure out of their natural habitats at the stunningly beautiful Maligne Lake, followed by the Bald Hills and Little Shovel Pass. He took a break from collecting at the end of August for a month of travelling by car with Carrie to visit family in Winnipeg and Calgary.

In 1967 the Sopers enjoyed a long drive through the Maritimes, with a stop for one day at Expo 67[5] on the way home. Dewey did not seem impressed. His only comment on the Montreal World's Fair was that "[it was] a most unusual and bizarre experience."

A few years later he would enjoy Disneyland, which he described as a "fantastic environment." A visit to Las Vegas on the same tour brought forth, "Las Vegas is a fantastic, glittering and malevolent receptacle of gambling casinos, booze and other vices enshrouded in beautiful buildings costing untold millions of dollars."[6] He did admit that he enjoyed the stage shows, however, his favourite being the *Folies Bergere*. He wasn't much more complimentary about Edmonton's Klondike Days: "[We] took in Klondike Days at the Exhibition Grounds with its numerous attractions and distractions. One would not want more than a few hours of the crowds, congestion and noise in any one year."[7]

Writing of his busy work schedule, even in retirement, Dewey shared his simple philosophy: "It's better to wear out than to rust out." He added, "Ever since my retirement, in 1952, I have found so much to accomplish that it has rarely been a question of not knowing how to pass the time, but rather to find enough time to succeed in doing what I want to do."[8]

In June 1968, while on a collecting trip to the Alberta locations of Saunders Lake, Medicine Creek, and Muriel Lake, Dewey found his seventy-five-year-old body starting to complain. He felt unwell and, as a result, he stopped fieldwork for the rest of the summer. The heat particularly had begun to affect him. By autumn, though, as the air cooled, he was ready for his annual hunting, fishing, and trapping excursion with Roly. He always looked forward to those few days together, as did Roly. Perhaps in recognition of Dewey's age, they did not take tents. Instead they camped in the comfort of Roly's camper trailer near Dutch Creek on the Oldman River, in the foothills of the mountains. It was, Dewey noted, "A delightful few days."

Retirement from public service had changed little in Dewey's life or work patterns. He spent the balance of that year working on manuscripts, apparently determined to get everything on paper for posterity regarding his hundreds of field trips taken over a span of six decades. Even that daunting task could not keep him from his annual holiday. In January he and Carrie sailed from Vancouver on the SS *Oriana* for a month-long South Pacific cruise. En route they visited a variety of ports which, with the exception of San Francisco, Dewey reported on with one-line observations: Honolulu ("Hawaii — charming in the extreme"), Fiji ("notably exotic and stimulating but too hot for comfort!"), New Zealand ("an especially captivating country with which we fell in love without qualification").

On the return journey, this time aboard the SS *Canberra*, they stopped in Tonga, where Dewey found the heat "depressing." He also did not enjoy the long days at sea out of sight of land. That meant no wildlife sightings. He complained, "Under such conditions a long ocean voyage can become tedious in the extreme!"

Finding it uncomfortable to work in the field during the summer heat, Dewey restricted his collecting to the Albertan spring and fall. Then his body complained again, and June 1971 was another let-down: "Owing to an onset of arthritis some weeks earlier, I failed to get out on wildlife observing and collecting trips for the Department of Zoology. The handicap was too much and quite impractical in the light of all circumstances."

After five months of treatment, and feeling much better, he managed some collecting, mostly of birds, then set off on his annual outdoor foray with Roly. In 1971 they went pheasant hunting with Roly's English pointers. Time was definitely taking its toll on the old naturalist: "By the end of October with my final collecting trip … I had taken a total of only 28 specimens." And that total, he pointed out with evident disappointment, included the hunting trip with Roly.

With snow falling and another winter gripping Edmonton, Dewey went back to his office work in the basement, answering correspondence, updating wildlife records, and tidying his library. He accepted that his serious writing, in the form of wildlife articles and books, was also over. A talented artist who had experimented with hand-tinting his black-and-white photographs for many years, he now began painting watercolours of wildlife and scenery from the eastern Arctic, based on his black-and-white photographs from nearly fifty years earlier. He started the project in December 1971 and had completed forty-seven small paintings (eight by eleven inches in size) by the end of February 1972. He had also produced five larger ones, twice the size, two of which he donated to the Arctic Institute of North America.

For the next two years his memoirs are filled with notes about occasional short collecting trips close to Edmonton, family details, and the annual travels with Carrie. A real highlight was a Government of Alberta banquet held at the McDonald Hotel on October 28, 1972. Dewey was one of a special group of Albertans honoured with achievement awards. He was thrilled to receive his certificate from then premier Peter Lougheed, and a commemorative gold lapel pin from the lieutenant governor, Dr. Grant McEwen.

A few weeks later, in a sign that he, perhaps, accepted that his life was winding down to its inevitable conclusion, he sold his complete library of

A Second Attempt at Retirement

Dewey Soper with Alberta premier Peter Lougheed at an awards banquet in Edmonton, October 28, 1972.

wildlife research books and pamphlets to the Department of Zoology at the University of Alberta for the lowly sum of four hundred dollars. Despite the fact that he would probably never have read any of them again or used them for research, he was sad to see them go: "Disposing of the above certainly left a large vacancy in my reference library; some had been close companions for over 50 years and I saw them go with a certain feeling of regret."[9]

February 1973 brought more health problems. Dewey, keeping it low-key, said, "Fatigue and general indisposition set in." He was wrong. By mid-month his heart had developed an irregular beat and his blood pressure was low. The combination of those two issues, plus his age, put him into hospital in an intensive care unit for a week, followed by two weeks recuperating in a private room. Throughout March and April he rested, making "a slow and steady recovery." Then his doctor advised him to stop driving.

For most of his adult life, Dewey had driven many thousands of miles each year on wildlife pursuits and on family pleasures; he always enjoyed driving. Losing his car would restrict his activities in an abrupt and possibly painful manner. Perhaps surprisingly, therefore, Dewey agreed to give up his licence without a fight. He gave the car, a Chevrolet, to Betty Soper. This effectively put paid to any further solo wildlife collecting and camping field trips. He wrote, with a sad acceptance of the facts, "It was hard to adjust to these circumstances after over 60 years of exciting work in the field — the penalty of growing old!"[10]

No longer able to go collecting by himself, he recorded that he had taken his last specimen, a yellow-rumped (or Myrtle) warbler (*Dendroica petechia*) at Ord Lake, Alberta, on September 26, 1972. That marked a total of 10,033 specimens of birds and mammals taken since his first, a swamp sparrow (*Melospiza Georgiana*), taken at the farm near Preston, Ontario, on April 26, 1915.[11]

In May he celebrated his eightieth birthday at a party organized by Carrie, who, Mary Lou said, "was a fabulous cook and loved to entertain." Carrie proved the worth of that statement by bringing a large number of relatives together to fill the house with fun for an evening, which Dewey thoroughly enjoyed. He received another birthday present, of sorts, when a cheque for $250 arrived from *The Beaver* as payment for publication of his article "The Conquest of Pangnirtung Pass."

That article was followed by two more pieces for *The Beaver*: "Kingnait Pass" was published in the Winter 1973 issue, and "Baffin Island — The Mysterious West Coast" appeared in the autumn of 1974.

While Dewey was taking life comparatively easy, writing occasionally and working in the garden when the weather permitted, Carrie, too, was beginning to feel her age. In March she fell ill and entered hospital for an operation (Mary Lou thought it was to have a pacemaker installed). Carrie was home in ten days, followed by weeks of recuperation before she was fully recovered. Those gentle weeks were probably good for them both. From Dewey's point of view, "Because of my old 'ticker' I could spend only limited hours per day [working in the garden], to be on the safe side. In between intervals of work I had many leisurely hours in a long chair on the patio reading, bird watching and perhaps a little snoozing, particularly in warm weather."

Writing the three Baffin Island articles for *The Beaver* magazine and seeing them in print reminded Dewey of an idea that had been germinating in his mind for some time. Over the winter of 1974–75 he wrote furiously on a new project, spending six or more hours per day documenting his experiences on Baffin Island between 1923 and 1931. The plan was to create a book he wanted to call *Arctic Dawn*. It took him six and a half months to produce 76,000 words and to sketch eighteen pictures for illustrations. This book, when eventually taken from its rough, original state to publication, became *Canadian Arctic Recollections*.

A highlight of that summer (1975) was a late-season visit to a friend's cottage on Skeleton Lake, near Boyle, about seventy miles north of Edmonton. There Dewey went out in a canoe a few times, prompting a not unexpected bout of nostalgia: "In earlier years I had been very fond of travelling by canoe and of late times I had often missed it. This was one of the nicest weekends of the season."[12]

After writing a couple of magazine articles about his early collecting and exploring days at the beginning of winter, he wrote, "Now and again I get mild spells of nostalgia for the camp life and the collection of specimens of Natural history."

He completed *Arctic Dawn* in 1975, but then suffered disappointment when it was rejected by two publishers. He put the manuscript to one side and continued with his gardening and his other writing projects. In the summer he donated his Arctic books, three Arctic photo albums, and a large painting of the CGS *Arctic* to the Boreal Institute of the University of Alberta. He also handed over all his wildlife field notebooks, journals, and specimen catalogues, plus his field equipment, to the Department of Zoology for the sum of $1,500. As an additional vote of thanks, the department honoured him with a special party at the Museum of Zoology on October 10. Many of the items he had donated were on display that night and he was happy to discuss them with old colleagues and newer department members.

The year 1978 sent Dewey what should have been a wakeup call to do less and less. His own paragraph on the subject is an eloquent statement about his age and his health:

Then in early May ... while working at my desk, I fell over unconscious with a moderate stroke on the right side, complicated by very low blood pressure. This called for a stay of about 10 days in hospital during which, fortunately, [the] effects of the stroke almost entirely passed away. I was still left with some light-headedness and unusual fatigue; use of a cane was recommended. This certainly made me feel like an old man![13]

It was now time for Dewey and Carrie to accept that they could no longer look after their own home. With that in mind, they prepared to move again, this time to a seniors' residence. Dewey was unable to help in the preparation of the house and garden for sale. Carrie and Mary Lou took care of that. Dewey actually spent more time in the hospital while his wife and daughter did the work. At the end of October they moved in. A somewhat disgruntled Dewey wrote, "We found it a very definite inconvenience to go from our roomy home on 81 Street to the much smaller space available in the one-bedroom apartment."

Dewey's grandson, Philip Soper, recalled a humorously positive side to the new arrangement, remembering that, even late in his life, Dewey was a ruggedly handsome man with a perpetual tan from months in the outdoors each year, topped by a shock of snow-white hair, and of course, those blue eyes. "He was an absolute chick magnet," Philip said with a laugh. He then explained that his grandfather painted many of his Arctic watercolours outside on a public terrace at the apartment complex where Dewey and Carrie lived. That terrace was right outside the Sopers' door. While Dewey worked on his paintings he was usually surrounded by a small crowd of elderly ladies. That, of course, caused a reaction in Carrie.

"Grandma had a bit of a sharp tongue. She would come out and shoo the women away, telling them Dewey had to work, or he wanted to talk to me. Of course, really, she was just jealous," Philip said.[14]

During his student years at the University of Alberta, Philip Dewey Soper became president[15] of the Students' Union. When that body opened a new bar, they held a "name the bar" contest. The final choice was "Dewey's." Whether that was in honour of Dr. J. Dewey Soper or his grandson, Philip

Dewey Soper, is not known, but Philip said, "Dewey's became the place to hang out."

It still is, but it wasn't somewhere that Joseph Dewey Soper would have chosen to spend much time. He preferred the outdoors. In an interview for the *Edmonton Journal* in 1978, the then eighty-five-year-old Dewey remarked, "I've been a wilderness man almost all my life. Some of the happiest days were spent in a tent."[16]

A pipe smoker for much of his adult life, Dewey eventually gave it up on the advice of his doctor. As the autumn of 1982 progressed, Dewey's physical condition deteriorated. He was hospitalized in Edmonton for a few weeks, and perhaps knew deep down that he would never again walk the fields and woods in search of birds. Roly went to see his father twice during those final weeks. He recalled that "the second time I knew his time was drawing near. He was very tired, scarcely moved and whispered to me that he 'wanted it to be over.'"

A few days later his wish came true. Dewey Soper passed away at the age of eighty-nine in November 1982. Carolyn Soper outlived her husband by twenty years, although for well over half that time she lived in a dark world dominated by Alzheimer's disease.

In a fitting posthumous gesture to their distinguished late colleague, two years after Dewey passed away the Alberta Society of Professional Biologists established the Dr. J.D. Soper Award for presentation to Canadian biologists who have made an outstanding contribution in the field of biology.

A collection of Dewey's lovingly painted watercolour paintings toured Arctic communities in 1988–89 and received a warm reception, and in 1988 many of them were exhibited at the Calgary Olympic Winter Games. The complete collection of some two hundred framed watercolours is now stored in the archives at the Arctic Institute of North America in Calgary.[17]

Dr. Dewey Soper's reputation as a field naturalist and as an explorer was assured. Others felt he deserved more — much more. In the spring of 1972, without his knowledge, members of his family and associates made a series of representations to Government House in Ottawa to have Dewey appointed to the Order of Canada. Despite the importance to Canada, and the world, of Dewey Soper's lifelong scientific work, the efforts came to naught. In 1980 additional names were added to the list of nominators and a new application submitted. Once again, the Chancellery of Honours

Dewey Soper at home in Edmonton, aged eighty-seven, July 1980.

failed to recognize the importance of the nomination or the man. Roland Soper made a final effort to get Dewey's name accepted in July 1982, when his father was eighty-nine and quite frail. As with previous attempts, this last was also unsuccessful.[18]

In an era when pop-music stars and sports personalities, as well as politicians, among others, are welcomed into the Order, it is difficult to understand the rationale of an intelligent advisory council that would fail to see the

A Second Attempt at Retirement

justice in appointing a man of science who had given a life of exemplary work on behalf of the natural sciences and his country.

Perhaps the best possible ending to the Dewey Soper story was written by Dewey himself as long ago as December 1915, at the age of twenty-two, two years after he and Jack Coker had returned from their hunting and trapping expedition to the foothills of the Rockies.

In his own haunting words: "Almost certainly the strange lure of the wilds would strike again and the subtle call, with all its implications, answered once more."[19]

Hopefully Dewey Soper heard that call again in his next life.

Appendix I

Awards and Honours

Awards and honours received by J. Dewey Soper:

1929:	The Geographic Board of Canada designated a high area west of the northern part of Nettilling Lake, Baffin Island, as the Soper Highlands.
1931:	The Geographic Board of Canada designated a river (known as the Koukdjuak by the Inuit) near Lake Harbour, Baffin Island, as the Soper River.
July 1957:	The federal government established the Dewey Soper Bird Sanctuary immediately to the north of Bowman Bay on southern Baffin Island. By Order-In-Council, P.C. 1957-862.
May 1960:	The University of Alberta conferred an Honorary Doctor of Laws degree, *Honoris causa*, in recognition of Dr. Soper's personal contribution to the knowledge of Canadian fauna and general Arctic explorations.
May 1961:	Appointed Honorary Research Associate in Zoology, Department of Zoology, University of Alberta, Edmonton.
January 1967:	Dr. George Ball, entomologist at the University of Alberta, named a new Aklavik beetle *Pterostichus (Cryobius) soperi*

	in honour of Dewey's extensive wildlife investigations in the western Arctic.
August 1969:	Elected as a Knight of Mark Twain by the Mark Twain Society, Kirkwood, Missouri.
October 1972:	Alberta premier Peter Lougheed presented Dewey with a Personal Achievement Certificate at the annual Alberta Achievement Awards dinner. At the same time he received a gold lapel emblem from the lieutenant governor of Alberta, the Honorable J.W. Grant MacEwen, for a lifetime achievement in wildlife research and conservation.
November 1978:	The Government of the Northwest Territories presented Dewey Soper with the Commissioner's Award for his work in exploration, mapping, faunal research, and botanical collections in the Canadian eastern Arctic.
1980:	Received the Douglas H. Pimlott Conservation Award. Presented by the Canadian Nature Federation, it is Nature Canada's most prestigious award, recognizing outstanding contributors to Canadian conservation.

Appendix II

Scientific Discoveries

The following is a list of scientific discoveries made by J. Dewey Soper:

June 1925:	Discovery of a new subspecies of the ringed seal (*Phoca hispida soperi* Anderson) at Nettilling Lake, Baffin Island, Northwest Territories.
August 1927:	First positive Canadian record of the pallid meadow vole, also known as the sagebrush vole (*Lagurus curtatus pallidus* Merriam), Lodge Creek, Alberta.
August 1927:	First positive Canadian record of the black-tailed prairie dog (*Cynomys ludovicianus ludovicianus* Ord), Val Marie, Saskatchewan.
October 1927:	Discovery of a new subspecies of the Manitoba short-tailed shrew (*Blarina brevicauda manitobensis* Anderson), Max Lake, Turtle Mountain, Manitoba.
June 1929:	Discovery of a new subspecies of the willow ptarmigan (*Lagopus lagopus leucopterus* Taverner) at Camp Kungovik, Bowman Bay, Baffin Island, Northwest Territories.
July–August 1929:	Discovery of the breeding grounds of the blue goose (*Chen caerulescens*), Bowman Bay, Baffin Island, Northwest Territories.

May 1935: First positive record for Manitoba of the Wisconsin woodland jumping mouse (*Napaeozapus insignis frutuctanus* Jackson), Caddy Lake, Manitoba.

June 1939: First positive Canadian record of the mountain plover (*Eupoda montanus* Townsend), Bracken, Saskatchewan. In June 1941 Dr. Soper collected two specimens, the first to be taken north of the international boundary between Canada and the United States.

September 1940: Discovery of a new subspecies of the prairie dusky shrew (*Sorex vagrans soperi* Anderson), Lake Audy, Riding Mountain National Park, Manitoba.

June 1941: Discovery of a new subspecies of the Phenacomys vole (*Phenacomys ungava soperi* Anderson), Swanson Creek, Riding Mountain National Park, Manitoba.

May 1943: First positive Canadian record of the Mississippi Valley pocket gopher (*Geomys bursarius* Shaw), eleven and a half miles east-northeast of Emerson, Manitoba.

Appendix III

Clubs and Associations

J. Dewey Soper was a member of the following clubs and associations:

Fellow, Arctic Institute of North America
Fellow, American Ornithologists' Union
Honorary Member, Ottawa Field-Naturalists' Club
Charter Member, American Society of Mammalogists
Member, Edmonton Bird Club

Notes

In addition to the sources noted below, valuable information and anecdotes came from face to face conversations with Roland and Trent Soper at Roland Soper's home in Calgary on Thursday October 29, 2009, and from emails and telephone discussions with them and other Soper family members over the winter of 2009–10.

Introduction

1. Foxe Basin, Foxe Channel, and Foxe Peninsula are named after an Englishman, Captain Luke Foxe, who circumnavigated Hudson Bay in 1631 in his ship *Charles* and penetrated north into the large sea basin that now bears his name.
2. Anthony Dalton, *Adventures with Camera and Pen* (Toronto: BookLand Press, 2009), chapters 1 and 2, 9–23.
3. Anthony Dalton, *Alone Against the Arctic* (Victoria: Heritage House, 2007).
4. *Ibid.* Also Anthony Dalton, *Baychimo: Arctic Ghost Ship* (Victoria: Heritage House, 2006).
5. Information on many HBC ships, including RMS *Nascopie*, can be

found in "Ships Histories," at the Archives of Manitoba/Hudson's Bay Company Archives in Winnipeg.
6. J. Dewey Soper, *Canadian Arctic Recollections* (Saskatoon: University of Saskatchewan, 1981).
7. J. Dewey Soper, "Autobiographical Sketch" (Edmonton: University of Alberta Archives, J. Dewey Soper fonds 78-108-1/1).
8. J. Dewey Soper, "Dr. Joseph Dewey Soper — An Autobiography" (Calgary: Roland Soper).
9. Dr. J. Dewey Soper, *The Mammals of Alberta* (Edmonton: Hamly Press, 1964), 14.

Chapter 1: A Young Naturalist

1. The CGS *Arctic* was a German-built steamship carrying auxiliary sails. Originally named *Gauss*, she had a flared, rounded hull which was ideal for use in polar ice. Captain Bernier purchased her on behalf of the Canadian government for seventy-five thousand dollars in 1904. Her intended role, and Bernier's, was to attempt a passage to the North Pole on behalf of Canada. In any event, that ambitious expedition was cancelled soon after. T.C. Fairley and Charles E. Israel, *The True North: The Story of Captain Joseph Bernier* (Toronto: Macmillan, 1957), 63–66.
2. Joseph Elzear Bernier (1852–1934), born in L'Islet, Quebec, was a sailor all his life. He captained his first ship at the age of seventeen and first served in Arctic waters when he was fifty-two. He was captain of the CGS *Arctic* from 1904 to 1925. *Ibid.*
3. In the nomenclature of polar ice, "bergy bits" are large pieces of floating glacier ice, smaller than icebergs, but with up to five metres showing above the sea level and from one to three hundred square metres in area. Smaller pieces are referred to as "growlers." *Pilot of Arctic Canada*. Vol. 1, 2nd ed. (Ottawa: Canadian Hydrographic Services, 1970), 81, 84.
4. *Iceblink*: A whitish glare on low clouds above an accumulation of distant ice. *Ibid.*, 85.
5. J. Dewey Soper, *Canadian Arctic Recollections* (Saskatoon: University of Saskatchewan, 1981), 2.

Notes

6. Information on the winter of 1892–93 in southern Ontario is from *www.halinet.on.ca/greatlakes/documents/Brookes/default.asp?ID=Y1893*. Accessed January 23, 2010.
7. J. Dewey Soper, "Dr. Joseph Dewey Soper — An Autobiography" (Calgary: Roland Soper), 2.
8. *Ibid.*, 3.
9. J. Dewey Soper, "Boyhood Reminiscences" part of "Wildlife and Wilderness Adventures, 1912–1914" (Edmonton: University of Alberta Archives, J. Dewey Soper fonds 87–17–2/19), 51.
10. J. Dewey Soper, "Autobiographical Sketch" (Edmonton: University of Alberta Archives, J. Dewey Soper fonds 78–108–1/1), 3.
11. J. Dewey Soper, "Dr. Joseph Dewey Soper — An Autobiography," 5.
12. J. Dewey Soper, "Boyhood Reminiscences," 49.
13. *Ibid.*, 45–46.
14. *Ibid.*, 46.
15. American polar explorer and naval officer Robert Peary claimed to have stood at the North Pole on April 6, 1909. Whether or not he actually did so has long been in doubt. Source: Frank Rasky, *The North Pole or Bust* (Toronto: McGraw-Hill Ryerson, 1977), 294–327.
16. Dr. Frederick Cook, an American from Brooklyn, claimed to have reached the North Pole on April 21, 1908, almost one year before Peary. *Ibid.*
17. The controversy as to whether Peary or Cook was first to the North Pole, or in fact whether either of them actually achieved their goal, continues today. Frank Rasky's book gives brief but telling details. For a more in-depth study of the subject, see Wally Herbert, *A Noose of Laurels* (London: Hodder & Stoughton, 1989).
18. Norwegian explorer Roald Amundsen and a team of five other men arrived at the South Pole on December 14, 1911. His rival for the Antarctic prize was the British naval officer Robert Falcon Scott: he arrived at the pole one month after Amundsen. Scott and his team of four were found frozen to death in February 1913. For more details see Max Jones, *The Last Great Quest: Captain Scott's Antarctic Sacrifice* (Oxford: Oxford University Press, 2003).
19. J. Dewey Soper, "Boyhood Reminiscences," 46.
20. J. Dewey Soper, "Autobiographical Sketch," 6.

21. *Ibid.*, 7.
22. *Ibid.*, 7.
23. Wild rabbit was a popular meat in the first half of the twentieth century. The farm boys would have taken the rabbits for family consumption in stews and pies.
24. Historical details on Edmonton available from *www.edmonton.ca/city_ government/edmonton_archives/city-of-edmonton-archives.aspx*. Accessed January 24, 2010.

Chapter 2: Into a Western Wonderland

1. By 1924 McKernan's Lake had been mostly drained. It was eventually filled in and, with the surrounding area, probably used for agriculture initially. Later still it was built over with family dwellings. By then its once resident wildlife had migrated to more peaceful settings. Source: *Lost Creeks and Wetlands of Edmonton: www.ualberta.ca/ERSCO8/ water/urban/lost3.htm*. Accessed January 4, 2010.
2. J. Dewey Soper, "Autobiographical Sketch" (Edmonton: University of Alberta Archives, J. Dewey Soper fonds, 78–108–1/1), 5.
3. J. Dewey Soper, "Chickadee and Shreike [sic] December 1914," part of "Wildlife and Wilderness Adventures" (Edmonton: University of Alberta Archives, J. Dewey Soper fonds 87–17–2/19), 32.
4. Dewey's first camera was an Eastman Pony Premo No. 6.
5. The newspaper was based in Montreal, Quebec. Known as "Canada's National Farm Magazine," it was published by the Montreal Star Company. Source: *www.philsp.com/data/data121.html*. Accessed January 24, 2010.

Chapter 3: First Expedition: Into the Foothills of the Rockies

1. Details on Mount Columbia are from *www.peakfinder.com/peakfinder. asp?PeakName=Mount%2BColumbia*. Accessed January 24, 2010.
2. J. Dewey Soper, "An Amateur Naturalist in the Wilds of Western Alberta, October to December, 1913" (Edmonton: University of Alberta

Notes

   Archives, J. Dewey Soper fonds, 78–108–1/2), 2.
3. Information on Dewey Soper's physical size supplied by Roland Soper, October 29, 2009.
4. J. Dewey Soper, "An Amateur Naturalist in the Wilds of Western Alberta, October to December, 1913," 2.
5. Funsten Brothers of St. Louis, Missouri, were well-known for their fur-trapping equipment and for buying raw furs.
6. J. Dewey Soper, "An Amateur Naturalist in the Wilds of Western Alberta, October to December, 1913," 3–4.
7. Ibid., 9.
8. Ibid., 12.
9. Ibid., 13–15.
10. Ibid., 15.
11. Squaw bread (also known as Indian Maiden bread) is a tasty fried bread cooked crispy on the outside and should be light and fluffy on the inside.
12. Mountain Cree are now the Aseniwuche Winewak Nation of Canada. Source: *www.aseniwuche.com*. Accessed January 24, 2010.
13. J. Dewey Soper, "An Amateur Naturalist in the Wilds of Western Alberta, October to December, 1913," 40.
14. Ibid., 43.
15. Ibid., 43.
16. Ibid., 44.

Chapter 4: Ontario Again

1. A copy of this article, along with others, is held in the University of Alberta Archives, J. Dewey Soper fonds, 87-17-3/44.
2. The First World War began on August 4, 1914, and lasted until November 11, 1918.
3. Dewey Soper found the poem in a 1912 issue of *Redbook* magazine. He reproduced it in its entirety in a short typed collection of poems and anecdotes, filed in with: J. Dewey Soper, "Wildlife and Wilderness Adventures, 1912–1914" (Edmonton: University of Alberta Archives, J. Dewey Soper fonds, 87-17-2/19), 28.

4. *Ibid.*
5. *Ibid.*, 29.
6. The original notes, written in pencil, had become faded with time. Some had become almost illegible. In December 1970, Dewey rejuvenated everything he could read by typing the notes onto the loose-leaf pages of new pocket-sized notebooks. These are now held in the University of Alberta Archives in Edmonton, J. Dewey Soper fonds, 87-17-1/1.
7. Ernest Thompson Seton (1860–1946), author and wildlife artist.
8. William Edwin Saunders (1861–1943), ornithologist.
9. Dr. Rudolph Martin Anderson (1877–1961), mammalogist and zoologist.
10. Percy Algernon Taverner (1875–1947), ornithologist.
11. J. Dewey Soper, "Notes on the Wildlife of Wellington and Waterloo Counties in Ontario, Canada, During 1915 to 1918" (Edmonton: University of Alberta Archives, J. Dewey Soper fonds, 87-17-1/1), 24.
12. *Ibid.*, 28.
13. *Ibid.*, 38.
14. *Ibid.*, 59.
15. *Ibid.*, 59.
16. In his unpublished autobiography, Dewey Soper either forgot about or ignored this expedition and only reported on a repeat visit to the Ridout area in September 1918, although he noted it as October 1918. See J. Dewey Soper, "To the Wilds of Northern Ontario" (Edmonton: University of Alberta Archives, J. Dewey Soper fonds, 78-108-1/3), 94–109.
17. *Ibid.*, 96.
18. *Ibid.*, 100.
19. *Ibid.*, 100.
20. *Ibid.*, 104.
21. *Ibid.*, 105.
22. *Ibid.*, 106.
23. *Ibid.*, 107.
24. *Ibid.*, 109.
25. J. Dewey Soper, "Dr. Joseph Dewey Soper — An Autobiography" (Calgary: Roland Soper), 21.
26. Now the Royal Conservatory of Music in Toronto.

Chapter 5: Building and Learning

1. J. Dewey Soper, "Dr. Joseph Dewey Soper — An Autobiography" (Calgary: Roland Soper), 23b.
2. *Ibid.*, 23.
3. *Ibid.*, 23 (footnote).
4. *Ibid.*
5. *Ibid.*, 24.
6. J. Dewey Soper, "Field Notes on the Birds and Mammals Observed and Collected at the Bettschen Ranch, Near Broadview, Saskatchewan, and in the Islay, Alberta, District Including Laurier, Whitney, and Kenilworth Lakes in the Years 1919, 1921, and 1965" (Edmonton: University of Alberta Archives, J. Dewey Soper fonds, 78-108-1/2), 13.
7. J. Dewey Soper, "The Lore of the Wild" (Edmonton: University of Alberta Archives, J. Dewey Soper fonds, 87-17-2/20).
8. "National Conference on Conservation of Game, Fur-Bearing Animals and Other Wildlife Under the Direction of the Commission of Conservation in Co-Operation with the Advisory Board on Wildlife Protection" (Ottawa: Commission of Conservation, Canada, 1919), 2.
9. J. Dewey Soper, "The Edmonton and Kiscoty Districts and East to Ottawa and Quebec City for Departure to the Eastern Arctic, October 6, 1922, to July 9, 1923" (Edmonton: University of Alberta Archives, J. Dewey Soper fonds, 78-108-1/3), 73.
10. *Ibid.*, 81.

Chapter 6: Expedition to the Eastern Arctic, 1923

Note: Dewey Soper's official report to his employers, "Report of the C.G.S. Arctic Expedition of 1923," consists of a letter to expedition commander J.D. Craig, an introduction, itinerary (the basic details of the voyage), a memorandum on Arctic settlements visited, ethnological remarks, a record of sea and air temperatures, notes on mammals, and a record of birds seen and/or collected, plus a recommendation for further zoological and other scientific work on Baffin Island and other areas visited. The report is held in the

Library and Archives Canada/Department of Indian Affairs and Northern Development fonds /RG85-D-1-A Vol. 349, File 203.

1. John Davidson Craig was commander of Canadian government expeditions to the Arctic in 1922, 1923, and 1924.
2. The legal team was sent north to Pond Inlet to handle the trial of three Inuit men accused of the murder of Robert S. Janes, a fur trapper and, coincidently, formerly Second Officer on the CGS *Arctic* during its 1910 voyage to the Arctic under Captain Bernier. Shelagh D. Grant, *Arctic Justice* (Montreal: McGill-Queen's University Press, 2002), 156.
3. Third mate Wilfred Caron was swept overboard. Desmond O'Connell, working from the rescue boat, jumped in and died while trying to save him. Both bodies were reported washed up on shore at different locations and times. *Ibid.*, 157, and notes to pages 158–60, item 23.
4. The most direct route to the Atlantic, and subsequently the Arctic, from Quebec City would have been through Jacques Cartier Passage, between the north shore of Anticosti Island and the Quebec coast.
5. J. Dewey Soper, "Report of the C.G.S. Arctic Expedition of 1923," Itinerary, 2.
6. *Ibid.*, 4.
7. *Ibid.*, 6.
8. From a letter Dewey Soper sent to J.D. Craig from Edmonton, dated April 8, 1924. J. Dewey Soper, "Report of the C.G.S. Arctic Expedition of 1923."
9. J. Dewey Soper, *Canadian Arctic Recollections* (Saskatoon: University of Saskatchewan, 1981), 2.
10. Shelagh D. Grant, *Arctic Justice*, 158, note 27.
11. J. Dewey Soper, "Report of the C.G.S. Arctic Expedition of 1923," Itinerary, 12.
12. The RCMP post had been established the previous summer and was named for J.D. Craig, who had been commander of the 1922 expedition as well as the 1923 voyage.
13. LOA = Length overall.
14. Captain MacMillan (1874–1970) was an American, and an Arctic

explorer of considerable note. In forty-six years he made more than thirty expeditions to the Arctic. Source: *www.bowdoin.edu/arctic-museum/biographies/macmillan.shtml*. Accessed January 23, 2010.

15. The Greely Expedition of twenty-five men, under the command of U.S. Navy lieutenant Adolphus Greely, left St. John's, Newfoundland, in 1881, to establish a scientific base on Lady Franklin Bay on the northeast coast of Ellesmere Island. Only six men survived a dreadful ordeal in the northern ice. Leonard F. Guttridge, *The Ghosts of Cape Sabine* (New York: Putnam, 2000).
16. The *Arctic* was 165 feet long.
17. J. Dewey Soper, "Report of the C.G.S. Arctic Expedition of 1923," Notes on Mammals, 6.
18. J. Dewey Soper, *Canadian Arctic Recollections*, 7.
19. It is possible that this is the same abandoned camp that Dr. Frederick Cook said he wintered in only twenty years before, after his much questioned "successful" dash to the North Pole.
20. Ernest S. Dodge, *The Polar Rosses, John and James Clark Ross and Their Explorations* (London: Faber & Faber, 1973), 67.
21. J. Dewey Soper, "Report of the C.G.S. Arctic Expedition of 1923," Itinerary, 20.
22. Between 1984 and 1986, Dr. Owen Beattie conducted autopsies on the three sailors from the Franklin expedition and determined they had probably died from a combination of lung disease and lead poisoning from ill-made cans of food. Scott Cookman, *Iceblink* (New York: John Wiley, 2000), 78–82.
23. J. Dewey Soper, "Report of the C.G.S. Arctic Expedition of 1923," Itinerary, 20.
24. Ernest S. Dodge, *The Polar Rosses*, 235.
25. Not to be confused with the vibrant settlement of Eskimo Point on the west side of Hudson Bay, north of Churchill.
26. A foxtail is a spikelet or spikelet cluster of a grass that serves to disperse its seeds as a unit. Source: *en.wikipedia.org/wiki/Foxtail_(diaspore)*. Accessed January 24, 2010.
27. J. Dewey Soper, "Report of the C.G.S. Arctic Expedition of 1923," Itinerary, 23.

28. Thomas Button was sent to Hudson Bay in 1612 by a consortium of British merchants. His instructions were to sail west from Digges Island and search for the Northwest Passage. He failed in the attempt and he lost one of his two ships at the mouth of the Nelson River, but he did return with much useful information on the west coast of the bay, the islands within the bay, and the tidal ranges. *Pilot of Arctic Canada*, Vol. 1, 2nd ed. (Ottawa: Canadian Hydrographic Service, 1970), 42.
29. Bill (H.W.) Tilman was a mountaineer and a sailor who late in life combined his love of both with extreme expeditions to the polar regions. Born in Liverpool, England, in 1898, he disappeared at sea in the South Atlantic while en route to climb on Smith Island in the Southern Ocean. Tim Madge, *The Last Hero: Bill Tilman* (London: Hodder & Stoughton, 1995).
30. Arctic explorer P.D. Baird had made an attempt on a crossing of Bylot Island in 1937, but failed due to soft snow.
31. Therkel Matthiassen was a member of Knud Rasmussen's Fifth Thule Expedition. Knud Rasmussen, *Across Arctic America: Narrative of the Fifth Thule Expedition* (New York: Putnam, 1927), 17.
32. Peter Freuchen became famous as an Arctic explorer, author, filmmaker, showman, and the man who amputated his own foot in the Arctic. Peter Freuchen, *Vagrant Viking* (London: Gollancz, 1954).
33. The Fifth Thule Expedition was organized and led by the Dane Knud Rasmussen. Knud Rasmussen, *Across Arctic America: Narrative of the Fifth Thule Expedition*.
34. J. Dewey Soper, "Report of the C.G.S. Arctic Expedition of 1923," 25.
35. *Ibid.*, 27–28.
36. William Duval was a white trader who had been married to a Native woman for forty years and had lived in the Cumberland Sound area all of that time. J. Dewey Soper, *Canadian Arctic Recollections*, 9–10, and Ray Price, *The Howling Arctic* (Toronto: Peter Martin, 1970), 159–61.
37. J. Dewey Soper, "Report of the C.G.S. Arctic Expedition of 1923," Ethnological Remarks, 6.

Notes

Chapter 7: A Second Arctic Expedition

1. J. Dewey Soper, "Report of the C.G.S. Arctic Expedition of 1923," Introduction (Ottawa: Library and Archives Canada/Department of Indian Affairs and Northern Development fonds /RG85-D-1-A, Vol. 349, File 203), 6.
2. *Ibid*. Recommendation for further study.
3. *Ibid*. Letter to J.D. Craig.
4. J. Dewey Soper, *Canadian Arctic Recollections* (Saskatoon: University of Saskatchewan, 1981), 11.
5. J. Dewey Soper, "J. Dewey Soper — An Autobiography" (Calgary: Roland Soper), 31 (footnote).
6. J. Dewey Soper, *Canadian Arctic Recollections*, 11.
7. Information on Baffin Island is from *en.wikipedia.org/wiki/Baffin_Island*. Accessed January 19, 2010.
8. Bernard Hantzsch died on the shores of Foxe Basin as a result of his endeavours and was buried by his Native companions near the coast north of the river that now bears his name.
9. From the late eighteenth century to the early years of the twentieth, whalers, from Scotland and from New Bedford, Massachusetts, primarily, spent the summers hunting bowhead whales (*Balaena mysticus*) in Davis Strait, including Cumberland Sound and Baffin Bay. W. Gillies Ross, *Arctic Whalers, Icy Seas* (Toronto: Irwin, 1985).
10. As the number of whales decreased in the Davis Strait region many of the whaling stations were closed down, Kekerten Island being one of them. *Ibid*.
11. In *A Faunal Investigation of Southern Baffin Island* (page 5) Dewey said they travelled during the evening and night of July 30 and the early part of the following day. Many years later, in *Canadian Arctic Recollections* (page 16), he stated that they left Pangnirtung on the morning of July 29.
12. J. Dewey Soper, *Canadian Arctic Recollections*, 16.
13. *Ibid*., 17.
14. *Ibid*., 18.
15. *Ibid*., 18.
16. *Ibid*., 18.

17. *Ibid.*, 19.
18. Carron oil is a mixture comprising equal volumes of linseed oil and lime water that is used for the relief of burns. It is also known as lime liniment.
19. J. Dewey Soper, *Canadian Arctic Recollections*, 21.
20. Dewey Soper wrote of the Iceland (Kumlein's) gull, "This species was first discovered, not far from this locality, by Ludwig Kumlein, naturalist to the U.S. Howgate Arctic Expedition of 1877–78." J. Dewey Soper, *Canadian Arctic Recollections*, 21.
21. *Ibid.*, 21.
22. *Ibid.*, 22.
23. RMS *Nascopie* ran up on a rock within sight of Cape Dorset. She was abandoned by crew and passengers and subsequently sat on the rock for three months before sliding into the deep. "Ships Histories" (Winnipeg: Archives of Manitoba/Hudson's Bay Company Archives).
24. Major L.T. Burwash worked for the Canadian government in the Department of the Interior in the 1920s and 1930s. He was a meticulous explorer with experience across the Canadian Arctic.
25. J. Dewey Soper, *Canadian Arctic Recollections*, 25.
26. *Ibid.*, 29.

Chapter 8: Exploring Baffin Island

1. J. Dewey Soper, *Canadian Arctic Recollections* (Saskatoon: University of Saskatchewan, 1981), 27.
2. *Ibid.*, 30.
3. *Ibid.*, 31.
4. According to Dewey Soper's story, the white woman was a Mrs. Hayward. He offered no other details about her. *Ibid.*, 32.
5. *Ibid.*, 36.
6. The Inuit Dewey Soper referred to as Kilabuk was almost certainly James Killibuk. He was well-known at Pangnirtung as a good hunter and a naturally skilled mechanic; he eventually became a leader of the community. Ray Price, *The Howling Arctic* (Toronto: Peter Martin, 1970), 168–71.

7. It is probable that the "buffalo" meat was actually caribou as there are no buffalo on Baffin Island.
8. J. Dewey Soper, *Canadian Arctic Recollections*, 38.
9. *Ibid.*, 39.
10. *Ibid.*, 41.
11. *Ibid.*, 41.
12. *Ibid.*, 43.
13. *Ibid.*, 42.
14. *Ibid.*, 42.
15. *Ibid.*, 42.
16. *Ibid.*, 45.
17. *Ibid.*, 47.
18. Franz Boas (1858–1942) was a physicist and an eminent anthropologist, often referred to as "The Father of American Anthropology."

Chapter 9: The Nettilling Lake Expedition

1. J. Dewey Soper, *Canadian Arctic Recollections* (Saskatoon: University of Saskatoon, 1981), 52.
2. *Ibid.*, 52.
3. *Ibid.*, 53.
4. J. Dewey Soper, *A Faunal Investigation of Southern Baffin Island* (Ottawa: National Museum of Canada, 1928), 14.
5. J. Dewey Soper, *Canadian Arctic Recollections*, 66.
6. *Ibid.*, 58
7. *Ibid.*, 58.
8. The land beside the Koukdjuak River is only a few inches higher than the river itself.

Chapter 10: A Winter Traverse

1. In *Canadian Arctic Recollections* Dewey also refers to him as Newkega, although it is possible they are two different people. J. Dewey Soper,

Canadian Arctic Recollections (Saskatoon: University of Saskatchewan, 1981), 64, 68, 70, and 72.
2. German explorer Bernard Hantzsch was the first to cross southern Baffin Island to Foxe Basin in 1911. He died on the shores of Foxe Basin and was buried near there by his Native companions.
3. J. Dewey Soper, *A Faunal Investigation of Southern Baffin Island* (Ottawa: National Museum of Canada, 1928), 21.
4. J. Dewey Soper, *Canadian Arctic Recollections*, 67.
5. Douglas R. Stenton, "A Soper Record Cairn from Baffin Island," *Arctic* (March 1986), 92–94.
6. The spellings of the latter three Inuit names are estimates based on Dewey's handwriting. They do not agree with the names he used for these men in his *Canadian Arctic Recollections*, written more than fifty years later.
7. J. Dewey Soper, *A Faunal Investigation of Southern Baffin Island*, 23.

Chapter 11: Cape Dorset Summer

1. Major L.T. Burwash followed a similar route during one of his many Arctic expeditions.
2. All winter camps were in igloos, or snow houses, built by the Inuit as and when needed on the trail. Tents were only used in the summer months.
3. J. Dewey Soper, *Canadian Arctic Recollections* (Saskatoon: University of Saskatchewan, 1981), 72.
4. *Ibid.*, 74.
5. At that time the snow and blue geese were thought to be different species. It was later learned that the blue goose is simply a phase of the snow goose. Bruce Batt, *Snow Geese, Grandeur and Calamity on an Arctic Landscape* (Memphis, TN: Ducks Unlimited, 1998), 9.
6. J. Dewey Soper, *Canadian Arctic Recollections*, 75.
7. *Ibid.*, 75.
8. In *Canadian Arctic Recollections* Dewey Soper also refers to the Foxe Islands as the Tikoot Islands. Tikoot Island (singular) is on the southeast side of Chorkbak Inlet, about twenty-five to thirty miles away.

9. J. Dewey Soper, *Canadian Arctic Recollections*, 75.
10. In *Canadian Arctic Recollections* (page 75) Dewey Soper wrote that the river drops three hundred feet in the half-mile. That is incorrect and is probably a typographical error.
11. The hills range from two hundred to five hundred feet.
12. Information on SS *Bayrupert* and many other HBC ships can be found in "Ships Histories," at the Archives of Manitoba/Hudson's Bay Company Archives in Winnipeg.
13. Sydney R. Montague, *North to Adventure* (New York: Robert McBride & Co., 1939), 230.
14. The Newfie Bullet was a narrow-gauge steam train that ran across Newfoundland from St. John's to Port aux Basques. The railway was closed down in 1988.
15. Edward Preble was an American naturalist (1871–1957).
16. Arthur Cleveland Bent was an American ornithologist (1866–1954).

Chapter 12: A Brief Prairie Interlude

1. J. Dewey Soper, "Dr. Joseph Dewey Soper — An Autobiography" (Calgary: Roland Soper), 38.
2. J. Dewey Soper, "Unpublished Field Notes on the Birds Observed and Collected in the Province of Saskatchewan, Canada, in 1914, 1921, 1927, and from July 1937 to September 1947" (Edmonton: University of Alberta Archives, J. Dewey Soper fonds, 78-108-1), 2.
3. Dr. J. Dewey Soper, *The Mammals of Alberta* (Edmonton: Hamly Press, 1964), 81.
4. *Ibid.*, 231.
5. *Ibid.*, 389.
6. *Ibid.*, 175.
7. J. Dewey Soper, "Unpublished Field Notes on the Birds Observed and Collected in the Province of Saskatchewan, Canada, in 1914, 1921, 1927, and from July 1937 to September 1947," 3.
8. *Ibid.*, 3.

Chapter 13: Baffin Island 1928–29

1. There were no telephones on Baffin Island at that time and only infrequent contact by radio. The only way to receive and/or send mail was by sea, and the supply ship came in to most posts just once each summer.
2. J. Dewey Soper, *Canadian Arctic Recollections* (Saskatoon: University of Saskatchewan, 1981), 78.
3. The 1927 Putnam Expedition to Baffin Island, organized by publisher George Palmer Putnam, travelled under the sailing command of the redoubtable Newfoundlander captain Robert Bartlett on his schooner *Effie M. Morrissey*. This expedition forced its way across the Foxe Basin and attempted to push through Fury and Hecla straits to the Gulf of Boothia but was stopped by thick ice at the eastern entrance to the strait. Harold Horwood, *Bartlett: The Great Canadian Explorer* (New York: Doubleday, 1977), 139–45.
4. Dewey Soper used a Watt theodolite for surveying purposes. It was probably a Mark B, which was in common use in Dewey Soper's time.
5. The author ran into a similar situation in a small boat off the Arctic coast of Alaska in 1984. Anthony Dalton, *Alone Against the Arctic* (Victoria: Heritage House, 2007), 17–18.
6. J. Dewey Soper, *Canadian Arctic Recollections* (Saskatoon: University of Saskatchewan, 1981), 79.
7. Ibid., 80.
8. This offers another canoe route to connect with the Kommanik River for a crossing of the Foxe Peninsula on a slightly different route.
9. Inukshuk (singular) or Inuksuit (plural) are Inuit rock markers in the basic shape of a man.
10. J. Dewey Soper, *Canadian Arctic Recollections* (Saskatoon: University of Saskatchewan, 1981), 81.
11. A 1929 map that Dewey Soper used to plot the locations of his Baffin Island campsites shows limited knowledge of the west coast, with few islands depicted in Foxe Basin. (See page 204 in this book.)
12. J. Dewey Soper, *Canadian Arctic Recollections*, 83.
13. Ibid., 84.

14. A 1929 map that Dewey Soper used to plot the locations of his Baffin Island campsites shows Cape Dominion as a far less obvious geographical feature than it actually is. (See page 204 in this book.)
15. J. Dewey Soper, *Canadian Arctic Recollections*, 85.
16. In *Canadian Arctic Recollections* the date is noted as March 20, but that is a typographical error.
17. J. Dewey Soper, *Canadian Arctic Recollections*, 85.
18. Dewey Soper discovered the southern edge of the escarpment in 1926.
19. J. Dewey Soper, *Canadian Arctic Recollections*, 87.

Chapter 14: In Search of the Blue Goose

1. In Dewey Soper's Arctic era, biological evidence of the time suggested that the Blue Goose and the Lesser Snow Goose were different species. J. Dewey Soper, *The Blue Goose* (Ottawa: Department of the Interior, 1930). In 1961 scientists established that lesser snow geese and blue geese are a single species with a white and a blue colour phase. The "blue" is actually a combination of grey, silver, white, brown, and cinnamon feathers. When seen from a distance, the birds appear to be a metallic blue. Bruce Batt, *Snow Geese, Grandeur and Calamity in an Arctic Landscape* (Memphis: Ducks Unlimited, 1998), 9–10.
2. J. Dewey Soper, *Canadian Arctic Recollections*, 90.
3. *Ibid.*, 91.
4. *Ibid.*, 91.
5. *Ibid.*, 92.
6. Vilhjalmur Stefansson wrote a book called *The Friendly Arctic*. Dewey Soper disagreed that the Arctic could be friendly.
7. J. Dewey Soper, *Canadian Arctic Recollections*, 11.
8. *Ibid.*, 93.
9. *Ibid.*, 92.
10. *Ibid.*, 93.
11. *Ibid.*, 94.
12. *Ibid.*, 95.

Chapter 15: Lake Harbour, 1930–31

1. J. Dewey Soper, *The Blue Goose* (Ottawa: Department of the Interior, 1930).
2. Edward Beauclerk Maurice, *The Last of the Gentlemen Adventurers* (London: Fourth Estate, 2004).
3. Carolyn K. Soper, "A Nurse Goes to Baffin Island," *The Beaver* (Winter 1964), 33.
4. J. Dewey Soper, *Canadian Arctic Recollections* (Saskatoon: University of Saskatchewan, 1981), 98.
5. Ibid., 99.
6. Ibid., 100.
7. Dewey Soper met then RCMP staff sergeant A.H. Joy (1887–1932) at Pond Inlet on his first expedition to the Arctic in 1923. For a profile of Inspector A.H. Joy, see *pubs.aina.ucalgary.ca/arctic/Arctic35-4-558.pdf*. Accessed January 24, 2010.
8. The Soper River was designated a Canadian Heritage River in 1992.
9. Max Finkelstein, "The Soper River: Timeless Tails and Tuktu Trails," at *www.chrs.ca/Rivers/Soper/Soper-S_e.htm*. Accessed January 24, 2010.
10. *Pilot of Arctic Canada*, Vol. 1, 2nd ed. (Ottawa: Canadian Hydrographic Service, 1970), 134.
11. J. Dewey Soper, *Canadian Arctic Recollections*, 101.
12. The HBC had two vessels with the same name: SS *Ungava* and the motor schooner *Ungava*. Information on these and many other Hudson's Bay Company ships can be found in "Ships Histories," at the Hudson's Bay Company Archives, Winnipeg, Manitoba.

    In his unpublished autobiography (page 42) Dewey recorded that he and his family sailed from Lake Harbour, Baffin Island, to Churchill, Manitoba, on the HBC's SS *Bayeskimo* in September 1931. That is incorrect. *Bayeskimo* was crushed by heavy ice and sank in Ungava Bay on July 23, 1925, while on passage from Montreal to ports in Hudson Strait. According to *Canadian Arctic Recollections*, the Soper family actually sailed on the HBC's SS *Ungava* (not to be confused with the HBC motor schooner *Ungava*) at the beginning of August 1931. J. Dewey Soper, *Canadian Arctic Recollections*, 102.

Notes

13. The Winnipeg to Churchill railway line was completed in 1929.

Chapter 16: Two Decades of Stellar Service

1. J. Dewey Soper, "The Mammals of Southern Baffin Island, Northwest Territories, Canada," *Journal of Mammalogy*, 1944, Vol. 25, No. 3, 221–54.
2. J. Dewey Soper, "Ornithological Results of the Baffin Island Expeditions of 1928–29 and 1930–31, Together with More Recent Records," *The Auk*, 1946, Vol. 63, Nos. 1, 2, and 3, 1–24, 223–39, and 419–27.
3. The four sets of rapids that block vessel traffic on the Slave River between Fort Fitzgerald and Fort Smith are: Cassette, Pelican, Mountain, and Rapids of the Drowned.
4. Source: Parks Canada website: *www.pc.gc.ca/pn-np/nt/woodbuffalo/index_E.asp*. Accessed January 24, 2010.
5. J. Dewey Soper, "Dr. Joseph Dewey Soper — An Autobiography" (Calgary: Roland Soper), 44.
6. J. Dewey Soper, *The Mammals of Alberta* (Edmonton: Hamly Press, 1964), 117.
7. *Ibid.*, 189.
8. *Ibid.*, 189.
9. *Ibid.*, 206.
10. *Ibid.*, 263.
11. *Ibid.*, 327.
12. Source: *The Times Atlas of the World, Comprehensive Edition* (London: Times Books, 1967), xi–xv.
13. J. Dewey Soper, "Dr. Joseph Dewey Soper — An Autobiography," 45.
14. The Canadian Life Zone is the zone comprising the climate and biotic communities of the portion of the boreal life zone exclusive of the Hudsonian and Arctic-Alpine zones. Source: *www.answers.com/topic/canadian-life-zone*. Accessed January 24, 2010.
15. J. Dewey Soper, "Dr. Joseph Dewey Soper — An Autobiography," 46.
16. *Ibid.*, 46.
17. Not to be confused with Cameron Lake in Ontario.
18. J. Dewey Soper, *The Mammals of Alberta*, 153.

19. *Ibid.*, 160.
20. J. Dewey Soper, *Mammal Notes from the Grande Prairie–Peace River Region, Alberta.*
21. J. Dewey Soper, *Birds Observed in the Grande Prairie–Peace River Region of North-Western Alberta, Canada.*
22. Leonard Norris Elye (1884–1958), director of the Manitoba Museum from 1938 to his retirement in 1952. Source: *www.mhs.mb.ca/docs/people/norriselye_l.shtml*. Accessed January 24, 2010.
23. Criddle Farm size. Source: Lillian Gibbons, postscript by Alice Brown, "The Criddle Family," *Manitoba Pageant* (Winnipeg: Manitoba Historical Society, January 1961, Vol. 6, No. 2.)
24. Conversations with Roland Soper at his Calgary home on October 29, 2009.
25. The over and under pistol was a "Game Getter" manufactured by the Marble Safety Axe Company of Gladstone, Michigan. The barrel was ten inches to the receiver, sixteen inches overall. Dewey Soper also had a .22 pistol: a single shot with a ten-inch barrel, overall thirteen inches. Roland Soper said, "I believe he only used those two firearms in his youth. On the occasional field trip when I was with him, the only firearm he carried was a .410 double-barrelled shotgun. He used light loads for small birds and heavy loads for upland game birds, ducks, etc." Source: Roland Soper. Email to the author, November 1, 2009.
26. J. Dewey Soper, "Dr. Joseph Dewey Soper — An Autobiography," 46.
27. *Ibid.*, 49 (footnote).
28. Herschel Island, Yukon, was an important whaling station on the Beaufort Sea during the nineteenth and early part of the twentieth century. It was also the site of the first HBC post in the western Canadian Arctic.
29. Stanton was a small Inuit settlement that, apart from the Natives, consisted of a trading post and a Roman Catholic mission. *Sailing Directions, Arctic Canada*, Vol. III, 3rd ed. (Ottawa: Department of Fisheries and Oceans, 1981), 78.
30. J. Dewey Soper, "Dr. Joseph Dewey Soper — An Autobiography," 50 (footnote).
31. *Ibid.*, 50 (footnote).
32. *Ibid.*, 50.

33. The Alaska Canada Highway is also known as the Alaskan Highway, Alaska-Canadian Highway, or Alcan Highway.
34. The Klondike Gold Rush, also known as the Yukon Gold Rush, started in August 1896 and lasted until the summer of 1898. Source: *www.thecanadianencyclopedia.com/index.cfm?PgNm=TCE&Params=A1AR TA0004349*. Accessed January 24, 2010.
35. J. Dewey Soper, "Dr. Joseph Dewey Soper — An Autobiography," 51.
36. J. Dewey Soper, *Waterfowl and Other Ornithological Investigations in Yukon Territory, Canada*.
37. J. Dewey Soper, "Dr. Joseph Dewey Soper — An Autobiography," 51.
38. *Ibid.*, 53 (footnote).

Chapter 17: An Attempt at Retirement

1. The Korean War began on June 25, 1950, when North Korean troops invaded South Korea. The war lasted until July 27, 1953, when the armistice was signed at Panmunjom, in the demilitarized zone between North and South Korea. Source: *Chronicles of the 20th Century* (London: Dorling-Kindersley, 1995), 703, 748.
2. Email from Roland Soper to the author, December 22, 2009.
3. J. Dewey Soper, "Dr. Joseph Dewey Soper — An Autobiography" (Calgary: Roland Soper), 55.
4. *Ibid.*, 56.
5. *Hyla* can be translated from the Latin as "tree," or the name could be for tree frogs, genus *Hyla*.
6. Now CFB Uplands.
7. Hoyes Lloyd (1888–1978), ornithologist.
8. Dewey started his *Autobiographical Sketch* in the winter of 1955–56. That became the long synopsis for the eventual fifty-thousand-word autobiography, J. Dewey Soper, "Dr. Joseph Dewey Soper — An Autobiography," 59.
9. The year 1922 is probably a typo. It should read 1923, the year of Dewey's first Arctic expedition.
10. J. Dewey Soper, "Dr. Joseph Dewey Soper — An Autobiography," 61.

11. *Ibid.*, 62.
12. *Ibid.*, 62.

Chapter 18: Researching the Mammals of Alberta

1. J. Dewey Soper, "Dr. Joseph Dewey Soper — An Autobiography" (Calgary: Roland Soper), 63.
2. *Ibid.*, 63.
3. Roland Soper sent these two stories to the author by email on January 30, 2010.
4. J. Dewey Soper, "Dr. Joseph Dewey Soper — An Autobiography," 64, 65.
5. Part of the Waterton–Glacier International Peace Park, established 1932.
6. J. Dewey Soper, "Dr. Joseph Dewey Soper — An Autobiography," 67.
7. By road the distance quoted would have been closer to four times as far.
8. Snap-traps are similar in design to the common household mousetraps.
9. Dr. J. Dewey Soper, *The Mammals of Alberta* (Edmonton: Hamly Press, 1964), 62.
10. J. Dewey Soper, "Dr. Joseph Dewey Soper — An Autobiography," 70.
11. *Ibid.*, 71. The original manuscript, "Unpublished Records of Alberta Birds for the Years 1922–1961," is held in the University of Alberta Archives, Edmonton, J. Dewey Soper fonds, 78-108-1/5.
12. J. Dewey Soper, "Dr. Joseph Dewey Soper — An Autobiography," 72.
13. *Ibid.*, 72.
14. *Ibid.*, 72.
15. Conversations with Roly and Trent Soper in Calgary on October 29, 2009.
16. J. Dewey Soper, "Dr. Joseph Dewey Soper — An Autobiography," 75.
17. Dr. J. Dewey Soper, *The Mammals of Alberta*, 61, 62.
18. *Ibid.*, 59–61.
19. *Ibid.*, 62.
20. *Ibid.*, 15.

Chapter 19: A Second Attempt at Retirement

1. From a telephone conversation with Philip Soper on January 23, 2010.
2. Dewey Soper's recipe for good bait for small mammals can be found in *The Mammals of Alberta* (Edmonton: Hamly Press, 1964), 62.
3. Kangaroo mouse, also known as a jumping mouse. *Ibid.*, 241.
4. Professor Leslie Pengelly (1918–81), emeritus professor of wildlife biology at the University of Montana. His obituary can be found at *www.jstor.org/pss/3782771*. Accessed January 29, 2010.
5. Expo 67, or correctly, The 1967 International and Universal Exposition, was held in Montreal between April 27 and October 29, 1967.
6. J. Dewey Soper, "Dr. Joseph Dewey Soper — An Autobiography" (Calgary: Roland Soper), 103.
7. *Ibid.*, 105.
8. *Ibid.*, 88.
9. *Ibid.*, 108.
10. *Ibid.*, 110.
11. *Ibid.*, 114.
12. *Ibid.*, 118.
13. *Ibid.*, 126.
14. From a telephone conversation with Philip Soper on January 23, 2010.
15. Philip Dewey Soper was president of the University of Alberta's students' union in 1981 and 82.
16. Joanne Munro, "Career Spent in the Wilderness," *Edmonton Journal*, November 6, 1978.
17. Although Dewey Soper's Arctic-themed watercolours are stored at the Arctic Institute of North America for that organization's use, the copyright on all the paintings remains with the Soper family.
18. The letters of application to politicians and the relevant Canadian government offices regarding the Order of Canada are held by Roland Soper in Calgary.
19. J. Dewey Soper, "An Amateur Naturalist in the Wilds of Western Alberta, October to December, 1913" (Edmonton: University of Alberta Archives, J. Dewey Soper fonds, 78-108-1/3), 46.

Works by J. Dewey Soper

Published Works

Books

A Faunal Investigation of Southern Baffin Island. National Museum of Canada. 1928. Bulletin 53, Biology Series No. 15; 143 pages, 14 illustrations, 1 map.

Canadian Arctic Recollections, Baffin Island 1923–1931. Ed. Shirley Milligan. Institute for Northern Studies, University of Saskatchewan, Saskatoon, 1981.

The Mammals of Alberta. The Hamly Press, Edmonton, 1964.

The Mammals of Jasper National Park, Alberta. Department of Indian Affairs and Northern Development, 1970.

The Mammals of Waterton Lakes National Park, Alberta. Canadian Wildlife Service, Report Series No. 23, Edmonton, Alberta, 57 pages. Soper, J. (1973).

Articles

"Eskimo Dogs of the Canadian Arctic." *Canadian Geographical Journal*, 1940. Vol. XX, No. 2, 97–108.

"History, Range and Home Life of the Northern Bison." *Ecological Monographs*, 1941, Vol. 11, No. 4, 347–412.

"Report on Wildlife Investigations in Wood Buffalo Park and Vicinity, Alberta and Northwest Territories." Submitted to National Parks Bureau, Land, Parks and Forests Branch, Department of Mines and Resources, 1945.

"Birds Observed in the Grande Prairie–Peace River Region of Northwestern Alberta, Canada." 1949. *The Auk*, 663233.257.

"Bird Tragedies" (written for the Natural History Club of the *Family Herald and Weekly Star*, Montreal, April 8, 1914).

Unpublished Works

A Selected Bibliography of Unpublished Books and Articles by Dewey Soper (all held in the University of Alberta Archives, J. Dewey Soper fonds, Edmonton).

An Amateur Naturalist in the Wilds of Western Alberta, October to December, 1913.

The Lore of the Wild (1922).

Autobiographical Sketch (January, 1956).

Dr. Joseph Dewey Soper — An Autobiography (November, 1969).

Wildlife and Wilderness Adventures (1912–1914) Ornithology.

An Afternoon with the Willow Thrush in Alberta (Veery) (1912).

Outings Among the Native Waterfowl of Central Alberta (1913).

The Screech Owl and his Kindred (December 1912).

Winter Neighbours (1914).

Chickadee and Shrieke [sic] *Winter 1912–1913.*

The Destructiveness of the Sapsucker (December 1914).

The Goshawk (1914).

The Black-Capped Chickadee (Feb. 1914).

Works by J. Dewey Soper

Boyhood Reminiscences (January 1915).
To the Wilds of Northern Ontario (October 20 to November 2, 1917).

Arctic Publications by J. Dewey Soper

"Impressions of the Arctic." *The Edmonton Journal*, Edmonton, AB, December 29, 1923.
"Birds and Mammals in the Heart of the Polar Regions." *The Edmonton Journal*, March 1924.
"Discovery of the Nesting Grounds of the Blue Goose." American Game Protective Association, New York, December 1929. Vol. 18, 72–82.
"Discovery of the Breeding Grounds of the Blue Goose." *Canadian Field Naturalist*, 1930. Vol. 44, No. 1, 1–12, 6 illustrations, 1 map.
"Explorations in Baffin Island." *Geographical Journal*, London, UK, 1930. Vol. 96, 435–43, 5 illustrations, 1 map.
"Explorations in Foxe Peninsula and Along the West Coast of Baffin Island." *Geographical Review*, 1930. Vol. 20, No. 3, 397–424, 19 illustrations, 2 maps.
"Adventuring in Baffin Island." *Canadian Geographical Journal*, 1930. Vol. 1, No. 3, 191–206, 19 illustrations, 1 map.
"Explorations by J.D. Soper, 1924–26." In *Southern Baffin Island*, Department of the Interior, Ottawa, 1930. 67–83, 6 illustrations, 4 maps.
"Solitudes of the Arctic." *Canadian Geographical Journal*, 1933. Vol. 7, No.3: 103–15, 27 illustrations.
"Interesting Bird Records for Southern Baffin Island." *Canadian Field Naturalist*, 1934. Vol. 48, No. 3, 41–44; Vol. 48, No 4, 65–68; and Vol. 48, No 5, 79–82, 3 illustrations.
"Zoological Collecting and Research in the Arctic Regions." *Canada's Eastern Arctic*, Department of the Interior, Ottawa, 1934. Appendix A. 144–62, 4 illustrations.
"Fish of Southern Baffin Island." *Canada's Eastern Arctic*, Department of the Interior, Ottawa, 1934. 132–33.
"The Lake Harbour Region, Baffin Island" *Geographical Review*, 1936. Vol. 26, No. 3, 426–38, 9 illustrations, 1 map.

"Intimate Glimpses of Eskimo Life in Baffin Island." *The Beaver*, 1936. Vol. 266, No. 4, 34–39 and 64–65; Vol. 267, No. 1, 9–12 and 66, 19 illustrations.

"Bird Life in the Eastern Arctic." *The Beaver*, 1939. Vol. 270, No.1, 28–35, 12 illustrations.

"Local Distribution of Eastern Arctic Birds." *The Auk*, 1940. Vol. 57, No. 1, 13–21, 2 illustrations.

"Eskimo Dogs of the Eastern Arctic." *Canadian Geographical Journal*, 1940. Vol. 20, No. 2, 13–21, 14 illustrations.

"Life History of the Blue Goose, *Chen caerulescens*." *Proceedings of the Boston Society of Natural History*, 1942. Vol. 42, No. 2, 120–29, plates 15–26, 1 map.

"The Arctic Char at Nettilling Lake, Baffin Island, N.W.T." *Canadian Field Naturalist*, 1943. Vol. 57, 4–5.

"The Mammals of Southern Baffin Island, Northwest Territories, Canada." *Journal of Mammalogy*, 1944. Vol. 25, No. 3, 221–54.

"Ornithological Results of the Baffin Island Expeditions of 1928–1929 and 1930–1931, Together with More Recent Records." *The Auk*, 1946. Vol. 63, Nos. 1, 2, and 3, 1–24, 223–39, and 419–27.

Waterfowl and Other Ornithological Investigations in Yukon Territory, Canada. Canadian Wildlife Service, Ottawa, 1954. Wildlife Management Bulletin, Series 2, No. 7, 55 pages, 16 illustrations, 1 map.

"Netchilik." Chapter in the book *Discovery*. Ed. John Kenneth Terres. Lippincott, New York, 1961, 222–39. (A narrative concerning Nettilling Lake, Baffin Island.)

"The Conquest of Pangnirtung Pass." *The Beaver*, 1973. Vol. 303, No. 4, 40–48, 9 illustrations.

"Kingnait Pass." *The Beaver*, 1973. Vol. 304, No. 3, 41–47, 6 illustrations.

"Baffin Island: The Mysterious West Coast." *The Beaver*, 1974. Vol. 305, No. 2, 54–59, 6 illustrations, 1 map.

Selected Bibliography

Books

Batt, Bruce. *Snow Geese, Grandeur and Calamity on an Arctic Landscape.* Memphis, TN: Ducks Unlimited, Inc., 1998.

Burnett, J. Alexander. *A Passion for Wildlife: The History of the Canadian Wildlife Service.* Vancouver: UBC Press, 2003.

Cookman, Scott. *Iceblink: The Tragic Fate of Sir John Franklin's Lost Polar Expedition.* New York: John Wiley, 2000.

Corner, George W. *Dr. Kane of the Arctic Seas.* Philadelphia: Temple University Press, 1972.

Dalton, Anthony. *Alone Against the Arctic.* Surrey, BC: Heritage House, 2007.

_____. *Baychimo, Arctic Ghost Ship.* Surrey, BC: Heritage House, 2006.

Dodge, Ernest S. *The Polar Rosses: John and James Clark Ross and Their Explorations.* London: Faber & Faber, 1973.

Duffy, Ronald Quinn. *The Road to Nunavut: The Progress of the Eastern Arctic Inuit Since the Second World War.* Montreal: McGill-Queen's University Press, 1988.

Fairley, T.C., and Charles E. Israel. *The True North: The Story of Captain J.E. Bernier.* Toronto: MacMillan, 1957.

Federation of Alberta Naturalists, Fish and Wildlife Historical Society. *Fish, Fur and Feathers: Fish and Wildlife Conservation in Alberta 1905–2005*. Edmonton, 2005.

Freuchen, Peter. *Vagrant Viking: My Life and Adventures*. London: Gollancz, 1954.

Grant, Shelagh D. *Arctic Justice: On Trial for Murder, Pond Inlet, 1923*. Montreal: McGill-Queen's University Press, 2002.

Guttridge, Leonard F. *Ghosts of Cape Sabine: The Harrowing True Story of the Greely Expedition*. New York: Putnam, 2000.

Herbert, Wally. *The Noose of Laurels*. London: Hodder & Stoughton, 1989.

Hodgins, Bruce, and Gwyneth Hoyle. *Canoeing North into the Unknown: A Record of River Travel, 1874 to 1974*. Toronto: Natural Heritage Books, A Member of the Dundurn Group, 1994.

Horwood, Harold. *Bartlett: The Great Canadian Explorer*. New York: Doubleday, 1977.

Jones, Max. *The Last Great Quest: Captain Scott's Antarctic Sacrifice*. Oxford, UK: Oxford University Press, 2003.

Madge, Tim. *The Last Hero: Bill Tilman*. London: Hodder & Stoughton, 1995.

Martin, Constance. *Search for the Blue Goose: J. Dewey Soper, the Arctic Adventures of a Canadian Naturalist*. Calgary: Bayeux Arts, 1995.

Martin, Constance, Peter White, and Allotook Ipellie. *Recollecting: J. Dewey Soper's Arctic Watercolours*. Calgary: The Nickle Arts Museum, University of Calgary, 1995.

Maurice, Edward Beauclerk. *The Last of the Gentlemen Adventurers*. London: Fourth Estate, 2004.

Montague, Sydney R. *North to Adventure*. New York: McBride, 1939.

Moss, John George. *Echoing Silence: Essays on Arctic Narrative*. Ottawa: University of Ottawa Press, 1997.

Mowat, Farley. *Ordeal by Ice*. Toronto: McClelland & Stewart, 1960.

———. *The Polar Passion*. Toronto: McClelland & Stewart, 1967.

Owen, Roderic. *The Fate of Franklin*. London: Hutchinson, 1978.

Perrins, Dr. Christopher M. *The Illustrated Encyclopedia of Birds*. London: Headline, 1990.

Price, Ray. *The Howling Arctic*. Toronto: Peter Martin Associates, 1970.

Rasky, Frank. *The North Pole or Bust.* Toronto: McGraw-Hill, Ryerson, 1977.
____. *The Polar Voyages.* Toronto: McGraw-Hill, Ryerson, 1976.
Rasmussen, Knud. *Across Arctic America; Narrative of the Fifth Thule Expedition.* New York and London: Putnam, 1927.
Robbins, Chandler S., Bertel Bruun, and Herbert S. Zim. *A Guide to Field Identification: Birds of North America.* New York: Golden Press, 1983.
Ross, W. Gillies. *Arctic Whalers Icy Seas.* Toronto: Irwin Publishing, 1985.
Thomson, George Malcolm. *The Search for the North-West Passage.* New York: Macmillan, 1975.
Thoreau, Henry David. *Walden; or, Life in the Woods.* Boston: Ticknor and Fields, 1854.
Tilman, H.W. *Mostly Mischief.* London: Hollis & Carter, 1966.
Webb, R., A. Johnston, and J. D. Soper. Edited by W.G. Hardy. *The Prairie World in Alberta: A Natural History*, Edmonton: Hurtig, 1967.
Pilot of Arctic Canada. Vol. 1, 2nd ed., page 78. Ottawa: Canadian Hydrographic Service, 1970.
Pilot of Arctic Canada. Vol. 3, 2nd ed., page 32. Ottawa: Canadian Hydrographic Service, 1968.
Sailing Directions, Arctic Canada. Vol. 1, 3rd ed., page 71. Ottawa: Department of Fisheries and Oceans, 1982.
Sailing Directions, Arctic Canada. Vol. 3, 3rd ed., page 78. Ottawa: Department of Fisheries and Oceans, 1981.

Articles

Ferguson, Theresa A, "The 'Jarvis Proof': Management of Bison, Management of Bison Hunters, and the Development of a Literary Tradition." Instructor/Tutor, Athabasca University.
Finkelstein, Max. "The Soper River: Timeless Tales and Tuktu Trails." Accessed April 14, 2010, at *www.chrs.ca/River/Soper/Soper-S_e.htm*.
Höhn, Dr. E.O. "Dewey Soper, Veteran Arctic Naturalist." *The Beaver*. Fall 1980, 32.
Munro, Joanne. "Career Spent in the Wilderness." *Edmonton Journal*, November 6, 1978.

Nursall, Dr. Ralph. "Citation Address by Dr. Ralph Nursall, Director, Department of Zoology, University of Alberta, May 18, 1960." University of Alberta Archives, Edmonton.

Soper, Carolyn K. "A Nurse Goes to Baffin Island." *The Beaver*, Winter 1964, 33.

Stenton, Douglas R. "A Soper Record Cairn from Baffin Island, N.W.T." *The Arctic*, Vol. 39, No. 1, March 1986, 92–94.

Index

Entries in italics refer to images

Acton (Ontario), 23
Admiralty Inlet, 94
Aitken, Jim, 157, 159, 160, 170
Akatuga (Inuk), 118–23, 125–27, 129, 132–34, 137, 142, 144, 146, 149, 152–56, 179
Aklavik, 224–25, 228–29, 269
Alaska, 17, 216, 224, 226–28, 290, 295
Alaska-Canada Highway, 226, 295
Alberta, 2, 18, 33, 35–36, 39, 55, 57, 68, 73, 75–77, 162–67, 169, 192, 208, 214, 216–20, 222–23, 228, 237–40, 242, 244, 246–48, 250–54, 256, 259–62, 270–71, 278–79, 281
Alberta Society of Professional Biologists, 265
Allen, Herb, 62, 71
Amadjuak, 118, 155, 157, 160, 161, 170

Amadjuak Lake, 107, 111, 118, 147, 155, 198
Amadjuak River, 146–47, 153, 155
American Harbour, 113, 153
American Ornithologists Union, 161, 273
Amittok Lake, 148, 153
Amundsen, Roald, 30, 277
Anderson, Dr. R.M., 60, 68, 83, 106–07, 144, 167, 217, 235, 271–72, 280
Andrew Gordon Bay, 157–58, 172–74, 178, 183, 190, 192
Angmaluk Lake, 192
Anticosti Island, 282
Arctic, 14–17, 19, 21–22, 30–31, 68, 83–85, 87, 89–91, 93–95, 97, 98, 101–03, 105–07, 110, 112, 114, 116, 118–21, 126, 143, 145, 153, 158–60, 162–64, 167, 169, 173, 180, 187, 196–97, 202, 204–05, 207, 213, 217, 222, 225–26, 228–29, 232, 254, 257, 260, 263–65,

269–70, 275–76, 281–86, 288, 290–95, 297
Arctic (ship), 22, 84–93, 88, 96, 100–03, 106, 108–10, 116, 263, 276, 282–85
Arctic Circle, 15–16, 89, 100–01, 110, 113, 135, 178–80
Arctic Institute of North America, 14, 180, 186, 260, 265, 273, 297
Asgard, Mount, 129
Ashuna (Inuk), 185, 187–88
Athabasca River, 42, 52–53, 226, 246, 251
Atlantic Ocean, North, 22, 85–86, 89, 108, 205, 282
Attaguyuk (Inuk), 149
Austdal, Mary Lou, 13, 213–14, 218–21, 231–32, 234–36, 247, 251, 256–58, 262, 264
Austdal, Michael, 232, 234
Austdal, Michael Alexander, 235, 256–58

Baffin, William, 16
Baffin Bay, 21, 89–90, 112, 195
Baffin Island, 207, 211, 213, 216, 222, 236–37, 256, 262–63, 269, 271, 281, 285–93
Bailey, Reverend and Mrs., 196
Ball, Dr. George, 269
Barrow Strait, 93–94
Bartlett, Captain Robert, 290
Bathurst Inlet, 225
Battle, Mount, 129
Bayeskimo (ship), 292
Bayrupert (ship), 161, 289
Beaver, The (magazine), 196, 262–63, 292
Beck, Tom, 243
Beechey Island, 93–94, 102
Belle Isle, Strait of, 85, 101, 108

Bent, Arthur, 162
Beothic (ship), 154, 192
Bernier, Captain J.E., 22, 84–87, 85, 91, 276, 282
Bettschen, David, 56, 74–75
Blacklead Island, 112, 116–18
Blue goose, 157–58, 162, 169, 171, 176, 183, 184, 185–89, 195, 236–37, 271, 288, 291–92; breeding grounds, 169, 171, 176, 183, 185–93; Dewey Soper's search for, 157–58, 162, 169, 171, 176, 183–93, 237; first sightings, 145, 157, 158
Blue Goose River, 186, 188, 189
Boas, Franz, 136–37, 287
Bowdoin (schooner), 91, 283
Bowdoin Harbour, 159, 170
Bowman Bay, 158, 171, 177–78, 181, 185, 187, 189–90, 192, 236, 269, 271
British Columbia, 17, 39, 76, 217–18, 222, 247
Broadview (Saskatchewan), 55, 74, 281
Brock, General Sir Isaac, 23
Broughton Island, 132
Burwash, Major L.T., 118, 286, 288
Button, Sir Thomas, 95, 284
Bylot Island, 95, 105, 284

Calgary (Alberta), 13, 163, 231, 235, 244, 247, 249, 251–52, 255–56, 258, 265, 275, 292, 294, 296–97
Cameron, Gordon, 226
Camrose (Alberta), 75–76
Camsell, Harry, 228
Canada, 6, 14, 16–18, 22–23, 33, 42, 68, 83–84, 90, 102, 106, 145–46, 150, 152, 161, 164, 177, 200, 202–04,

Index

207–09, 219, 226, 232–33, 237, 239, 243, 250, 257, 265, 269–70, 272, 276, 278–80, 295, 297
Canadian Life Zone, 217, 293
Canadian Nature Federation, 270
Canadian Wildlife Service, 216, 237
Cape Bathurst, 225
Cape Dominion, 178, 291
Cape Dorchester, 170–71
Cape Dorset, 118, 154–58, 160, 170, 172, 174, 176–79, 181–83, 185, *188*, 190, 192, 195, 286, 288
Cape Farewell (Greenland), 89
Cape Weston, 170, 175
Caron, Wilfred, 84, 282
Chancellery of Honours, 265
Chorkbak Inlet, 156, 160, 183, 288
Churchill (Manitoba), 205, 283, 292–93
Coker, Jack, 40–46, *45*, 48–49, 51, 53, 56, 76, 78, 267
Cook, Dr. Frederick, 30, 277, 283
Cornwallis Island (Northwest Territories, now Nunavut), 17, 94
Craig, Commander John Davidson, 84, 87, 89, 107, 281–82, 285
Craig, Mrs. J.D. (Gertrude), 84, 93
Craig Harbour, 91–92, 102
Cree, Mountain (Aseniwuche Winewak Nation of Canada), 47, 49, 279
Criddle, Stuart (also Farm), 219–20, 294
Crowsnest Pass (Alberta), 217
Cumberland Sound, 15–16, 100, 106–08, 111–12, 121, 137, 154, 284–85
Cypress Hills, 165

Darling, Eric A., 56
Darwin, Charles, 18, 81

Davis, Captain John, 15–16, 112
Davis Strait, 22, 87, 89, 111–12, 132, 170, 195, 203, 285
Devon Island, 21, 92, 102, 105
Dewey Soper Bird Sanctuary, 19, 236–37, 269
Disco Island (Greenland), 87, 89
Discovery (ship), 15, 95
Douglas H. Pimlott Conservation Award, 270
Drumheller (Alberta), 164, 239
Duvall, William, 101, 107, 113, 119, 153, 284

Eagle Butte (Alberta), 165
East, Will (also Edith), 23, 33–34, 68, 162
Eastern Arctic expedition, 1923, 83–103
Edmonton, 13–14, 33, 35, 39–40, 53, 55, 68, 75, 81, 107, 114, 213, 222–23, 226, 228, 231–33, 236, 245–52, 257, 259–61, 263, 265–66, 269, 273, 278, 280–82
Edmonton Bird Club, 250, 273
Eliak (Inuk), 170
Elkwater (Alberta), 164–65
Ellesmere Island, 89–91, 102, 283
Elye, Leonard Norris, 219, 223, 294
Erebus (ship), 93
Erin County (Ontario), 23
Etah (Greenland), 91, 102
Expeditions:
　From Cape Dorset
　　To Foxe Basin, 147, 170–73, 177–78, 180–81, 185, 190–91
　　To Hantzsch River, 177–82

309

From Lake Harbour
    Hudson Strait surveying, 195, 199, 203–04, 207
    Soper River, 200–02, 207, 269
From Pangnirtung–Cumberland Sound
    To Foxe Basin, winter traverse, 111, 149–52
    To Issortukdjuak Fjord, 123, 125–26
    Kingnait Pass winter traverse, 128, 130, 133–36
    Nettilling Lake and Foxe Basin, 139–51
    Pangnirtung Pass winter traverse, 127–28, 130–32
Western Arctic
    Arctic flying, 223–25, 228–29
    Mackenzie River and delta, 39, 224, 228–29, 339

Fairbanks (Alaska), 228
Falardeau, Adrien, 84, 89
Family Herald and Weekly Star, 37, 55
Farley, Frank, 75
Finkelstein, Max, 203
Finnie, O.S., 169, 208
Fish Creek, 42–43
Foothills expedition, 39–53
Ford, Abe, 116, 199
Fort Assiniboine, 239, 252
Fort Chimo, 161
Fort Chipewyan, 226
Fort Fitzgerald, 208, 293
Fort Reliance, 225
Fort Smith, 208, 223–26, 293
Foxe, Luke, 275

Foxe Basin, 97, 111, 147, 149, 151, 170–73, 177–78, 180–81, 185, 190–91, 200, 275, 285, 288, 290
Foxe Islands, 158, 288
Foxe Peninsula, 154, 158, 160, 170–71, 173–74, 178, 182, 185, 190, 275, 290
Franklin, Sir John, 93–94, 283
Franklin Bay, 225, 283
Freuchen, Peter, 30, 97, 284
Frobisher, Sir Martin, 15–16
Frobisher Bay (now Iqaluit), 16, 111, 198, 200
Funsten Bros., 27, 41, 279
Fury and Hecla Strait, 170, 290

Gabriel (ship), 15
Gaspe, 85, 102
Geographic Board of Canada, 177, 200, 269
Georgian Bay, 73–74
Gibson, R.A., 207
Glacier Strait, 90, 92
Godhavn (Greenland), 87, 89–90, 102
Grand River, 61–62, 73
Grand Valley (Ontario), 26
Grande Prairie (Alberta), 42, 218–19, 226, 228, 294
Great Plain of the Koukdjuak, 178
Great Slave Lake, 209, 223–25, 228
Greeley Expedition, 91, 283
Greenland, 15, 21–22, 87, 89, 91, 102, 110, 118
Griffin, Arthur, 76–78, 80–81
Guelph (Ontario), 23–24, 31, 55, 59, 71, 73, 163

Index

Hamilton (Ontario), 22
Hamilton Inlet, 85–87
Hantzsch, Bernard, 111, 143, 177, 181, 285, 288
Hantzsch River, 177–79, 181–82
Harkness, Douglas, 236
Hay River (Alberta) (*see also* Wildhay River), 42, 45, 49–50
Hay River (Northwest Territories), 223, 228–29
Herodier, Georges, 100
Herschel Island, 224, 294
Hinton (Alberta), 40–43, 46, 48–50, 53
Hudson, Henry, 15, 95
Hudson Bay, 87, 205, 275, 283–84
Hudson Strait, 15–16, 106, 110, 118, 155–56, 160, 173, 176, 178, 183, 192, 195–96, 203, 205, 292
Hudson's Bay Company (HBC), 14, 16–17, 41, 112, 119, 208, 276, 286, 289, 292
Huntsville (Ontario), 23–24
Huronic (ship), 83

Imigen Island, 139–40
Inuit (Inuk), 92, 103, 113, 117–18, 120–21, 123–25, 127–28, 130, 139–40, 142–43, 146, 152, 155–58, 160, 170–77, 179, 183, 185, 187, 192, 196, 198–204, 229, 269, 282, 286, 288, 290, 294
Islay (Alberta), 68, 75–76, 281
Isoa, 142–43
Issortukdjuak Fjord, 113, 123, 125–26

Jasper National Park, 77, 245–49, 251–52, 258

Johns, Dr. Walter, 244
Jones Sound, 92
Joy, Inspector A.H., 202

Kangertukdjuak, 119, 139
Kangia, 142
Karmang Cairn, 152
Kassigiak Fjord, 117–18
Katannilik Territorial Park, 203
Kavivau (Inuk), 172, 174, 176–78, 185, 187–88, 192
Kekerton Island, 116
Kekertukdjuak, 132
Kilabuk (Inuk), 127, 129, 286
King William Island, 93
Kingnait Fjord, 112, 136
Kingnait Pass, 128, 130, 133, 134–36, 262
Kingodlik (Inuk), 134
Kingua, 113
Kivitoo, 132
Kjar, Them, 226
Klondike, 226, 259, 295
Kluane Lake, 227
Koksoak River, 161
Kolik River, 123
Kommanik River, 172–73, 190–92, 290
Kopik (Inuk), 134
Korean War, 229, 295
Koukdjuak River, 147, 149–50, 152, 177–79, 181, 236, 287
Kungesinil (Inuk), 142, 146
Kungovik, Camp, 185–86, 188–89, 192, 271

Labrador, 22, 85–87, 89, 102, 108, 110, 116, 145, 161, 170, 205

Lady Borden (boat), 115, 119, 148
Lake Harbour, 156, 192, 195–200, 203–04, 207–08, 269, 292
Lake of the Woods, 163, 166
Lancaster Sound, 21, 87, 92–96
Lewin, Vic, 248, 250
Linnaeus, Carl, 18
Lloyd, Hoyes, 235, 295
London (Ontario), 62, 67, 174
Lougheed, Peter, 260–61, 270

Mackenzie Delta, 224, 229
Mackenzie River, 39, 224, 228–29
Macmillan, Donald, 282
Manitoba, 14, 39, 163–64, 166, 205, 216, 219, 222, 271–72, 276, 286, 289, 292, 294
Manitoba Museum, 219, 223, 294
Margetts, Hugh, 116–17
Mark Twain Society, 270
Mary (yacht), 94
Mason & Risch Piano Company, 73
Mathiassen, Therkel, 95, 97, 100
Maurice, Edward Beauclerk, 195
McCall, Frank, 224
McEwen, Dr. Grant, 260
McKernan's Lake, 36, 278
McLaughlin, Ilona, 23, 71
McLaughlin, Nelson, 27
McNabb, Malcolm, 229
Melville Bay, 21, 90
Melville Island, 94
Merchant's Bay, 132
Meta Incognita, 15, 111, 200
Metik (schooner), 159
Midlualik Bay, 113–14, 119
Migratory Birds Convention Act, 216

Milk River, 165, 250–51
Miner, Jack, 68
Mitchell, South Dakota, 25
Montague, Sydney, 161, 289
Montreal, 17, 169, 205, 258, 278, 292, 297
Montreal River, 71–73
Moon River, 61, 73–74
Moosa (Inuk), 198–99, 201
Mount Columbia, 39, 278
Murray Maxwell Bay, 177
Muskoka, 23, 61, 73–74
Mutuse (Inuk), 201

Nascopie (ship), 17, 118–19, 160–61, 169, 192, 195, 275, 286
National Herbarium of Canada, 202
National Museum of Canada, 18, 33, 68, 83, 92, 101, 106, 118–19, 126, 145–46, 163, 167, 169, 189, 209, 235, 239, 241–42
National Museum of Natural Sciences, 163
Navy Board Inlet, 95
Nettilling Fjord, 119, 139–40, 142, 148–49, 153–54
Nettilling Lake, 107, 118, 125, 139–40, 142–43, 145–47, 149, 151–53, 155, 179, 200, 269, 271, 287
Newfie Bullet, 161
Newfoundland, 85, 161, 283, 289–90
Newkeguak (Inuk), 149, 153, 155–56
Niantelik Harbour, 112, 117
Noble, Crawford Jr., 143
North Pangnirtung Fjord, 127, 132
North Pole, 30, 276–77, 283
North Saskatchewan River, 33, 35–36, 82

Index

Northwest Territories, 39, 169, 207–08, 213, 222–23, 228, 270–71, 293
Nunasweeto (Inuk), 179
Nunatuk, 125
Nuwata, 160, 170–71, 174–76

O'Connell, Desmond, 84, 282
Olympic Winter Games, Calgary 1988, 265
Ontario, 23, 25–26, 29–30, 40–41, 48, 55, 59, 61–62, 67, 69, 71, 73, 83–84, 162–63, 174, 207, 229, 247, 262, 277, 279–80, 293
Order of Canada, 265, 297
Ottawa, 14, 33, 68, 83–84, 89, 101–02, 108, 114, 118, 144, 154, 158, 161–63, 169, 192, 198, 202, 205, 207, 213, 216, 222, 234, 236–37, 250 265, 273
Ottawa Citizen (newspaper), 237
Owl River, 130–31

Padle Fjord, 132, 134
Pangnirtung, 100, 106, 108, 112, 114–16, 118, 120, 125–27, 131, 133, 137, 142, 148 49, 151–54, 156–57, 195, 285–86
Pangnirtung Fjord, 15–16, 102, 107, 111, 115–16, 119, 126–27, 130, 132
Pangnirtung Pass, 17, 127–28, 130, 132, 135, 262
Parry, Sir William, 16
Patagook (Inuk), 179
Peace River, 39, 209, 218–19, 223, 226, 294
Peary, Robert, 30, 277

Pengelly, Leslie, 257
Penny Highlands, 114, 127
Peterhead boat, 156
Point Pelee, 68
Pond Inlet, 84, 89–90, 96–100, 102, 195–96, 282, 292
Poojut (Inuk), 149
Port Burwell, 161
Prairie expedition, 163–68
Preble, Edward, 162
Preston (Ontario), 59, 60, 262
Prince Albert (Saskatchewan), 167
Princess Patricia's Canadian Light Infantry, 229, 231
Putnam Expedition, 170, 290
Putnam Highlands, 181, 183

Quebec, 85, 87, 102, 161, 205, 276, 278, 282
Quebec City, 84, 101, 108–09, 205, 281–82

Rasmussen, Knud, 97, 284
Resolute, 17
Ridout (Ontario), 62, 67, 280
Ridout River, 61, 65, 67, 72
Rivet, Judge Louis, A., 84, 90
Rocky Mountains (also Rockies), 27, 39, 41, 49, 58, 64, 75, 77, 81, 163–64, 216–18, 250, 258, 267, 278
Ross, Captain John, 93
Rowan, Dr. William, 75, 233
Royal Canadian Air Force (RCAF), 232, 234
Royal Canadian Mounted Police (RCMP), 84, 88, 91–92, 96, 100, 106, 108, 112, 115–16, 119–20,

139, 148, 153, 161, 163, 197, 199–
200, 202, 244, 282, 292
Royal Navy, 93
Ryder, John, 250

Sabine, Cape, 91, 283
Saila (Inuk), 176, 183
St. John's, 161, 283, 289
St. Lawrence, Gulf of, 85
St. Lawrence River, 84, 101, 205
Saskatchewan, 14, 39, 55, 68, 74, 165, 167, 215–16, 222, 271–72, 281
Saunders, W.E., 60, 62, 67, 71, 174, 280
Scotland, 23, 89, 285
Scott, Robert Falcon, 273
Sermilling (Bay and River), 113–14, 120, 125–26
Seton, Ernest T., 27, 31, 60, 161, 280
Shackleton, Sir Ernest, 30
Shappa (Inuk), 170, 172–74, 176–80, 192
Sharon, "Mush," 224–26
Slave River, 208, 216, 224, 228, 293
Soper, Betty (nee Neil), 235, 249, 251–52, 256, 262
Soper, Carolyn (Carrie), 162–66, 169, 193, 195–97, 199–200, 205, 207–08, 213, 220–21, 223, 228–29, 231–36, 247–48, 251–52, 256–60, 262, 264–65, 292
Soper, Cecil, 23, 73–74
Soper, Edith (aka Mrs. Will East), 23, 33–34, 68, 162
Soper, Elizabeth, 251–52, 256
Soper, Joseph (Sr.), 23–26, 24, 34–35, 55, 59, 71
Soper, J. Dewey: as artist, *68, 80, 86, 99,*
111, 128, 135, 153, 171, 175, 180, 186, 201, 220, 235, *246,* 260, 263, 264, 265; awards and honours, 19, 81, 144, 244, 260–61, 263, 264, 265, 269–70; birth, 23; Blue goose, early interest, 107, 145, 157; conservation, 19, 226, 236–36, 270; death, 265; early life, 23–33; education, 24, 29, 32, 35, 75, 81, 107; as explorer, 19, 30–31, 111, 113, 169, 187, 213, 265; health, 48–49, 123–24, 198, 260–63; homebuilding, 35, 37, 73–75, 76, 196, 232, 233, 234–36; hunting, 27, 28–30, *40, 41, 144,* 192, 221, 243, 255, 294; mapmaking/surveying, 125, 126, 130, 134, 137, 139, 143, 147–48, 150–52, 161, 174, 177, 182, 207, 213, 232, 253; marriage, 163, 165; as pianist, 55–56, 58, 69, 73; published works, 14, 18, 162, 237, 239, 246, 252–54, 285; receives Honorary Doctor of Laws degree, 244–45, 269; relationship with children and grandchildren, 220–22, 233–35, 242, 255–56, 257–59; retirement, 232, 235–36, 237, 258–59; taxonomic honours, 144, 165, 269, 271–72; on trapping, 27–29, 31, 36, *40,* 45–47, 50, 91, 100, 204, 218, 235, 242, 253, 256, 258–59, 267; travel, 232, 258, 259, 260; as Zoology Research Associate, 269
Soper, Lew, 25
Soper, Mary Lou (*see* Austdal, Mary Lou)
Soper, Philip, 13, 251, 255–57, 264–65, 297

Index

Soper, Roland (Roly), 13, 167, 169, 193, 195–200, 207–08, 211, 213–14, 219–22, 229, 231–35, 242–44, 249, 251–52, 255–57, 259–60, 265–66, 275, 279, 294–97
Soper, Roy, 23, 248
Soper, Samuel, 23
Soper, Trent, 13, 251, 256–57, 275, 296
Soper Highlands, 179, 269
Soper River, 200–03, 207, 269, 292
South Pacific islands, 259
South Pole, 30, 277
South Saskatchewan River, 39
Spence, Harry, 78, 80
Spreu, Herb, 226
Stanton (Northwest Territories), 224–25, 229, 294
Stefansson, Vilhjalmur, 30, 187, 291
Sternberg, Charles, 164
Strathcona (Alberta), 33, 35, 40, 223
Strathcona Sound, 94
Sunwapta Pass (also River), 246, 249
Swindells, Brenda Lee, 236, 256–58

Takuirbing River, 142, 148
Taverner, Ida, 163
Taverner, Percy A., 60, 163, 271, 280
Taverner Bay, 179–81
Tellier, Leopold, 84
Temagami (Ontario), 61, 71–72
Temagami, Lake, 71, 72
Temiskaming, Lake, 71–72
Terror (ship), 93
Tessikdjuak Lake, 173, 178, 182, 190
Tête Blanche, Mount, 129
The Fly (sailboat), 139, 143, 147, 153–54
Thule Expedition, fifth, 97, 284

Tikoot Islands, 156, 176, 288
Tilman, H.W. "Bill," 95–96, 284
Toronto, 13, 22, 69, 231, 280
Trapping, 27–29, 31, 32, 36, *40*, 41, 46–51, 126, 166, 218, 242, 249, 253, 255–56, 279
Tredgold, Thomas, 88–89, 91–92, 94–95, 112–16, 119, 124, 139, 141–42, 183

Unga (Inuk), 119, 123, 153
Ungava (motor schooner), 113–14, 116–18
Ungava (ship), 205, 292
Ungava Bay, 161, 292
University of Alberta, 13, 75–76, 81, 107, 233, 244–45, 250, 257, 264, 269, 280, 296; Boreal Institute, 263; Department of Zoology, 245, 250, 261, 269; Students' Union, 264, 297
University of Montana, 257
University of Saskatchewan, 14, 18

Val Marie (Saskatchewan), 165, 271
Vevik (Inuk), 116–18
Victoria Island (Northwest Territories), 17
Victoria Memorial Museum, 108

Wakami River, 64
Walker, Bob, 250
Wanderlust (canoe), 61–62, 64, 66–67, 81
Wark, David, 156, 170
Warterton Lakes, 164, 217, 245, 247–49, 251–52, 258, 296
Weasel River, 127, 130
Wetaskiwin (Alberta), 162, *164*, 166–67, 213

Whitehorse, 226, 228
Whitemud Creek, 36
Wilcox, Inspector C.E., 91–92, 94
Wildhay River (*see also* Hay River), 42, 45
Winnipeg, 14, 17, 83, 205, 216, 219, 222–23, 251–52, 256, 258, 276, 286, 289, 292–93
Wood Buffalo National Park, 208–11, 213, 219, 226

Yellowknife, 14, 225
York, Cape (Greenland), 21, 90
Yukon, 169, 208, 222, 224, 226–28, 294–95

About the Author

Anthony Dalton is a fellow of the Royal Geographical Society and a fellow of the Explorers Club. He has spent much of his life in adventurous pursuits, during which he has roamed over much of the world's wilder landscapes, canoed turbulent rivers, and sailed stormy waters, including in the Arctic. He is an award-winning author of seven nonfiction books and has written and illustrated hundreds of newspaper and magazine articles based on his expeditions and photojournalism assignments. He is the national president of the Canadian Authors Association as well as a member of The Writers Union of Canada and the Welsh Academi. He divides his time between the mainland of British Columbia south of Vancouver and the nearby Gulf Islands.